Mameluke Ali

NAPOLEON AFTER THE CAMPAIGN IN ITALY

Mameluke Ali

With Napoleon from the Tuileries to St. Helena

Louis Étienne Saint-Denis

Translated by Frank Hunter Potter

LEONAUR

Mameluke Ali
With Napoleon from the Tuileries to St. Helena
by Louis Étienne Saint-Denis
Translated by Frank Hunter Potter

First published under the title
Napoleon from the Tuileries to St. Helena

Leonaur is an imprint of Oakpast Ltd

Copyright in this form © 2014 Oakpast Ltd

ISBN: 978-1-78282-393-3 (hardcover)
ISBN: 978-1-78282-394-0 (softcover)

http://www.leonaur.com

Contents

Introduction

Louis Étienne Saint-Denis was born at Versailles on September 22, 1788. His father, Étienne, had been *piqueur* [1] in the royal stables under Louis XVI. The connoisseurs of the noble art of equitation have spoken of him with lively admiration. He was, it seems, a "model of a fine position on a horse," and above all he struggled energetically for the French traditions against the "antinational" school of the Anglomaniac horsemen. He had married Marie Louise Notte, daughter of an officer of the royal kitchens. One of his great-granddaughters still recollects hearing Aunt Notte, an unmarried sister of Marie Louise Notte, tell proudly how her father had made a cage of nougat which had been placed on the table at one of the court *fêtes*. There was a bird shut up in it, which flew away when it was broken and in its flight perched on the head of Marie Antoinette. The Revolution cost Etienne Saint-Denis his place. He moved to Paris, where for more than fifty years (he died in 1843, at the age of eighty-nine years) he was a riding master. At seventy-six he still broke horses, preferably those which his enemies, the so-called innovators, had failed in training and had made unruly.

After good preliminary studies, to which the writing and spelling of all his papers bear witness, Louis Étienne Saint-Denis became a clerk in the office of the notary Colin, in the Place Vendôme, in 1802. He remained there four years. At the end of that time, taking advantage of former relations with the Duke of Vicenza, [2] the elder

---

1. There is nothing in the English stable which quite corresponds to the office of *piqueur*. He had all sorts of functions. Among other things he was a huntsman, also an outrider who preceded his master to order relays of post horses; he was an overseer of stables, and it was his duty to take large convoys of post horses, carriage horses, draft horses, or remounts from place to place. As horses supplied the only means of locomotion in the armies of that day, except the men's feet, great numbers of them were required, and the *piqueur's* duties involved heavy responsibility.
2. Armand Augustin Louis, Marquis de Caulaincourt.

Saint-Denis secured his son's admission to the emperor's household. The youth first spent a month in the business offices of the stable, no doubt as a supernumerary or probationer, then on May 1, 1806, he was placed definitively on the registers with the title of student *piqueur*. He became *underpiqueur* in 1808, and then, having been appointed Mameluke and decorated with the name of Ali, he became "assistant *arquebus* carrier" on January 1, 1812.

Indeed, he himself drew up the account of his services.

SERVICES

OF LOUIS ÉTIENNE SAINT-DENIS

ATTACHED TO THE HOUSEHOLD OF H. M. THE EMPEROR

NAPOLEON I

In May, 1806, he entered His Majesty's household as student *piqueur* in the department of carriage horses.

In March, 1808, he went to Bayonne and Spain.

In August he started for Erfurth. When he returned to Paris he was appointed *underpiqueur* and shortly afterward he was sent to Bayonne and Spain. He returned to France with the detachments which had remained at Valladolid.

In April, 1809, he started for Germany with a convoy of horses. He returned to France with his convoy. On his arrival in Paris he took a large number of draught horses to Bayonne and then to Spain.

In September, 1811, he made the journey to Holland and commanded the third service in the emperor's suite.

In December he entered the personal service of the emperor in the private apartments as second Mameluke and accompanied His Majesty during the campaign in Russia.

In 1813, during the first part of the campaign of that year, he remained on detached service at Mayence and then went to join the emperor at Neumark. In the second part of the campaign he accompanied His Majesty. After the passage of the Rhine he remained at Mayence and left that city only after the foreign armies had entered Paris.

When he returned to Paris he went to Elba to join the emperor.

In 1815 he was on board the *Inconstant*. He was on duty with the emperor the day he entered Grenoble. He was also on duty with His Majesty when he arrived at Fontainebleau, and during all the journey from Fontainebleau to Paris.

In June he was always with the emperor during the short campaign in Belgium, at the Battle of Ligny and at that of Waterloo. He had left the Élysée with His Majesty and he returned to that palace with him.

He accompanied the emperor from Malmaison to Rochefort.

At the Isle d'Aix His Majesty chose him to go to America when he intended to embark on a lugger.

On May 5, 1821, he was at Longwood.

It was he who made clean copies of the emperor's dictation. All the memoirs of St. Helena, with slight exceptions, are in his hand.

His protector was the Duke of Vicenza.

★★★★★★

Further, Saint-Denis forgets, in this *curriculum vitæ* (I do not know why), the title of which he was so proud, that of the emperor's librarian,

Saint-Denis had married Mary Hall at St. Helena on October 18, 1819. She was a young English Catholic, born in Birmingham on December 5, 1786, who was governess to Grand-Marshal Bertrand's children. There was born to him on July 31, 1820, a daughter, Clémence, whose godfather and godmother were General de Montholon and Countess Bertrand.

After the emperor's death the Saint-Denis family left the island. It embarked on the *Camel* on May 27, 1821, landed at Portsmouth on July 21st, and arrived in Paris on August 28th.

Saint-Denis had but little fortune and the legacy which the emperor had left him was not paid at once. He placed his wife and children temporarily at Versailles, with Grandmother Notte, and he himself lived with his parents, 34 rue du Dragon. He had found employment. He wrote to his wife, on May 28, 1822:

> I leave the house at five in the morning and I rarely get back to it before eight o'clock at night. The fact that I have occupation makes me feel more strongly the desire to have you with me. Still, we must both be reasonable. This state of affairs cannot last long. What I earn is but little, it is true, but it is a beginning. My pay will be greater as the number of pupils increases. This small sum (thirty *sous* a day) will pay for my lodging, which is something, and ultimately I can be head of the establishment if it succeeds, which is probable enough.

A few months later he was annoyed at not being able to find lodgings in the quarter near the Luxembourg. However, he was able to find a place to live in Paris, since his second daughter, Isabelle, was born there on June 11, 1826. Finally, whether the "establishment" did not prosper or whether Saint-Denis had left it, he decided to settle in the provinces, in order to live more economically. We do not know why he chose the town of Sens. Perhaps he was drawn there by a friend, a retired officer, Dufeu, who later made him his residuary legatee. Perhaps he wished to be near Marchand, his companion at St. Helena, who had settled not far away on his property Le Verger, in the commune of Perrigny, just outside of Auxerre.

Saint-Denis spent the remainder of his life there, first in the rue de Canettes, then on the Esplanade. He left there only for short trips to Paris—notably to hasten the tardy delivery of the emperor's legacy—and for the pilgrimage to St. Helena. When the question arose of bringing back the emperor's ashes to France, Saint-Denis claimed the honour of going on the mission. This favour was granted, thanks to the intervention of M. Thiers.

He had some slight inclination to ask for a place under the government of July. Perhaps he abandoned the idea; it was difficult for him to give up his liberty, and he asked himself—he even asked Grand-Marshal Bertrand—whether to accept a place from anyone but the emperor would not be to show disloyalty, in some sense, to his master's memory. He grew old amid the esteem of everybody in his adopted city; he was a censor of the savings bank. In 1841 he lost his wife, who had borne him a third daughter besides Clémence and Isabelle, Napoléone Mathilde, born in 1827. In 1854 he was made a knight of the Legion of Honour.

He died in 1856. He left to the city of Sens some of the articles which he had preserved in memory of his emperor, the two volumes of *Fleury de Chaboulon* with notes in Napoleon's handwriting which have been published by Senator Cornet, two atlases in which Napoleon had made some drawings or calculations in pencil, the folio volume of the campaigns of Italy, besides personal relics, a coat with epaulettes and the Star of the Legion of Honour, a cockade from a hat, a piece of the St. Helena coffin, and a bit of one of the willows which grew over the emperor's tomb. He also said:

> My daughters should always remember that the emperor was
> my benefactor and, consequently, theirs; the greater part of
> what I possess I owe to his kindness.

Saint-Denis left "Souvenirs" in manuscript. A legend on this subject has been given currency by Dr. Poumiès de la Siboutie. He says in his *Souvenirs d'un Médecin de Paris*:

I was for a long time physician in the Saint-Denis family. The father, who died some years ago at a very advanced age (this consequently must have been written after 1843) had gone from the stables of Louis XVI, where he filled the modest office of *piqueur*. The son was a member of the imperial household; he was a footman. His intelligence, his devotion, his good looks won for him the good graces of the emperor, who attached him more particularly to his person and chose him to go with him to St. Helena. Saint-Denis had received but little education, but he nevertheless had the idea of writing day by day what he saw and heard. His duty constantly brought him in contact with the emperor; he heard many curious things from his mouth. I have been able to run through them and they interested me greatly. Here is a quotation which I borrow from them.

Sire, qui dit Montholon, j'ai eu occasion de voir beaucoup les Anglais, de vivre au milieu d'eux, et je puis vous dire qu'ils sont bons enfants tout de même—Oui, qui dit l'empereur, mais leur gouvernement ne vaut pas le diable, et il savait bien ce qu'il faisait, en me donnant pour geôlier le plus grand canaille de VAngleterre.[3]

It is in this grotesque, often expressive, always energetic style that this journal is written from 1801 to 1821. It becomes, especially, more interesting from 1814, when the master, brought closer to the servant, has fewer secrets from him. It is Saint-Denis who rendered to Napoleon the last services as servant.

This, naturally, has been still further embellished. From this single page Napoleon's librarian at St. Helena has been represented as a sort of illiterate groom who succeeded, not without effort, in performing after a fashion a task which was far above his uneducated mind. It has been supposed that the emperor forbade him to publish his journal and that Saint-Denis destroyed it after utilizing it to give his "Souvenirs" their final form. This version is certainly spicy, but the evidence on which it rests is inaccurate.

I shall say nothing of the obvious mistakes, such as the date 1801.

---

3. The vulgar, uncultivated quality of the French would be lost in translating it.

which is absolutely impossible; that may be a mistake of reading for 1806. But the doctor's memory certainly misled him.

In the first place, there is nothing in the "Souvenirs" which corresponds, either in form or in substance, to the pretended extracts which he gives from it.

Then Louis Étienne Saint-Denis did not leave his father's stables or riding school to go into the imperial stables. He spent four years as a clerk in a notary's office. An intelligent young man, such as he was, must certainly have improved and, supposing that he did not know it already, have learned a little French in such surroundings. Furthermore, when he entered the imperial household, it was in the business office that he was first placed. We know that he was a great and attentive reader, and remained one till his death, and that he took notes on the most diverse kinds of books—mathematics, history, even exegesis. He was also interested in grammatical questions, and that without believing unreservedly the first book which fell into his hands. One day he wrote to his wife from Paris:

> I should like to have the grammar which refutes that of Noël and Chaptal; Clémence knows what it is.

Can a man who has been ignorant up to thirty-three years of age begin to interest himself in such things at that time of life? If the Duke of Vicenza chose him out of all his personnel to offer to the emperor, it was doubtless because he knew him to be sufficiently polished. If the emperor designated him to take care of his books, he must have known that he was sufficiently educated for the task; he would not have entrusted this work to a Santini or an Archambault. Saint-Denis made clean copies of the St. Helena manuscripts; when he could not decipher a word he would substitute one of his own for the illegible text, which the emperor sometimes accepted, sometimes corrected, but without forbidding him to take these liberties. His companions recognised his superiority: "You who have education for us both," wrote Pierron, the former *major-domo,* or this: "You must laugh at my style and my spelling, but you will be indulgent to a poorly educated man like me"

And yet Pierron's letters themselves are those of a man who has received a solid primary education. Finally, by the time he returned to Paris—that is, the time when Doctor Poumiès could have known him, his letters prove that he knew perfectly well how to spell and that he was incapable of the barbarous style which is ascribed to him.

I will add that Saint-Denis had a lively sense of his own dignity.

When the emperor went to Longwood he organized his household and directed that there should be two tables, one for the heads of the different services, the other for the remainder of the personnel. Saint-Denis, second *valet de chambre*, was designated to preside at the second table. He was wounded because "they showed him so little consideration as to make him live with persons with whom he was not accustomed to associate." He says:

> While waiting for an opportunity to speak to the emperor, I preferred to go to the kitchen to ask for something to eat rather than to take my place at the second table, where, for that matter, I was to be the first. The next day the opportunity presented itself. I spoke to the emperor and explained my reasons. His Majesty, seeing that my pride was deeply wounded, considered my request and readily consented that I should eat at the first table. 'The devil,' said His Majesty, looking me between the eyes, 'you are not like Desaix. He would not have objected if I had made him eat in the kitchen with the dog or the cat.[4] Well, go!' I bent my head slightly in sign of thanks and went away.

Since in 1822 he wrote in a very correct style, he certainly wasn't the man ever to have allowed anyone to see pages written in such a way as to cast ridicule on him, (see note following).

★★★★★★

Note:—Here is how this man, who must have remained in gross ignorance up to the age of thirty-five years, wrote to his

---

4. Napoleon's method of dealing with his generals is shown in the matter of Davout's marriage, as told by Madame Davout herself. At the time of the San Domingo expedition he gave the command of it to General Leclerc, husband of his sister Pauline, Leclerc objected to going because he had a tie and responsibility which kept him in France. "You mean your love for my sister Pauline? She shall go with you. Change of air will do her good." Leclerc explained that it was his sister to whom he referred. Napoleon replied, "We must have her married at once—tomorrow, say." Leclerc said that he had no dowry to give her. "Am I not here? Tomorrow your sister shall be married. I don't know exactly to whom." Shortly afterward Davout came in to tell Napoleon that he was going to be married. "To Mademoiselle Leclerc? I think it is a very suitable match." "No, general, to *Mademoiselle* ———." "To Mademoiselle Leclerc!" And Davout was obliged to comply. It is pleasant to record that the match turned out a happy one in the end. Napoleon married General Lavalette to Hortense's cousin, Emilie de Beauharnais, in pretty much the same way. It, too, was a happy marriage, and it was owing to his wife's devotion that his life was saved after the Hundred Days. He had been condemned to death for taking Napoleon's side at that time, when his wife visited him in prison, changed clothes with him, and he escaped disguised in this way.—Trans.

wife eight years later, offhand, in an intimate letter:

June 30, 1828.

My dear Mary:—Our carriage brought us to Montereau, as you know, and we arrived there at a quarter to eight. At eight o'clock precisely the boat started and went out into the middle of the river. It is the most agreeable manner of travelling that one can imagine. There are fresh views every moment; *châteaux*, houses, woods, mountains, meadows, etc., follow each other swiftly before the traveler's eyes; it is really enchanting. We reached Melun without thinking of it. We stopped there about half an hour. Some travellers left us, others came to replace them. A first stroke of the bell warns the travellers, then there is a second, then a third, which is the starting signal. New pictures come to present themselves to us. Our eyes, turned in the direction in which we were going, sought to discover new points of view at which we would speedily arrive.

We had already left Melun half an hour when an important piece of the machinery broke, and left us motionless, so to speak, in the middle of the river, going like a boat which is peacefully following the current. In these circumstances there was nothing better for us to do than to go to the bank and wait. There is a boat from Melun to Paris called the *Aigle*; it goes up and down the same day. It arrives at Melun at two o'clock and leaves at three; it was about eleven. At last, about three o'clock, we heard the bells, smoke came out of the chimneys, and joy reappeared on everybody's face.

The boat came up to us, the transhipment was quickly made, and we were under way again, leaving our unlucky cripple where its wings had been deprived of movement. If all that we had seen from Montereau to Melun had appeared admirable, it was very different from Melun to Paris. I have never seen anything more beautiful in my life, immense and magnificent *châteaux*, gardens, delicious parks, etc., in short, all that one could imagine cannot equal the reality. I was almost sorry, when we arrived at the landing place, not to have a longer trip to make."

And this is not half of the letter. There are careless passages, it is true, but the ease of the style and the agreeable quality of the story are quite sufficient to prove that he had known how to write French for a long time.

★★★★★★

14

Finally, and above all, this supposed journal never existed. Saint-Denis never varies on this point. He always declared, in the most categorical manner, that he never took any notes during the whole time his service with the emperor lasted, except the itinerary of the Russian campaign, and this was stolen from him with his baggage during the retreat. He did not say it only to people who, like Pons de l'Hérault, questioned him about the things which he had witnessed; this might be considered as an evasion. But he stated it many times to his family, regretting it, and reproaching himself for his negligence. As a consequence he scrupulously kept a journal of his trip to St. Helena in 1840. What is decisive, he repeated it to his companions at St. Helena, who must have known what to believe in the matter, and could, if necessary, easily have convicted him of falsehood.

Dr. Poumiès de la Siboutie could not, consequently, have read a journal which did not exist. I imagine that he must have been the victim of some superposition of recollections; what he saw in the rue du Dragon was perhaps the journal kept by some companion of Saint-Denis—Archambault, Noverraz, Santini or another—a journal which Saint-Denis may have had in his hands, and have consulted in order to verify his recollections.

For from the day that he returned to France those of his former companions who designed to write about the life of the emperor at St. Helena naturally turned to him to settle all sorts of matters of detail. Then he would draw up notes and send them, keeping his draft, for he was a methodical person.

It was only later, and, we believe, when he had settled at Sens that he began to write his connected *Recollections* for his family and also for Marchand. It is these *Recollections* extracts from which will be read later on. They fill 321 large pages in a small and closely written hand. He never stopped working at them till the end of his life. In this way he appended thirteen pages of additions, two pages of notes, nineteen pages of supplements. Figures for the additions and letters for the notes indicate clearly, except for some small errors easy to correct, the place in the text where these are to be placed. As for the supplements, he did not have time to perform this task. He also made a complete catalogue of the library at St. Helena. Finally, he left comments on the works devoted to the history of the emperor—Las Cases, Montholon, De Norvins, Méneval, De Beauterne, Fleury de Chaboulon, William Forsyth, (Hudson Lowe), Thiers, etc.

He had said in the codicil to his will:

As all I have written is very informal, and as there are things in it which are of no interest to anybody but myself, I desire that my papers shall not be communicated to anybody but M. Marchand.

Saint-Denis's daughters regarded this modest phrase as a categorical prohibition. From that time they opposed an absolute refusal to every request which was made to them to make them known. Moreover, knowing little of what had been published about the emperor, they believed that certain passages revealed secrets and that they might be reproached for causing their father to betray confidences. Consequently, their resolution remained inflexible.

But they preserved the Recollections piously, and they have come down to us intact. The descendants of the two elder daughters have disappeared; the third, Napoléone Mathilde, had two daughters and a son. The latter died without issue, and one of the daughters never married. The other is my mother-in-law; it is in this way that the honour has fallen to me to present these pages to the public.

I leave it to historians to judge the value of what they present which is new. But I believe that in reading them everyone will feel the accent of sincerity which speaks in them. Obviously, Saint-Denis's only concern was to be truthful. His very worship of the emperor evidently convinced him that his master could only gain by being painted as he really was. On the other hand, he does not seek to exaggerate his own part and to associate his person indiscreetly with the person of the emperor. It will even be observed with what scrupulous care he distinguishes what he saw or heard from what was told him. He may have been mistaken sometimes, but it is clear that he never departed from what he believed to be the truth.

Another guaranty of accuracy is that visual memory which seems to have been prodigious in him. It is sometimes capricious, and then he says, frankly, "I remember nothing of ——"; but ordinarily it is astonishingly exact. One seems to see him closing his eyes and calling up the scenes which have struck him and are engraved on his memory. He can draw, like a map, not only the rooms at St. Helena, where he spent so many months, but a town in Germany or Spain which he has only passed through. And when his memories are coloured by emotion the map becomes a picture which we in turn can see living before us.

Finally, what is perhaps needless to say, and yet what I should reproach myself for not saying, is how much honour these pages do to their honest and modest author. He has such a grateful admiration for his master, such a continuous, indefatigable, and, so to speak, irresistible devotion, that it compels sympathy. With the memory of the great emperor will be associated the memory of the servant, Saint-Denis, the librarian of St. Helena, or, to say with Napoleon, who always used his Mameluke's surname, the faithful Ali.

G. Michaut,
Professor of the Sorbonne.

GEORGE I.

PILLAR OF
HERCULES

Telegraph

Miss Masons

Miss Masons

Mr Leggs

Mr. Robinsons
the Nymphs

10 DIA
PE

11 BALCOMB'S Cott

HUTTS GATE

Telegraph
Guard-House

Marsh Valley of the Nymph Valley of Silence

TOMB
OF
NAPOLEON

12

PROSPEROUS BAY

LONGWOOD

The
Company
Garden

Dr Kaye

Alarm H of

MR B
Secretary

Francis Plain
Camp

BRIARS

Fisher's Valley

Stables

Hospital
Barracks
of the
Chinese

TURKISH PT.

Brew House

Camp
of the 53rd

Kitchen

BARN PT.

Signal House

Rupert's Valley

South Latitude
15° 55'

FLAG-STAFF
BAY

Fort
Rupert

Bank's
Bay

SUGAR LOAF PT.

Long W. from London

THE NEEDLES

MAP
OF THE
ISLAND OF ST. HELENA
DRAWN FOR THE
MEMORIAL DE SAINTE HELENE

By an Engineer formerly of
Napoleon's Cabinet from the information
contained in the work itself and
from particulars
furnished by
Messᵗˢ Marchand, St Denis, Pierron,
and others in Napoleon's Service.

ᴺⁿᴰʸ BAY

MINUTE BAY

W DOVETON
Member of the Council

S W POINT

G DOVETON

R LEACH
Member of the Council

The Old Woman's Valley

Thompson's Valley

PLANTATION House
13

EGG I

BIRD I.

1 BRIARS, NAPOLEON'S RESIDENCE ON HIS
   FIRST LANDING
2 THE LITTLE PAVILION WHICH HE OCCUPIED THERE
3 CASCADE NEAR BRIARS.
4 POINT FROM WHICH NAPOLEON USED TO
   VIEW THE ROADS
5 LONGWOOD FROM BALCOMB'S COTTAGE.
6 FIELD IN WHICH NAPOLEON PLOWED A FURROW
7 HUTT'S GATE, THE GRAND MARSHAL'S FIRST
   HABITATION
8 MR ROBINSON'S (WHERE THE NYMPH
   RESIDED)
9 BOG IN WHICH ALI'S HORSE SANK.
10 DIANA'S PEAK ABOUT 2468 FRENCH OR 2628
   ENGLISH FEET.
11 BALCOMB'S COTTAGE WHERE COUNT LAS
   CASES WAS DETAINED IN CLOSE
   CONFINEMENT FOR SIX WEEKS
12 TOMB OF NAPOLEON.
13 PLANTATION HOUSE, THE GOVERNOR'S RESIDENCE
14 JAMES TOWN
15 ALARM HOUSE

Berkeley Battery

S TOWN

CHAPTER 1

The Tuileries

When Roustan[1] was taken ill during the journey to Holland, the emperor asked the grand equerry whether there was not anyone among his young men who could do Roustan's work—that is to say, accompany His Majesty on horseback, ride on the box of his carriage, take care of his arms and know how to load them, and do the work of a valet. The Duke of Vicenza,[2] after answering in the affirmative, selected Meunier and me, and ordered us to go to M. Lepage's to learn to put guns and pistols together and take them apart, and clean and load them. We both spent a fortnight in passing the apprenticeship which they exacted of us, and then they made me go alone to the establishment of M. Lerebours, the optician, that I might learn to take telescopes apart and put them together again, and to clean the lenses. I soon mastered this little job.

Only one second to Roustan was needed, not two. When the final choice had fallen on me, the grand equerry had me dressed as a

---

1. According to Constant, Roustan, so well known as the Emperor's Mameluke, belonged to a good Georgian family. Carried off at the age of six or seven years and taken to Cairo, he had been brought up among the young slaves who served the Mamelukes while awaiting the time when they should be old enough to enter that warlike body themselves. The Sheik of Cairo, when giving General Bonaparte a magnificent Arabian steed, also gave him Roustan and another Mameluke, Ibrahim, who was afterward attached to Madame Bonaparte's service.

2. Caulaincourt, after serving in the lower ranks in the army, was appointed *aide-de-camp* to Bonaparte, who quickly discovered his talent for diplomacy. He filled various diplomatic posts, among them that of ambassador to Russia, from which he was recalled at his own request in 1811, having probably foreseen the storm which was gathering. He did his best to induce Napoleon to abandon this campaign. There was no one from whom Napoleon heard more bold and useful truths than from him. He often warned the emperor that if he did not renounce his system of shedding blood he would be abandoned by the French and driven from his throne by foreigners.

Mameluke and on the 11th of December, I think, I was presented to the emperor in the Bois de Boulogne, at the Circle of the Acacias. There was a hunt that day. As soon as the emperor had arrived at the rendezvous and had got out of his carriage the duke sent for me, and His Majesty, looking me over from head to foot, asked what I knew. When the grand equerry replied that I worked for four years in a notary's office the emperor said, "Ah! he knows more than I need." I was accepted. The next day I entered the service of the private apartments. The emperor wished me to wait on him at breakfast and dinner. It was with that that I began my work.

During the day I was engaged in helping the valet on duty, or in aiding him to dress the emperor.[3] I was taught to make the bed of the master of Europe, and to arrange everything that he needed, and which he might ask for in his apartment. At breakfast I waited on the emperor directly; at dinner I gave the pages who waited the plates, the knives and forks and the dishes which they had to hand. It did not take me long to master my new employment.

My life was wholly different from that which I had led. Instead of walking about a stable, directing the cleaning of horses, and taking convoys of horses from place to place, I was seated in a chair or on a sofa, talking or sleeping before a good fire, waiting till I was needed. I had no diversion but the pleasure of talking to the valet on duty or looking through the windows (the emperor was at the Tuileries at that time) to see what was going on in the garden. It was a very monotonous life to remain all day in the beautiful rooms. I never went out except to go and dine, toward five o'clock, when the emperor was not in his apartments. The time when I was free was in the evening, when Constant, (see note following), or Roustan had arrived for the emperor's *coucher*. Then I went off duty. I would go and undress in my room, which was in the stables, and go out in civilian's clothes to take a turn around the Palais Royal, after which I would go to bed.

★★★★★★

Note:—Benjamin Constant entered the service of Eugene de Beauharnais as valet and went thence into that of Napoleon. He remained with the latter, whom he accompanied through all his campaigns, until the banishment to Elba. He wrote very

---

3. At the Tuileries the emperor wore the dress of a grenadier, and everywhere else, at the Élysée, at Saint-Cloud, etc., and in his journeys or with the army, he always wore that of a *chasseur à cheval*. In ceremonies, with his military uniform, he would wear the Grand Ribbon of the Legion of Honour on his grenadier's coat.

amusing memoirs in which he proclaims the utmost devotion to his former master, but this is somewhat belied by the fact that he introduced unnecessarily into them many of the scandalous stories which were invented about Napoleon by his enemies, while loudly protesting that he did not believe them. The contrast with Saint-Denis's memoirs in this respect is very striking.

He explains in his book that the reason why he did not accompany Napoleon to Elba was his indignation at being charged with the embezzlement of 100,000 *francs* which he had buried by the emperor's orders, but Saint-Denis does not accept this explanation. Masson says that in 1814, when Maria Louisa was still hesitating whether to abandon Napoleon or remain loyal, Constant and Roustan were brought to shake her still further by stories of the emperor's intrigues and mistresses.

★★★★★★

One becomes accustomed to everything and I became accustomed to what my new employment demanded, which was to do nothing three-quarters of the day. In the morning, toward seven or eight o'clock, I went on duty. There were always two or three people in the ante-chamber, which was the bathroom, who were waiting for the emperor's *lever* to be announced. When the emperor's toilet was finished and he had gone into his study, all those who had been admitted went away, even Constant and Roustan, after which the valet and I went into the bedroom and put everything into place; then we made the bed. After that the cabinetmaker, the wardrobe attendant, and the floor polisher came, each one to do his work under the eye of the valet. As for me, I went into the *salon* of the underofficers to wait till the *lever* [4] was over, when I would go into the *salon* of the high officers, where the emperor took his meals.

When everybody had left His Majesty's room the table layer set the table on a small round table,[5] and arranged a serving table, and

---

4. The emperor adopted many of the forms of the Bourbon court, among them the ceremonious *levers* (risings) and *couchers* (going to bed). The court functionaries were much the same, including the "services." These were the different divisions into which the imperial household was divided. The *service de bouche*, for instance, included everything connected with the table, down to the cooks in the kitchen. This was divided into seven departments, in the *Services du Roi*.

5. The round table was placed a few steps beyond the fireplace, six or seven steps from the wall on that side and about the same distance from the wall at the back of the room, with the armchair facing the window. Behind it was the serving table.

at the appointed hour the *major-domo*, M. Dunant, arrived with the food. What was to be kept hot was placed in chafing-dishes heated by alcohol lamps. When everything was in order the table layer went away. The *prefect* of the palace knocked at the door of the *salon* and notified the emperor that he was served. I stood at the right hand of the armchair which the emperor was to occupy, all three of us waiting till His Majesty should come and sit down.[6]

If the emperor sometimes arrived at once, he occasionally made us wait for him for a long time. A few moments after His Majesty had sat down the empress would appear. She would give her husband a kiss and sit down at his right. It was my duty to place a chair for her. Most frequently when the emperor came out of his room he would be accompanied by some important person—a minister or someone—with whom he would continue his conversation till the empress arrived, for when she was present all serious discussion was banished and playful chat took its place. At dessert the King of Rome was announced and Madame de Montesquiou, followed by an undergoverness, would come in, carrying the young prince in her arms. The emperor would kiss his son and the talk would continue with the empress, Madame de Montesquiou, and the person who was present. When breakfast was over the emperor would take the little king in his arms and go to the window, to show him the people passing and a group of curious men and women who habitually stood under the window during breakfast.

The little scenes of paternal love did not cease till the emperor and empress returned to the *salon*. Madame de Montesquiou and the undergovemess would go back to the little prince's apartments with the woman whose duty it was to rock the cradle, and who had remained in the *salon* of the underofficers during the visit. As for me, I would return to the private apartments, where the valet on duty was.

I was very fond of this duty of serving breakfast, because of the conversations which I heard there. If I had kept a journal I should have had very curious reminiscences of people and things.

One day the emperor took the little king in his arms after his breakfast, as was his custom, caressed him, played some little tricks

---

6. When the emperor went out of his *salon* to go to table he would have his hat on his head or under his left arm. In that case he would hand it to the prefect of the palace, who returned it to him when he went back into his *salon*. He often kept it on his head during the meal. If he happened to take it off he would lay it on the ground, to his right, and pick it up again when he left the table.

Napoleon, Maria Louisa, and the King of Rome

on him, and said to the empress, turning toward her, "Here! kiss your son!" I do not remember now whether the empress kissed the prince, but she replied in a tone almost of repugnance and disgust, "I do not see how anybody can kiss a child." The father was very different; he never stopped kissing and caressing his beloved son. What must Madame de Montesquiou have thought on hearing such language on the part of the empress? What do mothers of families think of it? (This scene occurred at the Tuileries, in the bay window.)

Another day the emperor, after breakfasting and having kissed the little king, was starting to go into the *salon*, when he turned toward the empress,[7] looking at her with that amiable smile which was peculiar to him, and said to her the two following lines:

Je vais donner une heure aux soins de mon empire
Et le reste du jour sera toute à Zaire.[8]

When the little princes, the sons of King Louis, and the princesses, daughters of King Joseph,[9] accompanied by their governesses, came to pay court to the emperor, they kissed their uncle's hand and afterward kissed him. They also kissed the empress. It was usually at breakfast that the emperor received them. He was very fond of asking his nephews and nieces questions as to what they had learned since he had seen them, especially Prince Napoleon and Princess Zénaïde.

M. Denon, who came from time to time to pay court to the emperor, was received at breakfast, like a number of other people. One day he brought two little statuettes, seven or eight inches high; they were seated, and represented the emperor and empress in antique costumes. That of the emperor was almost naked, for it had only a cloak thrown over the shoulders; that of the empress was more fully dressed, but the robe allowed one breast and one leg to be seen. The emperor said:

Whatever idea the artist had in representing me in this way, he has done it too indecently. I do not like that. I much prefer to have people dressed as they are habitually rather than to have

---

7. *Marie-Louise and the Invasion of 1814* by Imbert de Saint-Amand is also published by Leonaur.

8. *I will give an hour to the care of my empire, And all the rest of the day shall belong to Zaire.*

9. The sons of Louis were Napoleon Charles, whom Napoleon loved very dearly and wished to adopt, Napoleon Louis and Louis Napoleon, afterward Napoleon IIL The daughters of Joseph were Zénaïde and Charlotte.

them tricked out in costumes which do not belong to them. Dress the Greeks and Romans as they were in ancient times, but dress the French of our day as they are in the nineteenth century. To do anything else is ridiculous and outlandish.

The statuettes remained on the mantelpiece through the breakfast, and disappeared afterward. This piece of flattery on M. Denon's, (see note following), part did not succeed. It was, I think, without the emperor's knowledge that the statue on the column in the Place Vendôme was cast and put in place. It seems to me that I heard him say so.

★★★★★★

Note:—Dominique Vivaret, Baron Denon, was artist, diplomat, and courtier. When he came to Paris he had few protectors, and he decided to gain another, no less than the highest, Louis XV. He won the king's graces by going and placing himself every day and everywhere on his road as he passed. At last the king noticed this face which stood out from the mass of others. "What do you want?" the king asked him one day. "To see you, Sire." This clever reply opened to Denon the most inaccessible paths.

He was made curator of the collection of engraved precious stones left by the Marquise de Pompadour to Louis XV, and afterward entered diplomacy; but when the Revolution came he emigrated and was condemned to death. He boldly returned, however, and was protected by Marat, who saved his life. He attached himself to the circle of Madame de Beauharnais, and so came to know Napoleon, whom he accompanied to Egypt. There he exhibited the most reckless gallantry while sketching under fire. On his return he published a book, *Expédition d'Egypte*, in which everything was from his hand—text and drawings—and it obtained a prodigious success. Napoleon made him the Director General of the French Museums, It has been said that he designed the column in the Place Vendôme.

It was his character as a courtier which gives point to the story which Saint-Denis tells about the statuettes.

★★★★★★

Monsieur David, the celebrated painter, came on one occasion at breakfast time to pay his court to the emperor. He brought a portrait made by one his pupils. I do not recollect whether it was a painting, a drawing, or an engraving. The emperor was represented in half length, wearing the uniform of a grenadier, with his right hand in his waist-coat. This portrait, which was engraved and which I saw in the shops of dealers in paintings and engravings, was handsome, but it had none of the characteristics of the emperor's face. It was only good-natured.

One day, it was also at breakfast, the emperor received Talma,[10] who had been announced. It was the day after a performance of *Tippoo Saïb*, at which His Majesty had been present. The emperor made a number of critical observations on the piece to the great tragedian, and told him to communicate them to the author. He even gave the plan of a scene, and showed Talma what gesture Tippoo ought to make and what attitude he ought to take as he rose from his throne to go to fight the English, I think. And the better to impress on the actor the action and the language of the sovereign of Mysore, the emperor sat down in a chair and rose from it with a most expressive gesture, full of nobility and resolution, speaking a few words suitable to the situation (1812 or 1813).

At half past six I would leave the private apartments to go to the emperor's dinner. The table was laid, as for breakfast, in the *salon* of the higher officers. The emperor's place was with its back toward the fireplace and the empress was opposite him. The persons on duty were the prefect of the palace, the controller, two grooms of the chamber, the head of the service, two carvers and the butler, a valet for the empress, and I for the emperor. Besides these there were four pages, two for the emperor and two for the empress, who stood at the sides of each chair. They served the emperor and empress directly. The King of Rome, carried by Madame de Montesquiou, accompanied by an undergoverness, came at dessert. When dinner was over the head server went and served coffee in the *salon* where the emperor had already gone. My service at table being finished, I returned to the private apartments.

Every Sunday there was a family dinner. The emperor enjoyed arguing various theological points with Cardinal de Fesch.[11] and it was

---

10. During the period when Napoleon was in partial disgrace, before the "whiff of grapeshot" episode, the great actor Talma formed a friendship with him, and shared his purse with him when the future conqueror of Europe was in actual want. When fortune had changed, he remained the friend of the First Consul and of the emperor.

11. Joseph Fesch, Cardinal Archbishop of Lyons, was half brother of Madame Mère. At the outbreak of the Revolution he was Archdeacon of Ajaccio, and had been helping the Bonaparte family since the death of Luciano Buonaparte, Napoleon's great-uncle, their first protector. But at this time, owing to the persecution of the Church, he retired to private life. In these troubled times (continued next page),

rarely that his arguments did not nonplus His Eminence.

At one family dinner the Queen of Naples, Princess Pauline, Queen Hortense, Madame Mère,[12] Cardinal Fesch, and perhaps some others were at table. The emperor had just received a letter from a prefect who told him that a man named Geoffrin had saved several workmen in a coal mine which had caved in. The letter was given to the Queen of Naples, who could hardly decipher it. The emperor, seeing his sister's embarrassment, said, "Give it to Hortense; she will read it to us." In fact, the Queen of Holland, holding the letter, read it quite fluently. This letter gave the details of all the incidents which had occurred before the rescuers reached the spot where the unfortunate workmen were buried. During the whole dinner they never stopped talking of this occurrence, and everybody praised the courageous self-sacrifice of Geoffrin. The emperor sent this brave man the Cross of Honour.

Once, to my knowledge, the emperor went to dine in the little kiosk at the end of the terrace by the side of the lake. This kiosk, which had just been built, was very pretty and conveniently arranged.

One evening a very fine set of jewels had been placed on the table in the emperor's bedroom, opals surrounded by diamonds. We of the private apartments did not fail to look at it and admire it. It made a very handsome effect, especially in the candlelight. When the emperor came in he saw it and probably sent it to the empress, for the next day it was not in his room.

In each room of the private apartments at the Tuileries there were valets and grooms of the chamber. Among the latter were young men who had received an education. These latter amused themselves by reading in order to pass the time, and to divert themselves from the tedium of staying in a room. It sometimes happened that at the moment when they least expected it the emperor would appear. The book would immediately be laid aside, but sometimes it was forgotten

he threw in his lot with the Bonaparte family, and rose with them. When Napoleon became First Consul, Fesch resumed the cassock and took an important part in the negotiations which led to the Concordat in 1801. In 1802 he was made Archbishop of Lyons and cardinal iu 1803. On the fall of the Empire he retired to Rome.

12. Madame Mère (Madame Mother) was the title generally applied to the Emperor's mother. She was a Corsican of the purest and most primitive type. But she was a woman of great strength of character, who held her family together after her husband's death, by the exercise of the most rigid economy. This economy bred in her the parsimony to which Saint-Denis refers later, and which was a source of mortification to the emperor. It has been suggested, also, that she recognised failing powers in Napoleon long before anyone else, foresaw the collapse of his Empire, and was laying up provision against the future.

on a chair, a camp stool, or some other piece of furniture. If the book fell under the emperor's eyes he would take it and look through it. If it was a good book he would put it back where he found it, but if it was bad he would show a lively displeasure at the fact that the reading of such books in his palace was permitted. I am not sure that he did not throw them into the fire. He did not like to see anything in his apartments which could offend the eyes of anyone at all. Consequently, these young men were careful not to leave their books around, especially those which were immoral.

About the month of February the emperor took up his residence at the Élysée. This dwelling suited him infinitely well. When he wished to talk to anyone he had only to open the door of his *salon* or his cabinet to go and walk in the garden. He could not have this advantage at the Tuileries, where he felt himself a prisoner. In order to be more private, he caused a wooden fence to be built on top of the stone wall on the side of the Hotel Sebastiani. He was very fond of the walk which runs along this wall because it is more quiet.

In the little blue *salon* there was a console on which was a bronze representing the emperor seated beside a table on which was a map which he was studying attentively. In this same room there was a door opening on a back stairway which ran to the first story. The empress used this stair when she came to the emperor's apartment or when she went back to her own.

Almost every morning, when the weather was good, the empress, accompanied by two of her women, would go down into the garden and walk in the alleys near the emperor's apartments. She amused herself picking the violets, of which there were a large number in the borders of the flower beds.

When the good weather arrived the emperor and empress went to stay at Saint-Cloud. Living there did not please me at all. I was condemned to remain all day in a bedroom which was between the *salon* and the study (on the ground floor), and it was only toward ten or eleven o'clock in the evening that I could go away—that is to say, when the emperor and empress came out of the *salon* to go to bed. A staircase which ran up to the empress's apartments ended in the bedroom of which I have spoken. At night the empress passed through this bedroom and went up this staircase to go to her apartments.

When the emperor was in his bedroom, which was upstairs, and the empress came to see him, I had to precede her when she went back to her apartments. There was a long corridor to pass through, at the end of which was a small staircase to descend, and at the bottom was a little door which opened into her private apartments. I was obliged to go thus far to announce her to her women.

They made a trip to the Trianon. There also the emperor had room to walk. His bedroom was on the ground floor, on the right-hand side, opening on a little inside garden.

One day when he wanted to ride in the middle of the day they brought the horses, which waited awhile in front of the steps of the *peristyle* on the side of the large garden. The emperor usually rode without being very careful; this time he was unlucky. The horse reared and wheeled and threw his rider. Happily the fall, which was on the sand, had no bad results. The emperor got up quickly, feeling that he was not hurt, and went for his ride.

After staying there ten days the emperor returned to Saint-Cloud, where he remained for some time. The departure for the campaign in Russia was approaching.

The emperor was at Saint-Cloud when he received General Lefebvre-Desnouettes, who had escaped from England. The emperor was at dinner. He received him rather coldly at first, and reproached him with having sacrificed his *chasseurs* in the affair at Benavente. The general defended himself as well as he could, and then told his experiences from the time he had been made prisoner till his return to France. I think I recollect that it was an English lady who aided his escape. The result of the general's visit was that the emperor restored him to the command of his *chasseurs*. At St. Helena an English officer who had been at Waterloo said, in speaking of the *chasseurs* of the Guard, that they had been the admiration of the English troops who were opposed to them, and he added, "These valiant soldiers were so many lions; they were commanded by General Lefebvre-Desnouettes."

Chapter 2

Moscow

I have no longer any recollection of what happened during the time which preceded the departure for the campaign of Russia. According to some notes which I have found, it was on the 9th of May, 1812, that the emperor started for Mayence with the empress. Roustan was on the box. I had been sent ahead to Metz, where the emperor stopped and passed the night. The next morning he started fairly early. That day I went with him. That night we arrived at Mayence. It was the first ride which I took on the emperor's carriage.

A few days after the emperor and empress arrived at Dresden the Emperor and Empress of Austria arrived there, as well as the King of Prussia and his son, the crown prince. Sénéchal told me that it was in his bedroom that the emperor received the last named. When the king presented his son he begged the emperor to receive him as an *aide-de-camp*. Sénéchal, who was going out at the moment, could not hear the emperor's reply to this proposition.

On the day after the arrival of the Emperor and Empress of Austria, M. de Neipperg,[1] the emperor's *aide-de-camp*, came from his sovereign to inquire after Napoleon's health. The emperor was at breakfast, and I

---

1. Adam Adalbert, Count Neipperg, Austrian field marshal. He was attached to Marie Louise's service after Napoleon went to Elba for the purpose of weaning her from the remaining sentiment of "connubiality" which still attached her to the emperor. This should not have been a difficult job for the man who had detached Bernadotte and Murat from Napoleon, to whom they owed everything, but Neipperg, who seems to have been a sort of Austrian Don Juan, deliberately set out to seduce her, according to Masson. "In six months I shall be her lover, and later I shall be her husband," he is reported to have said. He succeeded in his first design in less than six months, though he could not marry her, which he did morganatically, until after Napoleon's death. He had three children by her, and Chateaubriand characterized him as *"the man who dared to lay his eggs in the eagle's nest."*

think that the empress was present. M. de Neipperg, was a man in full manhood, and rather tall; he spoke French very well and appeared very distinguished. He was blind in one eye, over which he wore a bandage. He wore the uniform of a colonel of Hussars. I do not recollect whether the state dinner in the emperor's apartments was on that day.

When the hour of the state dinner had arrived the emperor left his apartments to go to meet his father-in-law and the empress of Austria. He came back soon afterward, holding the latter by the hand, and led her to the *salon*. The Emperor Francis came immediately after him, followed by most of the guests.

When everything was ready the prefect went to announce to the emperor that the dinner was served. Almost immediately the door of the *salon* opened and the emperor appeared, leading the Empress of Austria, the Emperor of Austria giving his arm to the empress. The latter placed her father on her right and the emperor placed the Empress of Austria on his. The King of Prussia was on Marie Louise's left hand. The King of Saxony, the Grand Duke of Würzburg, and all the other great personages, princes and princesses whose names I do not recollect, occupied the other places at the table. The assemblage was most brilliant and the table magnificently served. The emperor was especially amiable to the Empress of Austria and showed her all sorts of attentions. This princess had very beautiful eyes. I noticed that she did not take off her gloves to eat.

The conversation was sufficiently gay and animated. The emperor gave the guests time to swallow the pieces. The Emperor of Austria and the Grand Duke of Würzburg were not the fattest of the party; the two together, although both were very tall, did not weigh more 'than an ordinary man. Both had sharp faces like an eagle and legs like spindles. The Emperor Francis had a very long queue which reached almost below his waist. Roustan handed the dishes to the emperor's pages and I to the empress's. The Grand Duke of Würzburg, recognising me as having served him as outrider, looked at me several times and smiled like one seeing an old acquaintance again.

During the whole time that the emperor and empress were at Dresden there were nothing but *fêtes*, but then Napoleon was all-powerful and blazing with glory.

Before we arrived at Thorn we had a very sandy stretch of road to pass and the carriage went slowly. The emperor stopped it and got out. He asked for his boots, which I put on him, and he mounted the horse of one of his suite and galloped off, leaving me with the carriage, to get along as I could.

When the emperor left Thorn I accompanied him. His dinner was prepared in a little town through which he was to pass and which was several leagues from Thorn. When we reached the appointed spot the emperor, seeing a number of people around the carriage, got out to receive the notables, and immediately got in again, instead of going to the house where they were expecting him, and gave orders to drive on. The disappointment was probably great among the crowd, the larger number of whom had very likely come from a distance in order to have the pleasure of seeing him and of looking at him for a while. After going a league or a league and a half the emperor stopped before the house of a poor woman. He wanted to dine there.

The suite was large; besides his usual escort there were several general officers, including General Krasienski, colonel of the Polish lancers of the Guard. Everyone got down, and generals and officers hastened to carry the chairs and tables from the poor dwelling into the middle of the courtyard. I laid the table and put on it some bottles of wine. They made a fire, on which they placed a caldron half full of water. They asked the good woman for eggs, and as she had only a few she went to get more from the neighbouring houses. When the eggs were brought they were placed in the caldron, where they cooked after a fashion. This cooking was done two or three steps from where the emperor sat down. The eggs were a long time in cooking; too much water had been put in. Finally, when they were nearly right everyone sat down—that is, the principal individuals, for the others had to stand or sit on anything they could find.

When the meal was finished the emperor sent for the poor people who lived in the house and questioned them, through General Krasienski. Among other things he asked what their fortune was and of what it consisted. The poor woman, looking about her, showed the general the chickens which were scratching here and there, and said, "There is everything that I possess."

"If I gave her some money," said the emperor, "would she be pleased?"

"She could buy the house she lives in and buy more chickens."

The suggestion was too welcome to the woman for her face not to show gratitude and joy. The emperor had a thousand or twelve hundred *francs* in gold given her, and she threw herself at his feet, which she kissed to show her gratitude.

During the journey from Kovno to Wilna I heard of a great storm by which the army lost a large number of horses, which was said to amount to thirty thousand, but so far as I was concerned I saw nothing of it.

After spending a number of days at Wilna the emperor started for Vitebsk. When he arrived there, and as he went into his room to undress, the emperor said to Sénéchal, "We will go no farther. The campaign is finished; we will make our winter quarters here." Alas! why did this not happen?

The emperor learned of the death of General Dorsenne, and it was on the public square of Vitebsk that he named his successor, General Friant. The grenadiers and the *chasseurs* were assembled and in line of battle; the emperor drew his sword, something which he very rarely did, and pronounced in a voice loud but full of emotion, the formula, "Soldiers, you will know, etc." Then he warmly embraced the general, who, on receiving the accolade, could not prevent his tears from being seen. This nomination was too solemn and too rare not to produce a profound effect on those who took part in it as well as on the soldiers. From that day till the Battle of Waterloo this brave general was always seen at the head of the Old Guard.

Half an hour before we came to the first houses of Moscow we reached a height from which we I could see the town and its many belfries, those of the churches and of the Kremlin. These belfries have the form of a column, a pyramidal octagon, and are ornamented at the top with a sort of gilded pear surmounted by a crescent and a cross, fastened by small chains. We perceived a black smoke which rose from a point in the middle of the city; it was a burning house, but it was the only fire that we saw. At that time it might have been eleven or half past. In less than an hour we were in the city. We were surprised at not seeing any inhabitants, except some poor people whom we saw here and there. All the houses seemed deserted. We saw only Polish or French soldiers walking in the streets, and the nearer we got to the Kremlin the more their number increased.

As we turned the corner of a street we met a Pole of the Guard who had several bottles under his arms and in his hands. He offered us one, which we accepted, but as he had nothing to open it with we handed it back to him that he might knock off the neck against a stone. It was champagne. My companions and I poured it into our mouths. We found it very good. We continued on our way to the Kremlin, which we entered shortly afterward by the gate on the west side. A little way from the gate which we had just passed we saw three or four Mamelukes sitting near a wall which was on the left of the road; they were dismounted men, resting. We were not long in arriving at a sort of square which I shall call the Court of the West.

There we got down from the carriage and separated, each one going to join his fellows of the service to which he belonged. As I went to the place where my duty called me I looked about at what was around me. The palace is composed of different buildings making a whole, but of various styles of architecture. At the left of a large building in an Oriental style there is a broad staircase which ends in a paved interior court, extending toward the right, at the end of which was a door communicating with the emperor's apartments. There, in a large room, I found the members of the service to which I belonged.

The emperor, who had passed the night in the suburb named Dorogomilow, had come in during the morning to take possession of the palace of the *tsars*.

When night had come and the emperor had gone to his room each of us thought of going to bed. My companions, who had been the first to come to the Kremlin and had taken possession of it, had provided themselves with everything necessary to make a bed. I had nothing. They had kept nothing for me, but my bed was quickly made. In the corner of the room was a large flag the woollen material of which was thin and very light. I doubled it several times and found myself with a sort of mattress, a line or two in thickness, which I spread on the floor. For a pillow or bolster I had my portmanteau, and my cloak for a covering. I lay down with the hope of passing a good night.

All was calm in the palace of the *tsars*, all was silent, everyone slept deeply, whatever his bed. In the middle of the night I waked up; it may have been midnight or one o'clock. I heard nothing around me but the sound of sleep—breathing in and out. I opened my eyes and rubbed them; I saw the room brightly lighted. I rose and went to one of the windows to see what caused the brightness. I was not a little astonished to see the city on fire, at least the southern and western part, as our windows looked toward the Moskowa and the west. It was horrible! Imagine a city as large as Paris, I should, say, swept by the flames, and that one was on the towers of Notre Dame, watching such a spectacle at night. I waked my companions, telling each of them to open his eyes. In a moment they were all on foot and went to look through the windows at the immense conflagration which was devouring the city.

As it was urgent for the emperor to be informed of what was

happening. Constant decided to go at once into His Majesty's room. The first valet went out for a few minutes, and, as he gave us no order, everybody lay down again, having nothing better to do than to wait for day. We awaited it impatiently.

When day came the fire was as active as we had seen it to be during the night, and continued its ravages, but it did not produce the same effect on the eyes and on the senses, and then one becomes accustomed to everything. It seemed as though, having the emperor near us, we could have nothing to fear.

I was up early. As I like to go out in the air as soon as it is day, I left our room and went to the great eastern staircase, to go and walk in the Kremlin enclosure. The greatest disorder reigned everywhere; there were some detachments bivouacking in the vast empty space before the palace, but there were very few men in each of them. Some soldiers were lying down and others were smoking, crouching or sitting beside a few embers; some were walking about; others, again, were coming with unsteady steps to join their comrades. Empty bottles or flasks scattered about the fires showed clearly enough how the men had passed the night. Every one of the soldiers whom I met had lost something—some one thing, others another; a horseman was looking for his bridle or his saddle or his blanket, another did not know where to find his horse, etc.

Everyone was watching the progress of the fire, which was rapidly spreading to quarters which had thus far appeared to have been forgotten by the destroying element. Orders had been given to save different buildings from destruction, but what could be done in this general conflagration? Nothing! Where were fire engines to be had? They could not find one. Buckets? There were none. Water? How could it be found in this city which we did not know and which had no inhabitants? They let the fire burn on, dragging whatever was useful or necessary out of the houses.

The walls which enclose the Kremlin are high on the outside and built of brick. At intervals there are towers, some of which, those at the angles, are round, and the others square, these last surmounted by a construction somewhat similar to that of the little belfries on village churches, the form of their roofs being a quadrangular pyramid. In the centre is the palace, situated on a plateau which commands all parts of the city. As the palace was built of bricks and hewn stone, it was for that reason in less danger from the fire than the houses in the city, which were of wood for the most part, and, moreover, it was separated on almost every side from any building which was easily inflammable.

What must have been the emperor's thoughts as he contemplated the sublime but sad spectacle of this ocean of fire which surrounded him and which made an island of the Kremlin? His generals, seeing that the governor's house was only a heap of ashes and that the bell tower had. just caught fire, earnestly begged the emperor to abandon both the dwelling of the *tsars* and the old capital of their empire. He yielded finally to their earnest solicitations, but not without many objections. When he had breakfasted he considered the matter again, and at eleven or twelve o'clock he mounted his horse. Accompanied by his suite he left the Kremlin and Moscow and went to Petrowskoi, a *château* a league or two west of the city. The baggage of the household, that of the Guard, and the Guard itself went in the same direction. But as the preparations for leaving had taken some time, we could not set out till rather late in the afternoon.

It was with great difficulty that we succeeded in extricating ourselves from the city, whose streets were obstructed by burning beams, the ruins of fallen houses, and by flames which barred our way. We were continually being obliged to change our direction, and even to retrace our steps, in order not to get caught. The wind blew violently and whirled about, so that it raised a great amount of dust, which blinded men and horses. What created a further obstruction was a multitude of soldiers of all kinds who were carrying away in their arms, on their horses, in country carts, all sorts of provisions and booty which they had been able to pull out of the storehouses, the shops, the dwellings, and the cellars. All this presented a picture of the greatest disorder.

A little before nightfall we happily found ourselves outside of the city. Then we could breathe easily and not smell the bad odour which was exhaled by the burning houses. It was night when we arrived at Petrowskoi. The transport was parked near the *château*, where the emperor had been settled for several hours.

The following day, I think, the emperor, the Guard, the household, the carriages and wagons all returned to take possession of the Kremlin again. The calm of destruction reigned in the city. Everything which had been of wood was in ashes; what was of brick had fallen down in great part; the churches, being entirely of brick, had been spared by the fire. The ruins were still smoking on all sides, and the odour which escaped from them was most intolerable. It was estimated that two-thirds of the houses had been destroyed.

We found the Kremlin and the palace in the same state in which we had left them; probably a guard had been left there. The emperor remained in this residence during all our stay in Moscow, which was prolonged for thirty-nine days. This figure has been preserved in my memory and I do not know why, for ordinarily in time everything ends by being forgotten or by becoming extremely vague. I recollect that one fine morning when we got up I saw snow. There was about an inch of it, but it did not remain on the ground long.

Every morning there was a review or parade of the Old Guard. It was there that I saw how many men the Dutch had lost; their regiment was now composed of only a few companies. The fatigues of the route and the privations which they had undergone had decimated them more than the enemy's fire. These men were stout and full faced. I did not see one of them on the retreat.

Prince Eugene took his meals with the emperor at the Kremlin nearly every day, and the Prince de Neufchâtel [2] always did. At breakfast one day the emperor was talking to Grand-Marshal Duroc and the conversation turned on the most beautiful way to die. His Majesty said that he thought the most beautiful was to fall on the field of battle, struck by a bullet. As for himself, he should not be so happy. "I shall die," he said, "in my bed, like a d―― d――."

The emperor took a ride on horseback every day about two or three o'clock, accompanied by his officers and his escort. He rode about the city or the neighbourhood and only returned in time for dinner.

The emperor had a very large *salon* at the palace of the Kremlin. This room was divided into two parts by a beam or cornice supported by two columns, between which one passed from one part to the other. There was a tripod between the wall and the column on either side. This *salon*, which was probably the throne room of the *tsars*, was ornamented with gilding, but this had become blackened by time. It was the finest room in the palace in point of richness. I recollect having seen that there was a picture of the Madonna in several of the rooms in the left-hand corner at the end opposite the entrance, and I have heard it said that when a Russian, even the emperor, came into the room, the first thing that he did was to bow to the Madonna.

The windows of the bedroom opened on the Moskowa. It was a

2. Louis Alexandre Berthier, Prince of Wagram, Prince of Neufchâtel, Marshal of France.

large room, an oblong square, to the left of that which was occupied by the *valets de chambre*, from which it was separated only by a simple partition. In the left-hand corner, made by the partition and the side opposite the windows, there was a little cylindrical desk placed diagonally across the corner which was, I think, occupied by the fireplace. This desk had three screens of green silk—one pulled out to the right, another to the left, and the third upward.

The emperor would sit at this desk either to read or to write. This piece of furniture has stuck in my memory for this reason: the emperor, in his campaigns and even in his pleasure journeys, had a certain number of cases of books which were placed during the whole time of his stay either in his cabinet or in his bedroom. When he was bored or had nothing to do he would take a volume, and when he had finished with it would lay it on the piece of furniture which was nearest to him. Well, during nearly the whole time that he remained in the Kremlin the *History of Charles XII*, by Voltaire, a pretty little volume in 18mo, bound in morocco with gilt edges, remained constantly on this desk. The emperor was far from believing at that time that his history would have so much analogy with that of the King of Sweden.

A company of French actors (there were, I think, ten or a dozen of them) which was at Moscow had remained in the city after the Russians left. During the fire these poor people, most of whom had lost their luggage and had no means of existence, had come to the palace to ask for help. There were two women among them. When the Emperor was informed of their presence and their unfortunate position, he gave orders for them to be taken care of. From then on they had food. As from time to time there was a gathering or a *soirée* in the emperor's apartments at which the officers of the household and the principal officers of the Guard were present, the actors were admitted two or three times to His Majesty's *salon*. When the French evacuated Moscow these unfortunate people had nothing better to do than to go with us, and they marched with the baggage of the household. Two poor women had much suffering to undergo.

One of them, already advanced in years, was full of strength and energy, but the other, still young was delicate and affected. One day during the retreat I saw the former warming herself at a little bivouac of a few sailors of the Guard. The cold was then beginning to make itself felt. These men, who came from the south of France and were already badly demoralised, were complaining of the terrible position in which they found themselves. They laid all their ills at the door of the emperor, who had brought them into this infernal country; they manifested their anger at the emperor by the most virulent expressions. This woman was trying to revive their courage, and said to them, among other things:

> You complain of the emperor, but do you not believe that he has as much to suffer as you, and that he is not sorely afflicted by not being able to succour so many brave men who are here, like you, who surround him and follow him? Do you not see him constantly in the midst of you, marching on foot and sharing your fatigues? Show more courage; have more energy; stand up against all the rigors of adversity. Remember that you are soldiers and Frenchmen.
>
> And I, a poor woman, I who am already old, I who have lost everything and am now deprived of the barest necessaries, I who have no future, what is there that I have not to complain of? And yet in spite of my sufferings, which are renewed every hour of the day, I bear my ills with resignation and courage. What does weakness do but make us more miserable than we are? Let us hope then. Every day which passes brings us nearer to that good country which we shall reach, no doubt; but we need courage, perseverance. When one is young, as you are, you ought to face and bear everything; in short, you ought to live on hope.

When they left Moscow the young actress, who had the good fortune to save some of her property from the fire, had put it in a small carriage drawn by young Cossack horses.[3] She travelled sometimes on foot, sometimes on horseback, with the transport of the household. One day, going down a hill, some cannon shots were heard on our left and balls flew across the road, one of which, striking the carriage, broke it in such a way that it was quite useless. The poor woman, who at that moment was happily on foot, had to abandon her carriage and load her baggage as well as she could in the Household baggage wagons. A few days later I learned that she had lost all or the greater part of her property. I do not remember to have seen the unfortunate actresses or their companions either at Smolensk or at Wilna. Like many others, they probably perished or were made prisoners.

---

3. The word which Saint-Denis uses, "*cognats*," is quite unknown to the French language, and appears to have been used only by the soldiers of the Grand Army to designate the small horses ridden by the Cossack cavalry.

CHAPTER 3

The Retreat from Russia

During the stay of the emperor in the Kremlin there had been some conferences to begin negotiations with the enemy; every day they had been waiting for a favourable reply. But when one reflects a little, what could be hoped from an enemy who had delivered such a city as Moscow to the flames? What had that enemy to lose now? The sequel proved that they only wished to beguile the emperor and fill him with confidence until they should have reorganised and collected their army, to let us exhaust ours, to wear ourselves out in this city which was only a heap of ashes, or in cantonments where there was nothing to eat either for men or for horses, and finally to keep us in Russia as long as possible in order that winter, which was advancing with great strides, should surprise us during our retreat while still far from any help. This policy was, unfortunately, successful for the Russians, who made us pay very dearly for the glory which we had had in making the conquest of their holy city.

Time passed rapidly and no satisfactory reply arrived at imperial headquarters. At Moscow everybody appeared to feel in the most perfect security, when we learned that the Russians had suddenly attacked the French advanced posts. This unexpected news created a little anxiety.

The emperor promptly set about replying to this aggression. The day for departure was set and orders were given to the army to march toward the south. We abandoned Moscow and its ruins on October 19th, I think.

From that time the clear days disappeared and the nights began to grow longer. The sun was frequently hidden and the horizon grew blacker and blacker. Men's faces became serious; they seemed to have a presentiment of a disastrous future and to dread it.

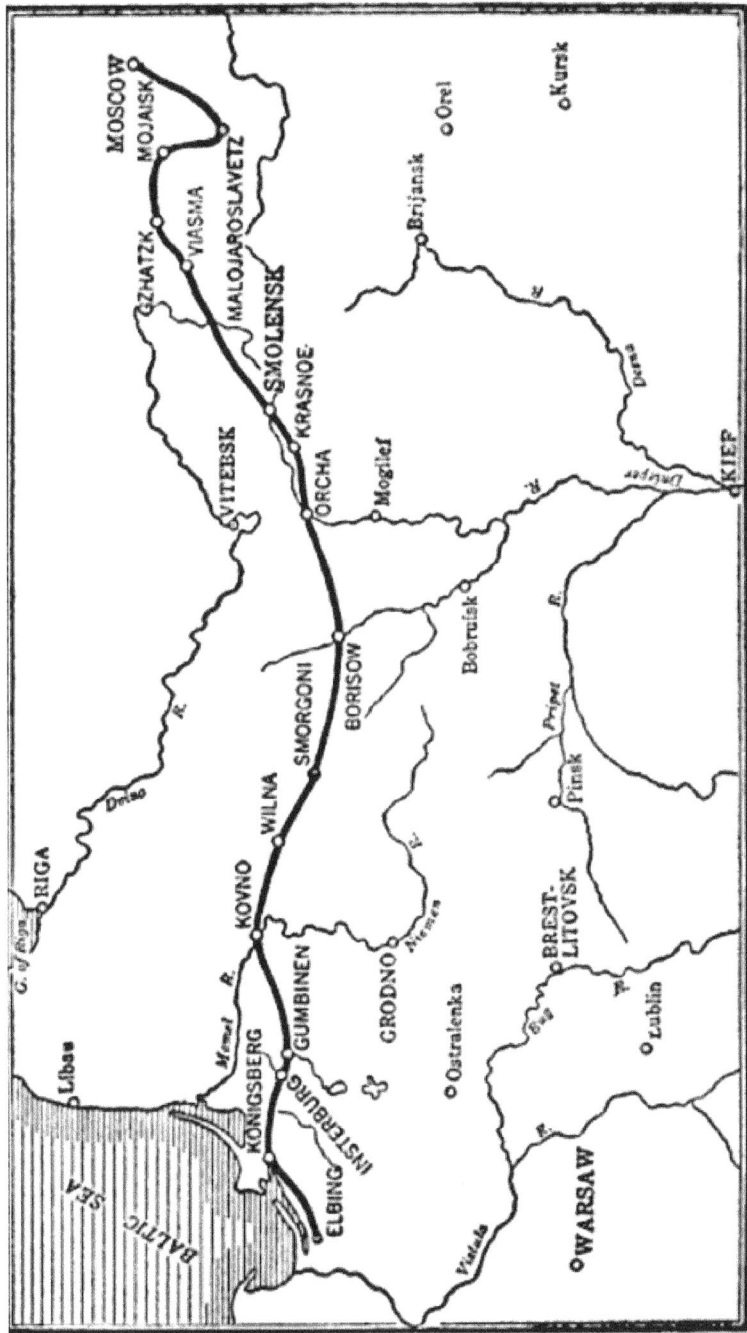

Line of Napoleon's retreat from Moscow

At Smolensk the cold was already somewhat severe. The disorganisation in the army began to show itself in a frightful manner. The size of the Guard was greatly diminished. In this same town, on the journey out, it was numerous and still possessed all its beauty, but then it had not met with perceptible losses. On the way back, what a difference!

After resting two or three days, the emperor and all the French in Smolensk marched on again. The cold was already sharp, the weather overcast, the days very short. As soon as we had left the town the rear guard blew up a great quantity of caissons which were parked outside of the walls on the right of the gate as we went out. We saw and heard the successive explosions. We had no horses with which to bring them away. There was something lugubrious about these explosions which made us feel that great disasters were coming. Every day we had less food and every day we abandoned cannon, caissons, and baggage. The corpses of men and horses began to mark the course of the road. The more we advanced the colder it grew. We marched slowly. After a number of days of fairly steady frost we had a thaw. More than once we saw the emperor, wearing his *pelisse*, with a stick in his hand, marching on foot with his staff.

We were going toward Orcha. To reach this town, where the emperor had arrived, it was necessary to march beside the Dnieper for a long distance. We could see the city on the right, and there was a long circuit to be made before we reached it. I saw soldiers of the line in considerable numbers who thought they would shorten the journey by going across the ice, which did not seem strong in many places. Some of these imprudent men probably perished. In spite of the fact that some of the generals forbade it, and the danger there was of drowning, when once the path was marked out other infantrymen were not afraid to take the risk, following the tracks of those who had preceded them.

Then we marched toward Borisow. We arrived there early and remained part of the day. Everyone believed that it was at Borisow that the passage of the Beresina was to be made. The day was far advanced when we received the order to go still further. During the evening, as we went along, we always heard a somewhat heavy cannonade. We were sent and thoughtful, hardly exchanging a word with a companion on our march. It was dark night and pretty late when we arrived at a hamlet composed of a few wooden cabins of the most wretched appearance, in one of which the emperor was lodged. It was at this spot that we were to pass the Beresina, beside which we had been marching since we left Borisow. The sound of the cannon had ceased with the day. We passed the night like many others—that is to say, badly enough. We did not sleep any more; we were eager for the morrow, in order to set out again.

The next day, the 3rd of December, I think, as soon as it was day, the order was given to pass the bridge. This bridge, which was on trestles, and the roadway of which was not more than a foot above the water, did not seem to me very strong, especially as it had to resist a great quantity of cakes of ice which the river was bringing down pretty rapidly. While several generals, sword in hand, were holding back the multitude who were pressing forward at the approaches to the bridge, the grand equerry, who had charge of policing the crossing, sent across in an orderly manner and successively the transport of the emperor's household and the artillery, directing the drivers to go slowly and at some distance apart in order not to strain the bridge. At the same time he made the grenadiers and *chasseurs* of the Old Guard march on either side of the vehicles. I was one of the first who went over. During the crossing I thought more than once that the bridge would break down under the weight of the cannon and the baggage wagons, but no accident happened. When once I was across I did not look behind me, too happy to have crossed this bridge, where so many others left their lives. I heard it said later that two or three other bridges had been thrown across. As for me, I saw only the one over which I passed.

Then we went through a swampy wood which lay along the left bank of the river. As the ground was frozen only a few inches deep, the track which we followed soon became nothing more than a long slough which we were obliged to cover with the branches of trees laid crosswise, so that the wheels of the cannon and the wagons might not sink in too deeply. We got out of this place with a good deal of trouble; the poor horses fell at every step, tripped as they were every moment by the branches on which they were walking. When we had passed this the road became a little firmer. We found three little bridges painted gray, of elegant construction, having on each side railings with turned pales. These bridges were a quarter of an hour from one another, and thrown over broad and deep brooks with swampy banks. One cannot understand how the Russians forgot to destroy these bridges; the disorder, which had already become great in the army, would have increased, for to repair or rebuild them would have retarded our march, and it is possible that if we had been attacked in this position a large part of the materiel which we still had would have been lost. It was at the passage of these bridges that I saw Marshal Lefebvre,[4] with a stick in his hand, strike several grenadiers in order to make them march faster and keep their ranks. Poor fellows! they were worn out.

The soldiers had been miserable for a long time, and it is only of the Old Guard that I am speaking. When they went to Moscow they had suffered great privations, but still they had something. When they came back they had to endure still greater wretchedness; they could find nothing. Fatigue, cold, and, still more, the lack of food deprived them of all courage, all energy. They retained scarcely the sentiment of self-preservation. They went on and on as long as they could and only stopped when their strength and their spirit failed. So every day their numbers grew less in an extremely perceptible manner, and we had not yet reached the end of the story.

I recollect that one day when we had arrived at the halting place, which was a convent in which the emperor was lodged, the grand marshal or the grand equerry commanded a number of carriages and baggage wagons belonging to the household to be burned. They also burned a number of boxes of books from His Majesty's library. Several people present would have liked to save a few volumes from the fire, but the order was that the cases should be delivered to the flames with their contents. It was in the court of the convent that this execution took place.

At the end of one of the following days the emperor found himself lodged in a little *château* which was furnished comfortably enough. There were divans around the room, which served as a *salon*. It was here that M. Gourgaud came to inform the emperor of the resurrection of Marshal Ney. This piece of news gave so great pleasure to the emperor that he showed an inexpressible joy throughout the whole evening. M. Gourgaud,[5] who was only a *chef d'escadron*, was made a colonel.

One evening, when the emperor was at dinner, he sent for Mar-

---

4. Pierre François Joseph Lefebvre, Duke of Dantzig, was an Alsatian and a man of the people. Although of great distinction in military affairs, he never succeeded in freeing himself of the plain and rustic manner of speech which he had originally. In this he was not assisted by his wife, who had been a laundress, and who was known in imperial circles as "Madame Sans Gêne." Under this title she was represented in a delightful comedy by Sardou.

5. Gen. Gaspard Gourgaud entered the artillery and served with credit in the campaigns of 1803 and 1805. For his services in the Russian campaign he was created a baron and made chief ordnance officer. He went to St. Helena with Napoleon, but his jealous disposition kept him in continual hot water with Las Cases and Montholon, which made his life so unhappy that he returned to France.

shal Bessières,[6] whom he had ordered to find out the condition of his Guard. "Well, Bessières, have my soldiers everything that they need? Are they comfortable?"

"Very comfortable, Sire," replied the marshal. "The spit is turning at a number of fires; there are chickens and legs of mutton, etc." If the marshal had looked with both eyes he would have found that these poor devils had little to eat. Most of them had heavy colds, all were very weary, and their number had greatly decreased. Everyone was silent. Then and for a long time before gayety had been banished from the bivouacs. The marshal was a Gascon and a courtier.

After a long and exhausting day the order was given for the transport of the household to camp in a spot which was away from any dwelling and even from any wood. A surprise was feared. In order not to attract the attention of hostile prowlers not a single fire was allowed to be made in the bivouac. Many people passed the night in their carriages, others slept under them, and some passed it partly in walking to keep themselves warm and partly lying down under a baggage wagon. This was the way in which I waited for the morrow. It was perhaps the worst night that I had passed in the whole course of the campaign.

Before Smolensk the army had already had a great deal to suffer, but after that town the suffering was considerably increased. We longed for Wilna; it seemed as though there our troubles must end. Although every day there remained a smaller distance to travel, it seemed as though we did not advance at all. We were cold, we were hungry, marching was painful. At each bivouac the number of men, of horses, of cannon, of caissons and of wagons was less than at the one before. It was thus that we reached Smorgoni.

Smorgoni was not a town, but a poor little village competed of the house of the lord of the manor, a sort of *château* which resembled a little Greek pagan temple, like those of which there are so many in Russia, and of a few peasants' huts. Before the *château* was a little square in which the transport of the Household was parked. This village must have been very pretty in summer, but in the winter there was nothing very attractive about it.

The emperor was lodged in the lord's house, as usual. When the bivouacs were established people began to whisper to one another; some unwonted arrangement was the object of the conversation of certain members of the household. I learned as a secret that the emperor was preparing to start for France, leaving the command of the

---

6. Jean Baptiste Bessières, Duke of Istria, Marshal of France.

army to the King of Naples.[7]

Toward eight or nine o'clock two travelling carriages drove up to the front steps of the *château* and after half an hour's waiting the emperor appeared with some other people. He got into the carriage with the Duke of Vicenza; Roustan and somebody else were on the box. The Grand Marshal [8] and two or three other superior officers got into the second, and the two carriages, lighted by their lanterns, immediately set out from the village. Everyone was saddened by this departure, but it was not approved of by the majority till after much reflection. [9]

When the emperor was no longer present it seemed as though everybody was left to himself. There was nothing to do but to go with the stream and to live as pleased Providence.

At Wilna I went to the house or palace where the emperor had lived. The headquarters of the King of Naples were installed in it. As soon as I had left my horse in the hands of a groom and had had my portmanteau carried to the room which was already occupied by my comrades of the service of the private apartments, I went to the kitchen, where I found a good fire to warm me, and bread, wine, and meat to satisfy my hunger. I refreshed myself thoroughly, of which I stood in great need. I went back to our common room to wash and to rest.

There had remained at Wilna a complete *service de bouche* and a number of baggage wagons containing the state tents and other luxuries which it had not been thought wise to carry further, as the baggage which they had already taken was considerable in quantity. There were also many troops in the city who were composed of different depots of the Guard, both foot and mounted, of the line and even of foreign soldiers, of the Confederation of the Rhine. It seemed that with this re-enforcement, weak as it was, we might count on some

---

7. Joachim Murat, King of Naples, husband of Napoleon's sister Caroline.
8. Gérard Christophe Michel Duroc, Duke of Friuli, Marshal of France and Grand Marshal of the Palace.
9. It is sometimes said that the reason for Napoleon's sudden return from Russia and his abandonment of his army was the discovery of the Malet Conspiracy. This was a plot to overthrow the dynasty by proclaiming the death of Napoleon before Moscow. Malet, a former officer, who conceived the scheme, succeeded, by means of a forged decree of the Senate, in getting possession of the persons of the Minister of Police and the Prefect of Police, and his accomplices were in possession of the Hotel de Ville, the Place Vendôme, the most important military posts, as well as the bank, the treasury, and the principal public offices. Before the scheme could be carried any further Malet and his principal supporters were arrested and shot.

days of rest which would permit the arriving army to be organised as it came, but that was not to be the case.

After dinner we went to bed. Being in a warm room, we had made ourselves comfortable, and so we spent an excellent night, although we had very bad beds, for we had only the bare floor, and I think a sort of mattress an inch or two in thickness. The next day we indulged in being lazy all the morning. We thought ourselves in the most perfect security. The day passed quietly and nothing made us think that the coming night might not be still better than the night before.

During the afternoon, not far from nightfall, at the moment when we least expected it, a rumour spread that the order had been given to prepare to leave, and shortly afterward we heard cannon fire, which made it clear that the enemy was not far from Wilna. This news filled us with consternation; we should have to start off again and spend the night as it might please heaven. People came, went, ran on every side. Everything was in motion both in the palace courtyard and in the city. Horses were saddled and bridled, the carriages hitched up, the palace guard had their knapsacks on their backs. We were all ready to start. We waited for a final order, which was a long time in coming. Finally it was given. We started, we reached the street, and we filed by; artillery, caissons and cannon, wagons of all sorts, and soldiers on foot and mounted were also on the march.

The streets which led to the gate by which we were to go out were crowded. The cannon still rumbled, and were intermixed with discharges of musketry. We advanced but slowly, with soldiers scattered through the city vainly looking for their regiments. Except for some platoons of grenadiers and *chasseurs* of the Guard and some slender scratch squadrons formed of officers of different cavalry corps, the rest were pell-mell and marched as they pleased, following the current. One saw a good number of men, but no army any longer. Many soldiers, worn out with fatigue, preferred to stay in the houses by the fire rather than go with their comrades. We had some difficulty in reaching the gate, but passed through it easily enough.

It was freezing hard, and the thermometer marked, I think, twenty-four degrees below zero. The road was extremely bad; the snow was so beaten by the feet of the travellers and hardened by the cold that it was transformed into ice. But we went on, though slowly. We reached the foot of the mountain. Here the road grows narrower and is not more than eight or nine feet broad and describes a hollow curve; the two sides are steep. As the horses of the first wagons, cannon, and caissons could not keep their feet, they fell at the first attempt to pull. When one got up the other fell; as the first and second wagons of the convoy stopped, all the others were prevented from advancing. Nobody could succeed in moving ahead a few yards. Men on foot, men on horseback, did the best they could to get out of the press, which grew worse from moment to moment and completely obstructed the entrance to the gorge. Some went to the right, some to the left, some passed through the wagons. I was one of the latter. When I reached the top of the mountain I let my horse have time to breathe, after which I went on.

I learned during the course of the evening, from the conversation of my friends, something of what had happened in the city and at the foot of the mountain. The Cossacks had entered the city before the soldiers had had time to evacuate it. The confusion, which had already been great before we started, had become much greater, consequently the enemy had nothing to do but to kill and make prisoners. A large number of soldiers who had suffered severely during the retreat, and others who were tired out, others again who had been wounded or had their feet frozen, unwilling to leave their beds or the fires by which they sat, had all been made prisoners or massacred. Soon afterward another party of Cossacks had come to make an attack on all the cannon, caissons, and baggage wagons, which had just left the city in long files or were crowded together at the foot of the mountain, increasing the disorder, which was already great before the enemy arrived. The baggage wagons had been opened and French and Russians had taken to pillaging them. One can imagine such a spectacle, lighted only by scattering musket shots and the whiteness of the snow.

The Russians must have seen the next morning, from what they had captured before and what they had just taken, how much of the French army must remain in men, horses, cannon, caissons, and baggage. They must have found in the wagons belonging to the emperor's household tents, harnesses, saddles, silverware, coined money, etc., etc., not only what had been left at Wilna during the campaign, but also what had been saved during the retreat. They must have found the whole or a part of the little which had been taken from them at Moscow and in the other cities, and probably their Cross of Ivan also, unless it had been thrown into some river or lake. Our losses in this affair of Wilna and of the mountain were immense, since everything was lost.

Although the army had suffered heavy losses since its departure from Moscow in men, horses, and materiel, there still remained, when we entered Wilna, a good nucleus, but in that city and at the foot of the mountain the pitiful but very precious fragments of our large and valiant army were annihilated. Many men succeeded in escaping, but how many stayed there!

After Wilna we had to pass over a long dike which crossed a great swamp. It was so cold that the greater number of the soldiers who had formed part of the detachments gathered at Wilna remained on the road, stricken by the cold. These men, who had not had to suffer like those who had come back from Moscow, would fall over forward, kick a little, and die. I have seen those who were nearest to them take off their greatcoats or their shoes, and they did not neglect to feel for their money belts. Everybody would step aside, going out of his way no more than not to walk on the dead or dying man, for fear of falling down himself. A perfect indifference, an extreme egotism, was in all hearts. Eh! what could they have done? To stop to help a poor devil meant losing time, getting oneself frozen. For woe to him who stayed still for a moment; he was quickly overcome. One had to keep moving all the time. Those who had made the campaign, being more accustomed to a cold temperature, stood it much better than the newcomers.

At one of our last halting places we were quartered in a good-sized farm. This farm, which was constructed of stone, had the appearance of a ruined castle. What was left of the foot guard, the grenadiers, and *chasseurs* had taken possession of the courtyards and had collected all the straw found in the barns, to make beds for themselves around the fires. The next day, when it was time to go, I saw grenadiers who had not the courage to rise in order to save themselves from the fire which was spreading to the straw on which they were lying. The laziness, or, to speak more truthfully, the weakness and exhaustion, were such that the greater part of these men had scarcely the strength to put their knapsacks on their shoulders and to take up their guns. How many arms must the enemy have found between Moscow and the Niemen! For all the soldiers, except a very small number, had thrown away their arms or had left them in their bivouacs.

During the whole day which preceded our arrival at Kovno the cold was excessively bitter. This showed in the marching column, which grew thinner as we advanced. Anyone who stopped, not having the strength to march, was a lost man, for the cold seized him quickly. How many soldiers were left on that road! I almost always went on foot, and only mounted my horse to rest a little, but I dismounted as soon as I felt my feet and hands getting numb. In spite of the pains I took to protect myself I had two fingers frozen—the first and middle fingers of my left hand.

At the entrance to Kovno there was no longer the compact crowd which I had seen at Wilna; there was only a group of two or three hundred individuals, so that we did not have long to wait for our turn to go in. All of us who belonged to the Household went to the place where the emperor had lived after the passage of the Niemen. We dined well and that night we slept very quietly. At last we were going to be outside of that Russia, that terrible country, which had just cut down pitilessly the finest army of modern times.

The next day, as soon as it was light, we left the city and went to the bridge, which was not far off, and crossed it. The Niemen was entirely frozen. Just as we crossed the bridge a detachment of some fifteen Poles of the Guard and a few foot soldiers also crossed it. They were all that I saw. After crossing the Niemen the Poles went to the left and we to the right, following some scattering soldiers who were a little way ahead of us. It was luck that guided us. At the end of the day we stopped at a sort of combination farm and country house occupied by the King of Naples. We spent the night there.

In this *château*-farm there was a lady who was probably the baroness of the place. She offered the French all the food that she had. I recollect that there we had extremely poor food; we ate meat almost without bread, for that, which was a combination of oats, bran, straw, and sand, did not permit our teeth to chew it. This stuff was called horse bread. Thank God! we had only a few days to pass before finding ourselves beyond this misery. The cold had become more endurable, although it was still severe.

The next day we stopped at Gumbinnen. I got half of a little round loaf of bread, I don't remember how, but it was made of so dense a dough and was frozen so hard that it took me more than an hour to gnaw it.

The next day we stopped at Insterburg. I had gone halfway when my horse stopped short and would not go any farther, in spite of all that I could do. It was nothing for me to walk, but how was I to carry my portmanteau, which was heavy and very unwieldy? I was looking for some way when a wounded soldier came by, mounted on a small Cossack horse. I offered to give him my horse's equipment if he would carry my portmanteau behind him to the town where we were going. The proposition was accepted. I saddled and bridled the little horse, and when the portmanteau was in place we started. I regretfully left my poor horse, La Panachée, to her sad fate. A few minutes earlier I had seen a Polish officer kill his horse, which could go no further, like mine.

After we had gone some five or six leagues, I on foot and my obliging soldier on his mount, we reached Insterburg. I stopped in an inn, where I found several members of the household and the *bouche*. I took my portmanteau and thanked my soldier, to whom, I think, I gave some money as a weak evidence of my gratitude.

A service of sleighs had been organised at Insterburg by the Inspector of Posts to carry the members of the emperor's household. That evening after supper I got into one of these sleighs. We set out for Konigsberg. During the night, when we arrived at the first relay, we could not get horses. Those which had been meant for us had escaped with their drivers. In our perplexity we felt obliged to compel the peasant who had brought us to double the length of his journey. We ordered him to feed his horses, and watched him for fear that he might escape from us, but to make it easier for him and to give him courage we promised him money, giving him some on account. The poor devil ended by yielding graciously to necessity. After he had drunk and eaten and had fed his horses he hitched up again and we went on.

It was about seven o'clock in the evening when we arrived at Elbing. We got out at the posthouse. This building was at the corner of a street, and one face, on which the entrance was, was on the principal street, and the other looked on a little street to the right of the building. There were three of four steps to go up before coming to the landing at the entrance door. When the sleigh stopped a man was coming out of the house. Thinking that he was one of the servants of the establishment, I gave him my portmanteau and got down, having my sabre under my arm. As the man went up the steps he fell on his knees, for there was a little ice on them. I passed ahead of him to accompany my companions, who had already entered the door, instead of waiting till he rose. I thought he was with me and would put my portmanteau with the other luggage, and without being concerned I went with my comrades into a room which had been pointed out to us, and we sat down at a table which was a little way from the door, behind which our baggage was piled up.

We asked for something to eat and they served us quickly. Beyond the room where we were there was another in which were a considerable number of people who talked very loudly, laughed, and smoked; joy was painted on every face and was revealed by a boisterous gayety. As neither my companions nor I knew a word of German, except enough to ask for what we needed, this joy, this gayety, this movement, this uproar, the cause of which we could not understand, was very disagreeable to us, and annoyed us to such an extent that we remained silent throughout the whole meal, saying what we had to say to one another in a low voice and cautiously. It was probable that they already knew the results of the campaign and, consequently, the annihilation of the French army. We ate heartily of what they served us.

It was about nine o'clock when we had finished dinner, and then each one thought of his things, to get ready to start. I had no trouble in finding my sabre, which was beside me; my companions found their baggage and portmanteaus, but it was impossible to find mine. The man who had carried it, instead of bringing it into the room where we were, had carried it off. It was useless to ask the postmaster, the waiters, the maids; no one had seen it. I looked, they looked again in all the corners of the passage and the room, but in vain. Much as I regretted it, I had to say goodbye to it. Poor portmanteau! I still had in it one white shirt from Paris which I valued especially, my shawls, all my linen, and many other things which I should greatly have liked to bring back; but it was lost beyond hope.

What I most regretted, and what I still regret, is a little notebook containing the itinerary of all my journeys and a portfolio in which there were letters and various other papers. I felt this loss very deeply. However, I had to be resigned to it. From that time I was free from all cares, but more than once I have cursed the village of Elbing, where they robbed me of my portmanteau which I had had so much trouble in saving in the different affrays that I had been in and in keeping safe during the whole retreat since Moscow. And still more I cursed my negligence and my lack of watchfulness. The sleigh was waiting; I had to go.

I arrived in Paris in the evening, and the next day I went to the Tuileries. I found my comrades in the private apartments. At breakfast time I went to the *salon* of the upper officers and waited on the breakfast. Finding myself at the palace, it seemed to me that the retreat from Russia had been only a dream. The bad news of our disasters was already circulating in Paris, but the details were very imperfectly known, and few people knew about this last defeat at Wilna. Many of my acquaintances, knowing that I had just arrived, overwhelmed me with questions, to which I had to reply to satisfy their curiosity.

Chapter 4

1813

A few weeks after my return (it was about the beginning of the second fortnight of January) the emperor went to Gros Bois for a hunt, to the Prince of Neufchâtel's. I had been sent ahead with an outfit in case His Majesty wanted anything or wished to change his clothes. Before the hunt there was a breakfast to which a number of people had been invited. I served the emperor. Contrary to his usual habit, he drank three quarters of his bottle of wine. As soon as breakfast was over I went up to the bedroom which had been prepared for him and where I had put his things in order to be able to give him anything that he might ask for. I had hardly entered the room when I saw him appear, followed by Grand Marshal Duroc. He asked me for paper, pens, and ink. When I had brought these things the grand marshal sat down at a table and wrote, from the emperor's dictation, a service order for a trip to Fontainebleau. I was in the room, not knowing whether I ought to go or stay. I decided to do the latter, drawing back. I heard the whole order dictated. When it was finished the grand marshal said to me:

> You have heard the order. Get into a carriage at once and say, when you arrive, that everything must be put in order for the emperor and empress, who will follow you very soon.

I packed up without losing any time, went and got my carriage, and started. When I got to the courtyard of the *château* I presented the grand marshal's order. Everybody was busy in a minute, trying to get everything in order for the arrival of the emperor and empress. There were carpets to be put down in the rooms, fires to be built in the fireplaces, etc. The bedroom was the first in order, and I arranged my little service so as to be ready on the arrival of His Majesty. Everything was prepared, so far as I was concerned, when I heard the rolling of the carriages and the noise of the horses. The workmen who had not finished their work had to postpone what remained to be done till the next day.

At the same time that I had left Gros Bois orders had been sent to Paris for the different services to go to Fontainebleau, where they arrived successively during the evening.

As soon as the emperor and empress had got out of their carriage they went to pay a visit to the Pope, a visit which the Pope returned immediately. The next morning the emperor had breakfast served in a room on the ground floor. As the upholsterers had not finished in this room, they were putting down the carpet when the emperor came in for breakfast. He seemed in a bad humour, probably annoyed at finding workmen in this apartment. He sent for the grand marshal, whom he reproved pretty sharply for the lack of diligence which had been shown in the execution of his orders. The latter, to justify himself, pleaded the short time which they had had in which to get everything ready.

When he was at breakfast the emperor called in the undergovernor of the *château*. He was a former captain of the *gendarmerie d'élite,* whom I had seen at Rio Seco. "Well, and the Holy Father?" The undergovernor gave an account of various things concerning the Pope's life, and of everything that was said by those about him. It was a long and very interesting report; unfortunately, my memory has not been able to preserve the details.

There was a small room between the emperor's bedroom and the salon. A *valet de chambre* remained in this, near the door of the large bedroom, to open the door of the cabinet or the *salon* for the emperor. I was on duty in this room during the discussions which took place on the occasion of the Concordat.[1] The discussions were very animated. The emperor spoke vigorously, half in French and half in Italian, and with an abrupt articulation which indicated impatience. I could not catch any phrase; the only word which I heard distinctly was *Santo Padre*, which the emperor repeated frequently in interrupting the long arguments which the Pope made to defend his interests. The voice of His Holiness was so low that I could hardly hear it. The discussions were animated and lasted a long time. From time to time M. Joanne, the stenographic secretary, would come out of the room and go down

---

1. In this Concordat, which was extorted from Pius VII at Fontainebleau, the Pope, among other things, abdicated his temporal sovereignty in Italy.

to his office, from which he would return almost immediately, I do not know whether it was that day that the Concordat was signed, and whether it was that day, also, that the banquet was to be.

The table was set for dinner as usual in a room which the emperor used as a dining room, and which was at the end of the *salons* and gallery of Francis I, but with this difference, that the table was much larger and more magnificently decorated. It was there that the great banquet, to which the Pope had been invited, was to take place. At the appointed hour the table was laid, the dinner was served, the servants were in their places, but the Pope, for whom they were waiting, did not appear. The emperor and empress were in the *salon*. A quarter of an hour, half an hour, passed in this way without the Pope's appearing. Finally the emperor, annoyed by such a delay, came out of the *salon* with the empress and took his place at the table. The persons who had been invited took theirs. The dinner was silent, few words were exchanged. The deepest displeasure was painted on the emperor's features. What could have prevented the Pope from coming? In the eyes of everybody it was a very great piece of impoliteness, a failure to observe the most ordinary decencies.

I learned that the Pope, who had a *service de bouche* from the imperial household, ate only boiled eggs. He was probably afraid that he would be poisoned. This was not the case with the prelates who composed his court; these gentlemen did justice to the good cooking.

It seems that during the first part of the Pope's detention the public was allowed to be present when His Holiness said mass. The attendance was so great that the government, fearing that under the appearance of a great devotion some intrigue hostile to it would be formed, thought wise to forbid the public to go to the chapel.

As soon as the emperor had finished with the Pope he returned to Paris. I do not remember whether he went to live in the Tuileries or went to the Élysée. If he did not go to the latter at once, he went there soon, liking to be free and to walk.

When the empress was made regent the emperor made her be present at the councils. I doubt greatly whether that was very agreeable to this princess, who, I fancy, more than once felt like dozing instead of listening to the deliberations of the councillors and ministers.

Ever since his return from Russia the emperor had been actively employed in creating a new army and new resources for himself, for all that had escaped from that fatal campaign was very little in comparison with what was necessary for him, in order that he might face the enemy with any chances of success. The best of the soldiers who had been saved from the shipwreck were in the fortified towns of Germany. All the material of the artillery had to be reconstructed, the cavalry to be remounted, the wagon train to be formed anew. The emperor was obliged to make very considerable sacrifices of money, and France of men. The emperor did not lose a moment; he neglected nothing to show that the Empire could still fight against the united forces of Europe.

As all the troops who were to constitute the new army had gone to their posts, the emperor left for Erfurth and was soon in contact with the enemy. I was left at Mayence, I do not know why. I should have much preferred to make the campaign.

Toward the end of May I received the order to join the emperor with a number of wagons which had remained at Mayence. When I reached Neumark, where headquarters were at that time, the armistice was on the point of being signed; one might say that it had been, for two or three days afterward the emperor left for Dresden and all the household and the guard went with him. The armistice had pleased everybody; they hoped that peace would follow. The emperor went to stay in the Marcolini palace, situated on the principal street of the suburb which was to the east of the city. This dwelling suited him from every standpoint, because, as his apartments were on the ground floor and he had the advantage of a large garden or park in which he could walk without being disturbed by anyone, he was as comfortable as he would have been at the Élysée or Saint-Cloud. Nearly every afternoon he would walk in the broad alley till evening.

In order to divert headquarters and the court of Saxony from serious thoughts of politics the emperor sent to Paris for the principal members of the *Comédie Française*—Fleury, Mademoiselle Mars, Baptiste Cadet, and others whose names I do not recollect. The morning they arrived he received the celebrated actress at his breakfast. She was almost ashamed at first to appear before him in the condition in which she was, as an accident had happened to her during her journey; her carriage had upset and in the fall she had received a blow on the eye which made it quite black. When she had told about her adventure, of which the emperor had already been informed, she recovered her self-possession, but still was her. She replied excellently to all the questions which the emperor put to her. She remained throughout the breakfast standing, and as the emperor was very amiable with her she must have been very well satisfied with the interview.

I was almost angry that he did not make her sit down; there are circumstances where etiquette ought to be banished. If Mademoiselle Mars's black eye somewhat affected the beautiful ensemble of her face, the agreeable quality of her voice fell deliciously on the ears of those who listened to her. On the stage a little white on the black spot caused most of the effect of the extravasated blood to disappear. I had never seen Mlle. Mars close to; I observed that she had a little scar on the middle of her forehead.

After the Battle of Leipzig I learned that the emperor was in a large town (the name of which is illegible.—Trans.). By asking soldiers and officers I succeeded in discovering the house which he occupied and which was situated at the back of a little place on the left of the road. The doors were open; everything indicated that the house was abandoned. It was almost without furniture, and I did not find a single person to speak to. I went into a first room, then into a second; I was about to go into the third when I saw in the fourth, facing the door, the emperor, seated on one of his folding armchairs. With his legs stretched out on a common chair, his hands folded on his stomach, his head sunk, and his eyes closed, he seemed absorbed in the most profound reflections.

Indeed, the terrible defeat which he had just suffered once more annihilated his material resources and deprived him henceforth of any chance of success. This attitude of the emperor wrung my heart and brought tears to my eyes. Never had I seen him in such a state of depression. I withdrew cautiously and returned to the first room, in order to prevent any strangers from reaching him, for there was not a single sentinel at the door.

The emperor crossed the Rhine, which he was never to recross, and took up his residence in his palace at Mayence. He remained in this town several days and there organized the remains of his army. Marshal Kellermann[2] was the governor of the place. Nothing had been done toward the provisioning or the defence. A considerable number of soldiers entered the hospital.

Every time that the emperor had passed through Mayence the Grand Duke of Baden had been in the habit of coming to pay court to him. His Majesty usually received him at his breakfast; but I think that this time the Duke dispensed with this act of homage.

I was designated to remain at Mayence, with which I was not at all

2. Francois Christophe de Kellermann, Duke of Valmy, Marshal of France.

pleased. Two *valets de chambre* of the private apartments and a *service de bouche* also remained.

The emperor departed for Paris, Marshal Kellermann went to take command of Metz, and General Morand became governor of Mayence. The storehouses were filled with food, the cannon which were in the yards were placed on gun carriages, and the place was organised for defence. The garrison was weak, being composed of some battalions and a regiment of guards of honour which was far from being full. Its colonel was M. de Pange, one of the emperor's chamberlains. The hospitals were full of sick. Typhus made frightful ravages. The poor wretches were only animated skeletons. At first a considerable number of them died every day, and large ditches to bury them were dug outside of the city to the southwest, not far from the road to Metz.

On the 1st of January, 1814, the Allies crossed the Rhine and soon after that the city was invested. From that time there was no news from the outside; we had to live by ourselves. Although there had not been much time to provision the city, food did not run short. The only discomfort which we had was to eat horse flesh instead of beef. Life was gay enough. We had theatrical performances several times a week, and during the carnival there were fancy dress and masked balls.

We were living in ignorance of everything when one morning we heard a somewhat vigorous cannonade. It was not from the city that this firing came, but from the enemy's lines. Shortly afterward an orderly arrived to tell the governor that there was a flag of truce at the advanced posts who wished to communicate with him or hand him dispatches. The flag of truce was received and we learned that the emperor had abdicated and that the Allies and the Bourbons were in Paris. This news came like a thunderbolt. We were far from expecting such an ending and such a catastrophe. There was sadness in all hearts, and more than one found his eyes wet with tears. General Morand himself was no more insensible than the others. A few days later a messenger came from Paris, charged with transmitting the orders of the new government, and it was then that the white cockade replaced the tricolour. Very few people had known this cockade, consequently it was worn with a sort of repugnance by the greater number, both soldiers and civilians.

When the troops learned the change which had taken place in the government of France they asked to be paid. There was but little money in the city treasury. The governor gave orders that all the gold and silver belonging to the emperor should be deposited with the receiver-general. The members of the *service de bouche* deposited the silverware which they had and I gave up some things which I had, among them two tortoise-shell snuff boxes lined with gold and ornamented with antique medals. I cannot now tell what induced me to give up these two articles of jewellery. What is certain is that almost as soon as I had handed them over I repented of it. I felt, too late, that they were purely the personal property of the emperor.

As there was nothing more for us who were attached to His Majesty's Household to do in Mayence, we asked the governor for money both to pay what we owed at our inns and to defray the expense of our journey to Paris. We had reason to be satisfied with the governor's behaviour toward us. When passports had been given us we took a *briska* [3] which had remained in the palace stables and set out for Paris, being careful, as we had been advised, to put white cockades in our hats, and I dressed in civilian's clothes in order not to attract attention.

The first person whom I went to see was the Duke of Vicenza. He received me very well at first, but when I told him that on General Morand's orders I had been obliged to deposit the snuff boxes and other articles which I had in my charge with the receiver-general he got so angry with me that he said the most abusive things to me imaginable, telling me that I never ought to have given up what belonged to my master. He seasoned the reproof with such energetic words and such sharp and scorching rebukes that my eyes overflowed with tears. I had perhaps obeyed too easily, but that was all I had been guilty of. The members of the *service de bouche* had done as I did, and I had done as they did. The position in which I found myself with the grand equerry hurt me all the more because he had always been extremely good to me and had taken me under his protection from my entrance into the emperor's household.

It was he to whom I owed all that I was and had. Such a scene, which I had never expected, upset me to such a point that I could not answer anything to justify myself, so that he said everything that he wished without my making the slightest reply. After a reception which affected me so painfully it was difficult to explain my intentions to him, which were to go and join the emperor. But, foreseeing all the unhappiness that I should have in setting foot in the duke's house after what had passed between us I decided, when I saw his words follow

---

3. A light, open travelling carriage.

one another with less rapidity, to tell him what I desired.

I was about to go down the first steps of the staircase when a pause occurred in which I was lucky enough to explain in a few words what my heart dictated. My words suddenly produced such an effect that the storm which had burst over me in so terrible a fashion grew calm at once; more moderate expressions took the place of those which had wounded me so badly. It was a beneficent balm which spread itself at the same instant through all my being. The duke had the goodness to say to me, though still somewhat coldly, that he would see to getting me a passport and that I should come to him in a few days. I saw, to my great satisfaction, that my generous benefactor had given me back a great part of his friendship and that a few visits would be enough to win it all back.

When I left the Duke of Vicenza I went to M. de Turenne's [4] hotel. I was fortunate enough to find him. I told him about the unpleasant scene which I had had with the Grand Equerry, and then his kindness in promising to get me a passport. "But by the way, my dear fellow," said M. de Turenne, "General Morand is in Paris; see him. It seems to me that I heard that he had bought the emperor's snuff boxes." I thanked him for the good advice which he had given me, and after a quarter of an hour's conversation, during which I gave him an account of the articles which I had belonging to His Majesty, I asked permission to take leave of him in order to go to see the general. I went at once to the latter's house. I do not recollect whether I found him during the morning itself or during the day, but I succeeded in reaching him. He lived in the rue Louis le Grand. I immediately explained to him the object of my visit, telling him that I had learned from M. de Turenne that he had bought the snuff boxes which I sought to recover, of course paying him the price which he had paid for them. Then I asked what had become of the bidet and another article which I had deposited with the receiver.

The general replied:

I have the snuff boxes, I paid two hundred and forty *francs* for them (the sum may have been more; I do not recollect); as for the other things, it was not I who got them. I shall be glad to give you the snuff boxes, since they are to be returned to the

4. The Count de Turenne was Grand Master of the Wardrobe. An inventory is attached to Napoleon's will of articles left in M. de Turenne's charge, which consisted mainly of the robes and decorations, such as the Grand Collar of the Legion of Honour and the Collar of the Golden Fleece, worn by Napoleon on state occasions.

emperor. I will see M. de Turenne.

You can judge of my joy. I was delighted with what I had done. I spared no pains to hasten the negotiations which were to place in my hands the two articles of jewellery which it was so agreeable to me to be able to replace in the emperor's hands. As soon as I had thanked the general I went at once to see M. de Turenne, whom I told what the general had said to me. Everything was arranged, and for the price for which they had been bought, which I paid out of my own pocket, I saw, to my great satisfaction, the snuff boxes in my possession. Without losing any time, I hastened to go to see the Duke of Vicenza, to whom I announced my good news. This action of mine pleased him so much that he entirely restored me to his good graces.

From that time on I had only to busy myself with preparations for the journey and the happiness of seeing the emperor again. I often went to see the Grand Equerry to learn when I could start, but there were new postponements, contrary to my wishes. Still, I took patience, hoping that at last the day of my departure would arrive. This long waiting annoyed me beyond expression. I learned that all these delays were caused by Madame Bertrand, who never got through with her preparations. The Duke of Vicenza wished me to go with her in order that the journey might be less expensive tome; it was a fresh sign of his goodness. But seeing that the countess seemed likely to be a great while longer without deciding to start, he said to me:

I think that it is as well that you should go by yourself; Madame Bertrand may delay many weeks more. I will see that you have a passport with which you will have nothing to fear. Get ready, for I hope to have it on such and such a day. Come and see me then.

As M. de Turenne had told me that he had some things to send to the emperor, I went to his hotel. He gave me some shirts, stockings, flannel waistcoats, etc., which I took to my father's lodgings and which I arranged in portmanteaus, adding to them various articles which I had brought back from Mayence. I shared with Sénéchal, who was in Paris, some clothes and a little linen which M. de Turenne thought best to throw away.

When the day arrived that the grand equerry had appointed I was promptly on hand. He gave me two passports, one from the French government and one from M. de Metternich.[5] As he gave them to me

5. Prime Minister of Austria, and after 1815 practically dictator of Europe.

he said: "Now you can go and reserve your place. Come back tomorrow and I will give you a letter for the emperor." I went to the Royal Posting Office and arranged for my departure in, I think, two days' time. As had been agreed, I went to see the duke. As soon as he was awake he had me come up to his room. "Here," he said, "this is the letter. You will lay at the emperor's feet the homage of my profound respect. I hope that he will receive you well."

After a few minutes' conversation, during which I told him that the next day I should be on the road to Elba, he gave me a hearty clasp of the hand, wishing me a good journey. My thanks were great. I expressed to him the gratitude with which my heart was full, not only for all that he had just done for me, but for what he had previously done in my favour.

As soon as I was sure of being able to go to the island of Elba I had bought all the pamphlets which had appeared since the installation of the Bourbon government, as well as a collection of newspapers. I had no doubt that the emperor, being far from France, would be very glad to read all these novelties, among which were a good number that were favourable to him.

Not wishing to arrive at His Majesty's like a pauper, I had put three or four thousand francs in my belt and my portmanteau was full of linen and all sorts of articles. Being well equipped and having everything which I could need for a long time, I went to the diligence accompanied by my mother and sister. The parting was painful; we all shed tears, for my absence might be a long one. After we had embraced I got into the wagon and started for Lyons on the road to Burgundy.

THE EMPEROR'S ATTEMPT AT SUICIDE

During the campaign of Russia and since then, during that of 1813 in Germany and that of 1814 in France, the emperor wore hanging around his neck by a thin cord a little bag of black silk in which was something which felt the size and shape of a clove of garlic. Whenever he stayed in Paris after his return from the Russian campaign the sachet was locked up in his travelling case. It was supposed that it was some amulet or talisman in which the emperor believed, or in which he had faith as something which could protect him from being struck by cannon balls or bullets, but in fact it was only poison, which he intended to use if he should be made prisoner by a party of Cossacks, so as to escape from his enemies by leaving in their hands nothing but a corpse.

At Fontainebleau, when he saw himself abandoned, not by his brave soldiers, but by the greater part of his general officers and by many others, the emperor tried to put an end to his existence. Those to whom he had distributed riches, honours, dignities in the time of his power, on whose fidelity he had a right to count, these had disappeared little by little and had gone to Paris, to salute the new power which had arrived at the tail of the baggage wagons of the enemies of France. Two of his servants, Constant and Roustan, to whom he had given all his confidence and whose fortune he had made, thought that they, too, would perform a praiseworthy act in imitating the great people who had deserted his cause. Both, on this occasion, showed to France and to the whole of Europe all that was meanest, vilest, and most contemptible in ingratitude.

In the silence of the night, passing in review all the events which had occurred and reflecting on the fate which was reserved for France and the fate of those who remained faithful, as well as his own, the emperor had at last only one idea, that of ending a life which would remove all pretext for vengeance from the foreign enemy and for the severities which would not fail to be practiced by those enemies who called themselves French and who for twenty-five years had not ceased to plot for the ruin of France, which had cast them out from her bosom.

It was four o'clock in the morning. The night had been calm, and probably the emperor had passed it, not in the torpor of sleep, but in the saddest reflections. Having decided to carry out his project, he called Hubert, who was on duty. The latter immediately entered the room carrying a shaded light; he asked for his dressing gown. Hubert, after placing the light on a table, helped the emperor to put on his dressing gown, his trousers with feet, and his slippers. Having done this, the valet uncovered the fire and fed it. The emperor, intending to write to the empress, told him to go and get some paper. Hubert hurried down to the study and brought back paper, pens, and ink, which he placed on the little table; he moved this up to the sofa which was before the fireplace and on which the emperor was sitting, and withdrew to the antechamber, but leaving the door ajar in order that he might hear the better if the emperor should happen to call him, and also in such a manner as to be able to see the emperor without being seen.

The emperor began to write, but, dissatisfied with the lines which

Attack upon Napoleon's life in the Rue Saint-Nicaise

he had written, he tore up the paper and threw it into the fire. He took up the pen again, wrote once more, and, as little satisfied as the first time, the leaf was likewise torn up and thrown into the fire. Finally, a third letter was begun and met the same fate as the two which preceded it. Shortly afterward the emperor rose and went toward the chest of drawers opposite the fireplace. At this moment Hubert, seeing the emperor standing up, closed the door a little further, in order not to be seen.

On this chest of drawers there were usually two glasses on a plate, covered with a napkin, a little teaspoon, a sugar bowl, and beside it a carafe full of water. But by chance the sugar bowl was not there, because, as the servant had delayed too long in having it refilled the day before, it was in the room where Hubert was. It should be added that there was usually melted sugar in one of the two glasses, but that from forgetfulness or some other reason there was nothing in the glass. While Hubert was listening in order to answer the emperor, he heard water being poured into a glass and then the noise of the little spoon which was being stirred about in order to melt something. Knowing that there was no melted sugar in the glass, Hubert could not imagine what it was that the emperor was stirring, but after a moment's consideration he thought that the emperor, not seeing the sugar bowl which was usually with the two glasses, had taken some sugar out of his dressing case.

When the emperor had stopped stirring the glass there was a moment of silence, after which the emperor came to the door and told Hubert to send for the Duke of Vicenza, the Duke of Bassano,[6] the Grand Marshal,[7] and M. Fain. At that moment, Hubert told me, the emperor's features were as calm as though he had just drank a glass of water. When these gentlemen arrived he told them that, not being able to survive the dishonour of France, he had yielded to the weakness of taking poison. As soon as the gentlemen had heard these words they promptly sent for M. Yvan, that he might administer an antidote. M. Yvan came at once and immediately gave the emperor a drink which quickly produced its effect.

The emperor vomited all the deleterious substance which he had swallowed, but not without violent efforts which fatigued him greatly.

---

6. Hugues Bernard Maret, Duke of Bassano. He was a confidential agent of Napoleon and conducted his official correspondence.

7. Count Henri Gratien Bertrand, who succeeded Duroc as Grand Marshal of the Palace. He accompanied Napoleon to St. Helena.

Toward six o'clock, as he felt better, he went down into the interior garden, where he walked with the other gentlemen for a long time. It is to be supposed that time and the emanations of his body had impaired the strength of the poison, for it must be believed that if it had retained its original strength death would have been instantaneous. The emperor was disappointed in his attempt.[8]

---

8. Napoleon is said also to have attempted suicide after his defeat at Waterloo. Professor Sloane says of the night of June 21st:

Early in June the court apothecary, Cadet de Gassicourt, had been ordered by the emperor to prepare an infallible poison. This was done, and during this night of terrible vacillation the dose was swallowed by the desperate fugitive. But as before at Fontainebleau the theory of the philosopher was weaker than his instincts. In dreadful physical and mental agony the would-be suicide summoned his pharmacist and was furnished with the necessary antidotes. *Napoleon Bonaparte*, Sloane. IV.

In spite of this second failure, Napoleon appears to have a third time prepared for suicide. After his abdication in 1815, one of his last visitors at Malmaison, before he left for Rochefort, was Doctor Corvisart, the emperor's favourite physician. When the famous doctor had left him Napoleon is said to have handed Marchand a small bottle filled with a reddish liquid. "Arrange matters," he said, "so that I may always have this on me, either in my vest or in some other part of my clothes, but so that I may get hold of it quickly."

Chapter 5

Elba

As soon as the ship was moored to the dock at Elba and I had paid the captain I made haste to land, to load a porter with my luggage and to take the road to the palace, which I reached in less than half an hour, after passing through a street with few people in it which had been pointed out to me.

The emperor's house, or palace, seemed to me of very ordinary appearance. I went in and saw Marchand, Gellis, and some other persons whom I knew. We shook hands, embraced, greeted one another warmly. I asked where the emperor was, whether he was at home. "No," they told me, "he is not; he is at Saint-Martin." Without losing any time, I put on my Mameluke's costume and went to the stables, where they got a horse ready for me.

Half an hour later I was in the emperor's presence. His Majesty was not a little surprised to see me. He received me kindly. I handed him the grand equerry's letter, saying that the duke laid at his feet the homage of his respect. The emperor no sooner had the letter in his hand than he unsealed it and read it. He seemed satisfied with its contents. Then he asked me all sorts of questions, which I answered according to my knowledge of the different things which I had been able to see or hear.

At last I had reached the goal which I had set for myself! I was happy. I learned later that when the emperor had been abandoned by Constant and Roustan he had asked where I was, and on being told that I was shut up in Mayence he had asked the grand equerry for someone to go with him and ride on the box of his carriage. The grand equerry had suggested Noverraz, his footman. Noverraz, having been accepted, had made the journey with him from Fontainebleau to Elba, and went with him on all his journeys. Noverraz was a Swiss by nationality. I had known him in the stables, where he had been a harness groom. Having been admitted to the emperor's household service, he went to St. Helena, where he remained till His Majesty's death. The emperor had always been grateful to him for his conduct at Orgon or Saint-Cannat in Provence, where his carriage had been attacked by a very ill-disposed crowd. Noverraz, being a tall and very strong man, had, happily, held back this vile populace, which, with insults in their mouths, uttered threats of death, throwing stones into the carriage.

When the emperor had breakfasted and undressed he sent for me. He was in his shirt, lying on a sofa. He asked me questions about people and things. In my replies I told him everything that I had learned about the Allies and the Bourbons and what the Parisian public said of either party. I did not forget to speak of the conduct of certain persons whom I had seen at his court and who had deserted his cause, etc. In short, I told him all that I knew. When I had finished answering all the questions which it had pleased him to ask me I presented him with the package of pamphlets and newspapers which I had collected during my stay in Paris. This attention on my part gave him pleasure, and I was pleased with myself for having had the idea of bringing all these writings, since they interested him. The emperor, having said "go" to me, I withdrew, and he amused himself turning over what I had given him.

The emperor's palace was situated on the highest point of the city on which one *façade* looked, while the other looked toward the shore of the Strait of Piombino. On that side there was a garden of an oblong square shape before the house, surrounded by a parapet built on the rock. A walk ran along its whole length, and outside of the parapet was a rough and steep hillside which ran down to the sea. The emperor walked on this terrace every morning and evening. From there he could see the arrival of the ships which came from the mainland.

The house was of only one storey, but at each end there was a little upper storey which made a small room. In order to join these together the emperor had a large room built between them, to complete an apartment which he meant for the Princess Pauline, (see note following), who was to come to Porto Ferraio and live there.

★★★★★★

Note:—Napoleon's sister, married to Prince Borghese of Rome. She was very beautiful and was said to be the model for some of Canova's nudes.

Here is a little picture of her vanity:

Princess Ruspoli knew how frivolously vain the imperial princess was, and did not forget to go into raptures over her foot. 'Would you like to see it?' said Princess Borghese, quietly. 'Come tomorrow at twelve.' Princess Ruspoli presented herself at the Palazzo Borghese and was ushered into an exquisite *boudoir*. The princess was reclining at her ease in an invalid's chair, her little feet well in view. A page, pretty as Cupid and dressed as pages are in medieval pictures, entered, bearing a costly ewer, a silver-gilt basin, a napkin of fine cambric, perfumes, and other cosmetics. He drew a velvet hassock up to the chair, the princess graciously put forth one of her legs, the little page took off the stocking, the garter, too, I think, and began to massage, to rub, to wipe, to perfume this beautiful foot, which really was incomparable. The operation was a lengthy one. , . . While the little page drew off and on her stockings, perfumed her beautiful foot and filed the nails, she was chatting, to all appearances quite devoid of self-consciousness.

It has been suggested that it was this same lack of self-consciousness which induced her to grant to Canova those famous, much-discussed sittings for the Venus which immortalised both artist and model.

★★★★★★

He had this room decorated so as to make it a large and handsome *salon*, the finest room in the building. The emperor occupied the whole ground floor, which was composed, what with the garden side as well as that on the square, of eight or nine rooms, the largest and most spacious of which were a *salon* and bedroom. Both were furnished, as were the other rooms, with very ordinary furniture which came from the Princess Eliza, Grand Duchess of Tuscany.[1] The furniture in the *salon* was light blue. The seat of the sofa had so little stuffing that one could feel the cross pieces and the straps. The mantelpiece was of white marble and was semicircular in shape. The upper part, or shelf, was supported by two fluted columns. This mantelpiece was of a

---

1. Anna Maria Eliza Bonaparte was the eldest of Napoleon's sisters, and the most ambitious. She was made Grand Duchess of Tuscany. She was hard and selfish, traits which were indicated in the quality of the furniture which she sent to her brother, to whom she owed everything.

beautiful model. On a console opposite it was a fine bust by Canova; it was of the Princess Pauline. I recollect that the candelabra in the *salon* were of wood painted to represent bronze, ornamented by a few gildings. As they used the ends of candles from economy, whoever was on duty had to be careful not to let them burn down to the end in order that the candelabra might not catch fire.

The emperor thought that the walls of the dining room and *salon* were too bare (the walls of all these rooms were painted in fresco after the Italian fashion—that is to say, with a border and an elegant painting in the large panel over the doors) and saw fit to frame in black wooden frames a number of engravings which he had taken out of a large work on Egypt. The island was so poor in glass that it was necessary to put two pieces over each engraving. The bathroom was decorated with little pictures, coloured Italian engravings on a black ground, representing the principal pagan divinities as they are described in Ovid. The furniture of this room was composed of some chairs and a wooden bathtub of the shape of our wine vats. The library, which also served as an office, contained a considerable number of volumes, which was increased later. The emperor did not allow anyone to go into his library; nobody was excepted but M. Nattier, his secretary, and the floor polisher. The bedroom, though very simple in its furnishing, was nice enough; it was supplied with everything necessary.

Running the whole length of the house on the garden side was a long walk, shaded against the rays of the sun by an awning of the same length. In the morning, when the weather was fine, this awning was unrolled so that the emperor might walk in the shade, and it had at the same time the advantage of preserving His Majesty's rooms from too great heat. In the eastern part of the garden, on two pilasters which served as the entrance to the little garden, there were two alabaster vases, rather large, in which lights were placed when night came. The emperor liked this soft light. As the temperature was pleasantest during the evening, he often dined on this walk. They used to place two little alabaster vases in which there were candles on the table, to light it. This had the advantage of not tiring the eyes and also of protecting the light from the wind.

Before the arrival of the Princess Pauline a number of cases of furniture, porcelain, glass, and an infinite quantity of pretty, useless things had been unloaded at the port and transported to the palace. The emperor, curious to see what these cases contained and wishing to be the first to see them, had them opened before him. When the box contained porcelains, glass, or bronzes he would have the pieces taken out one by one, have them handed to him, amuse himself by taking off their wrappings, and, after having looked at them and examined them on every side, he would place them on a table or some other piece of furniture within his reach. This form of distraction pleased him so much that not a box was opened unless he was present.

When the emperor knew of the arrival of the princess, his sister, he made all the arrangements necessary to receive her. The rooms in the upper story, which were designed for her, and which had been decorated and almost furnished, were put in order. The emperor himself saw to everything. As soon as the ship which carried His Majesty's sister entered the port and had anchored, the artillery of the place saluted the princess. The troops, I think were under arms during her landing. As soon as her carriage was ashore she got into it and drove to the palace. When I arrived Madame Mère was already settled at Porto Ferraio; she occupied a house in a street near the palace.

A short time after the arrival of the Princess Pauline the emperor's guard was increased by a detachment of mounted Polish lancers. These men, after accompanying the empress, had, it was reported, received orders to go to the island of Elba. I think that they gave themselves this order. There were a considerable number of officers among them. Consequently the cavalry, which had before that time been composed of only a few Mamelukes, was considerably more numerous. But as there was little forage in the island, about half the men were dismounted and their horses sold. It was a matter of economy.[2] Fifteen or twenty mounted men were enough to furnish the escorts, which were composed of only four or five men.

During the emperor's stay on the island of Elba, Corsican or Italian officers frequently arrived, asking for employment. Several entered the Corsican battalion. The emperor gave the others a pension which allowed them to live. Among these officers there was a Frenchman named Roul who had been in the *chasseurs* of the Guard when that body was formed, and I think that he had even been one of the guides in Egypt, since when he had served in the *carabiniers*. He held the rank of *chef d'escadron*. This fine fellow was very devoted, but he had no fortune but his sword. The emperor, who had known him, attached him to his person and made him his first *aide-de-ca*mp and appointed him commandant of his escort. M. Roul always accompanied him on

2. Napoleon asserted that the reason he left Elba was because the Allies failed to pay the income they had agreed to give him.

his rides.

The life at Porto Ferraio was lively enough; there were the soldiers of the battalion whose barracks were near the palace, the workmen who worked here and there, people coming and going, some strangers landing every day. On Sundays everybody, civil or military, wore his best clothes. There was a mass at the emperor's palace. It was said in the little waiting room by the archpriest, the *curé* of Porto Ferraio, a sort of bishop, I suppose, as he was dressed in violet; he was a Corsican of the old stock and some sort of relation to the emperor. Those who served the mass were Abbé Buonavita and a young priest. The Grand Marshal, General Drouot, and General Cambronne were to the right and left and a little behind the emperor. The officers of the Guard and the principal functionaries were behind and took places as they could. As the room was small, the greater part remained outside. At the end of the mass there was a reception in the salon. All the military were in full uniform. Madame Mére had mass said at her house. M. Buonavita was her chaplain. As for the Princess Pauline, she always found some way to escape being at divine service.

On that day the emperor always had a grand dinner—that is to say, a few more people than usual. Madame Mére was usually there, General Drouot, two or three officers of the Guard, and two or three others.

The emperor had one day in the week when he went to dine with his mother. The dishes served were cooked in the Italian manner; they recalled to him the meals which he used to take in his father's house. Her Highness's *major-domo* was a Corsican named Cypriani, who died at St. Helena. He enjoyed the confidence of the emperor and all the other members of the imperial family. He was often entrusted with important missions.

After he got out of bed in the morning the emperor used to take a cup of chicken broth and afterward a small glass of Constance wine. As the broth was very good and the quantity that they sent from the kitchen was much more than the emperor needed, the *valets de chambre* would take it when the emperor had gone into his study, and, like their master, they would each drink a drop of Constance. They thought that what the emperor liked they also ought not to dislike. It prepared their stomachs to receive their breakfasts.

The emperor was accompanied on his rides, either on horseback or in a carriage, by an escort of four or five men, Poles or Mamelukes, under the charge of M. Roul, of a *chasseur*, Noverraz, or me, and of

Amandru, his *piqueur*. The rides took place in the cool of the morning, up to nine or ten o'clock. At three or four in the afternoon, when the sun began to lose its strength, the emperor would go, either on foot or in his carriage, to take his boat and row about the vast basin of the roadstead, stopping sometimes on one side, sometimes on the other, to visit people who lived near the shore. The carriage was often ordered to go and wait for him at such and such a spot. The boat was manned by sailors of the Guard. One, who had been boatman to Princess Eliza, held the tiller.

Princess Pauline went about in a sedan chair. She was accompanied by her ladies in waiting and one or two young officers. As for Madame Mère, I do not recollect that she went out much, except to see the emperor.

Madame Mère must have been a beauty of the first rank in her youth. Her face was well modelled, with regular features. Her mouth was neither too large nor too small, her lips were thin, her nose almost straight, her eyes brown, large, brilliant, and very expressive. There was always some haughtiness and severity in her look. But the beauty of her features lost part of its effect because of the thick layer of paint which she put on her cheeks. This did not harmonize with her age, which required greater naturalness in the colour of her skin. Too much rouge does not go well with wrinkles.

On ordinary weekdays her dress was simple, though rich. She ordinarily wore a little bonnet ornamented with flowers. On Sundays and holidays, when she was in full dress to come to the palace, she had on a toque with feathers. On these occasions she wore very fine diamonds.

I knew nothing about her household arrangements; I know that she was very religious and was said to be very miserly. When she spoke French she had a very marked Italian accent. She said very little. At Paris her place at table was on His Majesty's right; at Elba she sat opposite him.

Princess Pauline might have been from thirty to thirty-five years old when she was at Elba. Her person, from what could be seen, had all the beautiful proportions of the Venus di Medici. Nothing was lacking to her but a little youth, for the skin of her face was beginning to be wrinkled, but the few defects which resulted from age disappeared under a slight coating of cosmetic which gave more animation to her pretty features. Her eyes were charming and very lively, her teeth were admirable, and her hands and feet were of the most perfect model.

She always dressed most carefully, and in the style of a young girl of eighteen. She always said that she was ill, out of sorts; when she had to go up or downstairs she had herself carried on a square of red velvet having a stick with handles on each side, and yet if she was at a ball she danced like a woman who enjoys very good health. She dined with the emperor and he liked to tease and poke fun at her. One evening she was so angry with what the emperor had said to her that she rose from table and went away with tears in her eyes. The irritation did not last long, for the emperor went up to see her that evening or the next morning and the little feeling of annoyance quickly disappeared.

The emperor went to Saint-Martin nearly every morning. This was his country house. It was situated in a long valley facing the city, and distant from it about half a league. It was built at the end of the valley, and halfway up the hill. On the side looking toward the town there were two stories, and on the other side the upper story was on a level with the ground. Before this *façade* there was a sort of court, and on the other side was a terrace. Although the house was ordinary enough to look at, it was very well arranged; there was a large dining room opening on the court and a drawing-room of the same size which looked out on the valley. These two rooms occupied the middle of the house, and were each lighted by three windows. Five very little rooms, transformed into a bedroom, a study, etc., and the entry, made up the whole house. It was all very clean, but extremely simple and modest in its decoration and furnishing.

I recollect that the sofas and other furniture of the sort were stuffed with hay instead of hair; and the material which covered them was green cloth. The walls of the drawing-room were decorated with views of temples and other buildings of upper Egypt.[3] I seem to have seen on a chest of drawers in the dining room a marble bust of the emperor's mother. At the two ends of the building, outside, there were two flights of steps which went down to the terrace. At the bottom of that on the right was a door which opened into a very pretty bathroom; it was decorated with Egyptian views. One would have thought himself in a panorama; all around one were the pyramids, the Sphinx, obelisks, temples, etc. The painter who had the decoration of this room had arranged everything with much taste. The spectator was in the middle of a square room with Egyptian pillars. All the models

---

3. Napoleon had a large illustrated work on Egypt in his library and he caused a number of the pictures in this to be copied on the walls by an Italian artist named Ravelli.

had been taken from the great works of Egypt. The bathtub, which was of white marble, was vase shaped. The other rooms on the ground floor were for the kitchens, pantries, etc.

The emperor wished to have a little larger courtyard back of the house than that which originally existed and had had the mountain cut away. In the excavated portion was a little dripping spring. His Majesty intended to make a fountain and also a little basin, but, as the work presented many difficulties and would entail considerable expense, he thought it better to give up the plan.

The emperor's gate keeper at Saint-Martin was a woman named Mademoiselle Durgy, who was from twenty to twenty-five years old. He called her his madwoman. She was sort of a Napoleonic fanatic, and as such was wholly devoted to His Majesty. As she had nothing to live on, the emperor had given her this little job as a means of support. She had an extraordinary imagination; there was not a single time that the emperor went to Saint-Martin that she did not show us some verses written by her in the emperor's praise.

The emperor, who was very fond of movement, variety, diversion, planned a party in the country. Several people were invited to it, among them the Vantini family and General Drouot. When the appointed day had arrived the emperor embarked, I do not recollect where, with all his guests. His boat and that which accompanied it were full. The weather was magnificent and the sea very smooth. The place where we landed was a pretty and very picturesque beach; there were rocks, trees, stretches of green grass, and a little way off a charming stream which fell here and there in cascades was shaded by clumps of bushes. The emperor settled himself a few yards from the sea, and in order to shelter himself from the rays of the sun had them put up the little awning of his boat, under which he and his guests took their places around a rustic meal. They placed all the dishes which were to form the breakfast on a tablecloth laid on the ground, and everybody, seated or standing, began to eat.

The emperor waited on the ladies, according to his custom, and the men waited on themselves or were waited on by the butler. The meal was very gay, and what contributed not a little to make it so was that the emperor enlivened it still more by his flashes of wit and the little stories which he knew how to tell so well. Never in my life have I witnessed so agreeable a spectacle as that which this delicious morning offered to my eyes. When the repast, which lasted longer than ordinary meals, was finished, the emperor asked for a gun and went ahead of his guests to see if he could find any game to kill. As nothing appeared at which he could fire, although he walked for half an hour, he handed me his gun and went and sat down beside the stream under the shade of the bushes, and there he took pleasure in putting his feet in the water and moving them about while he talked to those near him. He remained about an hour in the same place. He liked to feel the coolness of the water through his boots without having his feet wet. The day was well advanced when he went to the boat and started back to Porto Ferraio.

Before I arrived at the island the emperor had been to visit the Pianosa; he wanted to see this part of his possessions again and made the trip. As I was not on duty with his person on this occasion I do not know whether it was the *Inconstant* which took him there, but I remember that I received orders to embark with the guns on a little vessel of His Majesty's navy. A considerable number of members of the household, as well as some grenadiers or chasseurs, had received orders to go there. There was no dwelling on this island; it was deserted. The only extraordinary thing about it is that it is flat and only four or five yards above the level of the sea. It has wild olives scattered over it, its soil is stony, as its name indicates, and it produces only a little grass which feeds a few goats which are left on it and which are its only inhabitants.

The emperor, who had his tent for a house, stayed on the island two or three days. The day we started to return to Porto Ferraio we had a headwind and a very rough sea; it was only late at night, toward morning, that we succeeded in entering port. The ship on which I returned was the same which took me to Pianosa. It had its bowsprit broken.

The emperor had a house at Longone. This house, of which I recollect nothing as to its situation or arrangement, had been repaired and cleaned from top to bottom. His Majesty lived in it for a few days. The only recollection which I have of it is that the rooms were floored with red tiles, so soft and so badly baked that we were always in a red dust.

It was in this town that the Corsican battalion had its barracks. M. Guasco was its commandant. General Cambronne often went to inspect it. It sometimes happened that in the drill or the manoeuvres the general would shake the soldiers who were awkward or who marched badly. One day the emperor, whom he was telling of the training of the battalion and to whom he narrated the blunders of the soldiers to whom he had given blows or whom he had struck with his sword on their shoulders or their stomachs, said to him: "Look out! Don't treat these men like that, or you may suffer for it: they are vindictive and never forgive anything. Believe me, don't trust them." I think that the general took his advice. The battalion numbered four or five hundred men, very well equipped and drilled. It followed the emperor to France.

In Corsica there was a man named Bralard, commander, I think, of the military division. At Porto Ferraio he was said to be an enemy of the emperor and it was suspected that he had been sent to Corsica by the royal government to try to make some attack, in order to surprise the emperor, to carry him off or to make away with him. The position of the emperor's garden and the arrangement of his dwelling were such that it was not very difficult to get into it because the slope from the foot of the wall to the seashore could be easily climbed in spite of the rocks with which this part of it was strewn. As the wall was not very high, it would be easy to reach the top by means of a rope ladder armed with hooks. Moreover, there was a postern gate which was open or badly fastened, by which anyone could get into the garden. It is to be noted that, so far as I know, there was not a single sentinel in this part of the fortifications.

It was important, then, in order to prevent a surprise, to keep one's eyes open on the whole length of the parapet, and one's ears for the slightest noise. One night, which they believed chosen for the attack, I carried a mattress in the evening on the walk under the emperor's window and lay with my *poignard* in my belt and my sword by my side. I spent the whole night in this way, being all eyes and ears. My vigil was useless, for not the slightest thing happened. I do not know why they had not put a sentinel at the wall or even on the terrace. Perhaps they did not care to make public what was only simple suspicion. I do not recollect whether Noverraz or I spent the following nights out of doors.

One morning, pretty early, there was a high wind, and I heard, in the midst of the noise which the waves made in breaking on the rocks which surround the fortifications, cannon shots which were fired from minute to minute. The emperor had not risen. Without losing a moment I ran to the terrace to learn where the shots came from. The sea was so furious that the waves, after breaking with a loud noise, fell in a fine rain on the terrace and the garden. Through the thick drizzle in which I found myself I saw a ship ashore on the little beach which is only a few gunshots to the right of the mountain where the telegraph is. I saw two masts; it was a brig. More cannon shots were fired; I could see them. The ship was calling for help. No one knew what it was; it had not hoisted its colours. The emperor was told, and he came wrapped in his dressing grown, with a handkerchief around his head. He fixed his telescope on the ship which was in such a perilous position, and after looking at it for a long time thought that he recognised the *Inconstant*. But whatever ship it was, he gave orders to go to its help as soon as possible. The wind was so strong that at one moment the emperor was obliged to stoop down in order not to be blown over, and when he stood up again he was careful to wrap his gown carefully about him so as not to give the wind any hold.

It was, in fact, the *Inconstant* which had gone ashore. It took a long time for help to get to it, because it was necessary to follow the wide curve of the roadstead, or at least a large part of it, before coming to the ship. It was learned that Commandant Taillade had preferred to beach his ship rather than to have it lost on the rocks of the fortifications. The brig was coming back from an errand; it had on board M. Ramolini, a very near relative of Madame Mère. This poor man had been so badly frightened that as soon as he got ashore he fell on his knees to thank Heaven for being out of danger.

To the west, before one reached the emperor's dwelling, there was a large unoccupied area bounded on the north and west by a wall which was the continuation of that of the garden. In this empty space there were two constructions of cylindrical form topped by low cones. They were close to each other and were the ruins of powder mills. The emperor, having conceived the project of clearing this space in order to make a garden, ordered the destruction of these two ruins and entrusted the undertaking to some grenadiers and *chasseurs*, who asked nothing better than to have the opportunity to earn a little money. When the bargain was struck these soldiers went to work, but they had a hard job; the stones adhered so strongly to one another that they were obliged to employ gunpowder in order to break them up. Finally, after some days of extremely trying work, they succeeded in removing the last of them. They had well earned the price which had been agreed upon.

The gardener, upon the emperor's orders, had constructed along the whole length of the wall a slope of rough stones, set dry, leaving a space between of about six feet to serve as a terrace or walk. When the ground had been levelled, cut up, and divided, a plantation of orange trees was made there. A wooden fence was built on a line with the *façade* of the house which gave on the square, and was carried on to the wall situated on the west. Thanks to this work, the surroundings of the place became neater.

In this space which I have just described they had reserved at a little distance from the house fifty or sixty square yards on which to construct a house, and in this house a little theatre. As soon as the new garden was finished the project of building was put into execution, and in less than a month, I think, the emperor had a very prettily decorated theatre. It was hardly finished when His Majesty wished to have a play in it, but first it was necessary to organise a company. The actors and actresses were found among the officers of the Guard and some young ladies. The parts were learned, the costumes were made, and a day was appointed for the first performance. The music was provided by the band of the battalion. I think the first piece played was the *Folies Amoureuses* of Regnard, in which Adjutant General Debelle and his daughter, who was a lady in waiting on the princess, each had a *rôle*, in which they acquitted themselves very well. I do not recollect the second piece.

Between the acts there were refreshments. The emperor appeared very well satisfied with his evening, and the actors and spectators were no less so. I think I recollect that there were two or three such evenings. Immediately after having his little theatre built the emperor felt the necessity of having one in the city to entertain the garrison, whose pleasures were very limited and monotonous. In the street which ran from the palace to the gate on the land side there was, on a little square, a good-sized church or chapel of which no use was made, either because it was in too bad a condition or for some other reason. The emperor allowed it to be transformed into a theatre. As soon as the permission was given the repairs were made at once, and in less than a month the church was changed into a playhouse, where the garrison, of course, and the inhabitants as well, did not fail to enjoy themselves. I think that later balls were given there.

When the most urgent repairs had been made in the rectory of the Madonna of Murciane, the rooms had been whitewashed; they had been cleaned as well as possible, and they had been furnished with some indispensable articles. The whole place was very neat. The different terraces and the little roads which the emperor had ordered had all been made. His Majesty decided to go and live in this place. I went ahead of him with a train of pack mules loaded with the tents, the camp beds, and different things, among which were fowling pieces. As one leaves the village of Murciane la Marine one takes a rising and winding road, cut out of the mountain. It leads beside a deep ravine to the spot called the Madonna, which is not reached without much hard work and not without sweating profusely. One finally sees the church, the apse of which appears on the left. On the right are the buildings, of only one storey, not very high, which may be called the rectory. The road which separates the church from the rectory, and which goes on up into the mountain, resembles a little street or lane. As one goes on he sees a little square place on the left on which, on the left side, is the door of the church, and on the right, facing that door, is a wall out of which run pipes from a spring which gives very cool and clear water.

Opposite the entrance there was another wall which, like the last, backs up against the mountain. The square or court is paved with pebbles laid symmetrically. The buildings of the rectory do not run as far as the church, but a supporting wall, which follows, extends some yards beyond it. If one continues to follow the road one turns obliquely to the right and reaches the head of the ravine, after which, still going up, he comes to the top of the mountains, where there is a large sloping plateau dotted with big trees. When one has come to the end of the plateau he can see the island of Corsica. There are many high and sharp rocks along this side, and they stretch out some distance into the sea.

Let us come back to the buildings of the rectory. They form a number of rooms one after the other; they have their entrances on the lane and have windows opening on this and on the ravine. The building is much taller on the side of the ravine, the ground there being much lower. What is the ground floor on the side of the church becomes the first floor on that of the ravine. In the lowest part are the cellars, one of which is occupied by the two sacristans. Before this *façade* there is a good-sized terrace, planted with trees. Not far from there, lower and a little in advance, is another terrace which extends to an ice house, the entrance to which faces the terrace. Little winding roads furnish communication from one place to another.

A day or two after my arrival at the Madonna a good many people connected with the service of the Household and a small body of *chasseurs* or grenadiers came to live there. The emperor soon arrived and occupied the rooms of the rectory. The kitchen was established in one part of the large terrace and near it a tent was set up to be used as a lodging for the members of the *service de bouche* and to put provisions in. The soldiers placed theirs before the apse of the church. As there was not room enough for everybody, they took possession of the sacristy, in which they made themselves as comfortable as they could. The emperor had his tent set up. It occupied the end of the terrace opposite the ice house. This place had been arranged to receive him. His Majesty had it furnished with a camp bed, some chairs, and a table. It was believed at first that the emperor had come because he liked to give himself the pleasure of sleeping now in one place, now in another, which, for that matter, he was fond enough of doing, but a few days later it was known why all these arrangements had been made and the reason for the trip to the Madonna. We had been at the Madonna for a few days when the emperor had the idea of enjoying the pleasures of the chase.

I took two guns and we went together to take the road which leads from our lane to the mountain, and even to the plateau dotted with trees of which I have spoken above. The ascent, like enough to a ravine, was difficult because of the great quantity of rolling stones on which it was necessary to walk. The emperor went slowly and often rested. Panting, we reached the top, and consequently the plateau. Then we walked on a short, thick grass, more agreeable to the feet than the best carpets of the salons of Paris. The emperor took his gun and went now to the right, now to the left, or straight ahead of him. I followed him at a little distance, ready to give him my gun if he should discharge his own.

We had been in search of game for a quarter of an hour and nothing had appeared, neither quadrupeds nor birds, although our eyes searched everything within their reach. The emperor, already fatigued from being on his feet and bored at meeting nothing, stopped beside a tree to wait for some head of game to pass; then he took a few steps and stopped to watch again. From time to time he would take his glass to look here and there, and not the most wretched animal let itself be seen. It seemed as though on our approach the beings which lived in this place had deserted it. Finally, when we had come to the last trees on the edge of the plateau he took his glass again to examine the rocks which were at our feet, the sea, which reflected the brilliant rays of the sun, and the island of Corsica, which looked like an immense gray rock. Bored, disgusted at not being able to fire a shot, he said to me:

What a difference there is between this hunt and those which

I had at Versailles, at Saint-Germain, at Fontainebleau, where I killed so many head of game! I see that we shall do nothing here. Come! Let us get out.

We went quietly back by the road by which we had come and we returned to the Madonna. He had his breakfast served.

We had been about a week at the Madonna when we learned that some people whose names we did not know were to come to see the emperor. I had, I think, heard the name of Madame Walewska pronounced. Almost secret orders were given that the rooms in the refectory were to be prepared and that the kitchen should have something ready. After his dinner, and when the sun had gone down, the emperor appeared on horseback, accompanied by some people, going in the direction of the Marine de Murciane, to meet those whom he awaited. He returned to the Madonna somewhat late, accompanied not only by those with whom he set out, but by two ladies and a young boy some ten years of age. They were Madame Walewska, her son, and the lady's sister.

The emperor had the newcomers enter his tent. Supper was quickly served. As it was an informal meal with no ceremony, it was the emperor who carved and served, giving one thing to one of the ladies and another to the other. The young boy was also at the table. During the whole time the supper lasted the emperor showed a gayety, an amiability, and a gallantry which were charming. He was happy. Marchand and I waited on the table.

The landing had taken place mysteriously, or it seemed so, but the few persons who had accompanied the emperor and then all those who were at the Madonna were quickly informed of the presence of the two ladies and the young boy, and the next day it must have been known in all parts of the island, and above all at Porto Ferraio.

The emperor had known Madame Walewska at Warsaw at the time of the campaign in Poland.

The young boy was the son of this lady and the emperor. It is he who is known in Paris under the name of Count Walewski.[4]

Madame Walewska must have been, in her youth, a very beautiful person. Although she was, at the time of her trip to the island of Elba,

---

4. Count Walewski, who must have been about four years old at this time, was brought up in Poland. He ran away from there at the age of fourteen in order to escape serving in the Russian army. He eventually became a naturalized Frenchman and had a distinguished career under Napoleon III, becoming a Senator and Minister of Foreign Affairs, and being created a duke in 1866.

thirty or perhaps more, she was still very handsome. What detracted a little from her looks were some spots of red which were on her face. For the rest, she was very white and with a colouring which revealed fine health. She had a handsome figure, with a reasonable stoutness. She had a very beautiful mouth, fine eyes, and hair of a light chestnut. She had a very sweet look and appeared to be an excellent person.

Her sister was charming, with very regular features. She had the appearance of a young girl of eighteen or nineteen years of age, and of dazzling freshness. She was a little shorter than Madame Walewska. The young Walewski was a nice boy, already well grown, with a somewhat pale face. He had something of the emperor's features; he had his seriousness.

The next day an officer came to the Madonna, a Polish *chef d'escadron* in the uniform of the lancers of the Guard; he was Madame Walewska's brother, or passed for such. The emperor invited him to dinner. During the evening this officer took leave of His Majesty and returned to the Marine de Murciane and perhaps to Porto Ferraio.

While these ladies stayed the emperor dined with them on the terrace before his tent. He also took breakfast in the open air.

At the island of Elba the emperor was surrounded by many people who, being but newly attached to his service, did not know what it was to be close mouthed, and who had nothing more important to do than to go and tell what they saw and heard to anyone who was willing to listen to them. The emperor himself, though he was fond of mystery, acted incautiously, thinking himself still surrounded by people who were not talkative. At night he went out of his tent in his dressing grown and went to the ladies' apartment, which he did not leave till near daybreak. The sentries knew perfectly what to think of these comings and goings. In love affairs the simplest man is much more adroit than the emperor was and than great lords are in general.

In a small country everything is known, is learned. It is enough that two eyes have seen something, that two ears have heard some remark, for all the world to have seen and heard it. But things are often so badly reported, so inaccurately repeated, that they are wholly changed when they pass through several hands. The report was current that the empress and her son were at the Madonna. Even the officer of *gendarmerie* who had brought the son of Madame Walewska from the Marine de Murciane to the Madonna thought that he had brought the King of Rome.

Madame Walewska remained at the Madonna some twelve days,

I think, after which she prepared to leave. The emperor, wishing to give her some money, asked Marchand for some, but, as the latter had not enough, he came to me. He knew that my money belt was pretty well filled. He told me in confidence that the emperor, not having any money at the Madonna, he, Marchand, asked me to lend him a certain sum (two or three thousand *francs*, perhaps) for Madame Walewska, and that he would give it back to me when he got to Porto Ferraio. I immediately handed him what the emperor wanted to give.

A few days after Madame Walewska's departure the emperor left the Madonna to return to Porto Ferraio, and was accompanied by all the members of his suite whom he had taken with him, as well as by the little detachment of grenadiers or *chasseurs* who had guarded him.

Most of the land about the house at Saint-Martin belonged to the emperor and was planted in vines. When the vintage came a certain number of willing grenadiers and *chasseurs* were told off to gather the grapes. While the soldier workmen were busy they were visited by comrades who thought they would come and help their friends. But in spite of the larger number of workmen the work did not progress either faster of better than before. Everybody filled his stomach and carried away such a quantity of grapes that in the end very few reached the vats. The soldiers found it entirely just that what belonged to their father should belong to them, too. When the emperor learned how the vintage had been made he could not help laughing. "Ah! the rascals!" he said, "they have robbed me."

CHAPTER 6

The Flight of the Eagle

After the accident which had happened to the *Inconstant* she had gone into the port to be inspected and repaired. I do not recollect that she went out of the harbour before February 26th, the day of the emperor's departure for France. As soon as she had been made fit for service cases of arms and many other things had been carried on board of her, one thing today, another tomorrow, and so on, so that neither the people in the harbour, nor the inhabitants of the city, nor the soldiers had the slightest suspicion of the emperor's plans. So far as I am concerned nothing had attracted my attention as yet, although His Majesty went to visit his brig pretty frequently. But what set me to thinking, later, was the errands which I ran to Longone, to Colonel Germanowski and to Rio to M. Pons, and some words which the emperor let fall in my presence.

All these things together made me think that the emperor had some plan in his head. That which later came to increase and strengthen what at first had been only a simple supposition was that two small guns were put on board, with their limbers and caissons. Few people outside were in the secret, and if some of those inside knew something, it was because it is difficult for a man, no matter who he is, to conceal himself completely from those who are about him, so that they shall not guess something from the smallest of his actions, his gestures, his looks, etc. What is certain and positive is that the secret had been so well kept that the time for the expedition to start arrived without having the people of the island or even the garrison suspect up to the last day the project which the emperor had been entertaining for a long time.

A few days before February 26th the emperor had had orders given to the Guard to make a garden of an empty piece of ground adjoining their barracks on the west. This land was dug, broken up, levelled, the walks marked out, and the trees planted. Although it was a considerable piece of work, it was done in three days. When the emperor asked something of his soldiers nobody was ever lazy; everybody, without distinction, laid his hand to the work, nobody spared himself. It was a pleasure to see with what zeal everyone worked, and the gayety which prevailed among the workers. This occupation which the emperor gave them was not without ulterior objects; at the same time that it would deceive spies and lead them off the scent, it would wake the soldiers out of their sluggishness and put them in training.

The last day that the soldiers were working on the garden, or the day before that, the English corvette came into the roadstead of Porto Ferraio. Its arrival at such an inopportune moment was very disturbing to the emperor; he was afraid that the preparations which he had been making for so long might have aroused the suspicions of the English spies. Happily this was not the case. The corvette sailed away again on the 24th or 25th without suspecting what was in preparation, and as soon as she was seen in the open sea there was no longer any reason for anticipating the least trouble from her. For that matter, the emperor had decided, if she had remained at her anchorage until the day which he had fixed for his departure, to aim his cannon at her and sink her if she attempted to resist.

A number of ships of the island, both those belonging to the emperor and others which he had hired, had received orders to anchor at such and such a spot on the 26th, at a given hour. During the middle of the day the Guard, infantry, cavalry, artillery, and the Corsican battalion were told that everyone was to prepare his knapsack and his arms and to be ready for orders at any minute. This order was given at about six o'clock in the evening, and by nightfall everyone started. Each company was at the place appointed for it, and the embarkation began immediately. As many troops as possible were put on board the brig. When the *Inconstant* had its full complement the emperor did not delay in coming on board. About nine o'clock the fleet left the harbour. During the night the ships which had the Corsican battalion on board came and joined it.

The dismounted Poles had been made to bring saddles and bridles in order that they might be mounted at the earliest possible moment. Some of the emperor's horses had been put on board, as well as his carriage. Those on duty either in the bedchamber or in the *service de bouche* were in the brig or the other boats. As for the stable service, men, horses, and carriages, everything remained at Porto Ferraio till further orders, except what was absolutely necessary, which had been put on board.

The princesses remained on the island, awaiting the result of the expedition. Monsieur ———— (I do not recollect the name of this person), who was commander of the National Guard, had been appointed governor of the island.

I learned later that after the departure of the little fleet the English corvette, which had Colonel Campbell on board, had returned to Porto Ferraio. On being informed of what had happened the colonel had immediately gone to the princesses and vented his ill temper in the most indecent language, both against the emperor and against the princesses themselves. It was said that, having his handkerchief in his hand, he tore it with his teeth, and that what enraged him the most was the calmness with which Madame Mère replied to him. He was in despair because his active surveillance had been so completely baffled.

During the night of the 26th-27th we made little progress; the wind hardly blew at all, the sea was calm. During the night the wind freshened a little. At nine or ten o'clock that night we sighted a vessel which we knew for a French brig which was going in the opposite direction from ours. It was commanded by Captain Andrieux. We spoke to each other; I heard the words, "How is he?" which probably referred to the emperor. I do not remember what was said afterward, except to wish each other a good journey. As the vessel had passed very close to us, the grenadiers had been told to stoop down, so as not to be seen. This was the only ship which we met during our voyage. The weather remained fine throughout.

The 1st of March, early, we made out the coast of Italy, near that of France, and the latter during the forenoon. Then the emperor ordered us to take off the cockade of Elba and replace it by the tricolour (that of Elba was red and white, with the red in the centre; there were three bees on the white part). At the same time that the soldiers put on their tricolored cockades M. Pons de l'Hérault read in a loud voice the emperor's proclamation, which was received with transports of joy and repeated cries of "*Vive l'Empereur!*" During the day, at two or three o'clock in the afternoon, we dropped anchor in the Golfe Jouan. We immediately disembarked and encamped in a square meadow close to the road from Fréjus to Antibes. The emperor's bivouac was established in the middle of the meadow, which was bordered on the right and left by quickset hedges and on the north by the road.

Before the disembarkation of the bulk of the little army the emperor had sent some twenty men to Antibes, grenadiers commanded by an officer, to take possession of the place. This officer acted imprudently. Instead of leaving part of his men to guard the gate of the town he took with, him his whole squad, so that the commandant of the place, seeing so few men inside and being informed that there was no guard outside, raised the drawbridge, and our officer and his men found themselves caught as if in a rat-trap. This little miscarriage annoyed the emperor greatly. It was a bad beginning.

As soon as the emperor was settled in his bivouac he had his table set up and began to work over a map which he had opened. He then dictated different orders and instructions relating to the operations of the campaign which he had thought out and in which he had just taken the first steps. When he had finished his work he went to walk about while waiting for his dinner, stopping at the bivouacs of the soldiers, while he talked to them, or turning his steps toward the road which ran beside the meadow on the north side; there he talked to the people who passed, of whom there were but few, and asked them questions. When the dinner hour arrived he sat down with his generals. When the meal was over he walked about again, talking sometimes with the grand marshal, sometimes with General Drouot or some other member of his suite.

During the evening the advanced post on the road to Cannes stopped a courier who was brought to the emperor's bivouac. This man said that he was in the service of the Prince of Monaco, whose carriage he was preceding, and that formerly he had been a *postilion* of the Empress Josephine. Some people connected with the stables recognised him as such. The emperor asked him about the public feeling at the capital and what was said about him, Napoleon, the Bourbons, etc. His Majesty appeared well enough satisfied with what this courier answered and dismissed him, telling him to go on his way. He was going to Monaco.

It was already late when the emperor, feeling the need of rest, wrapped his body in a coverlet knit of wool and very light, sat down in his folding armchair with his legs outstretched on a chair, and, covered with his cloak, tried to sleep for a few hours. He remained in this position till the hour of departure.

About one o'clock after midnight everybody was on foot again. Camp was struck soon afterward, and at two o'clock the troops

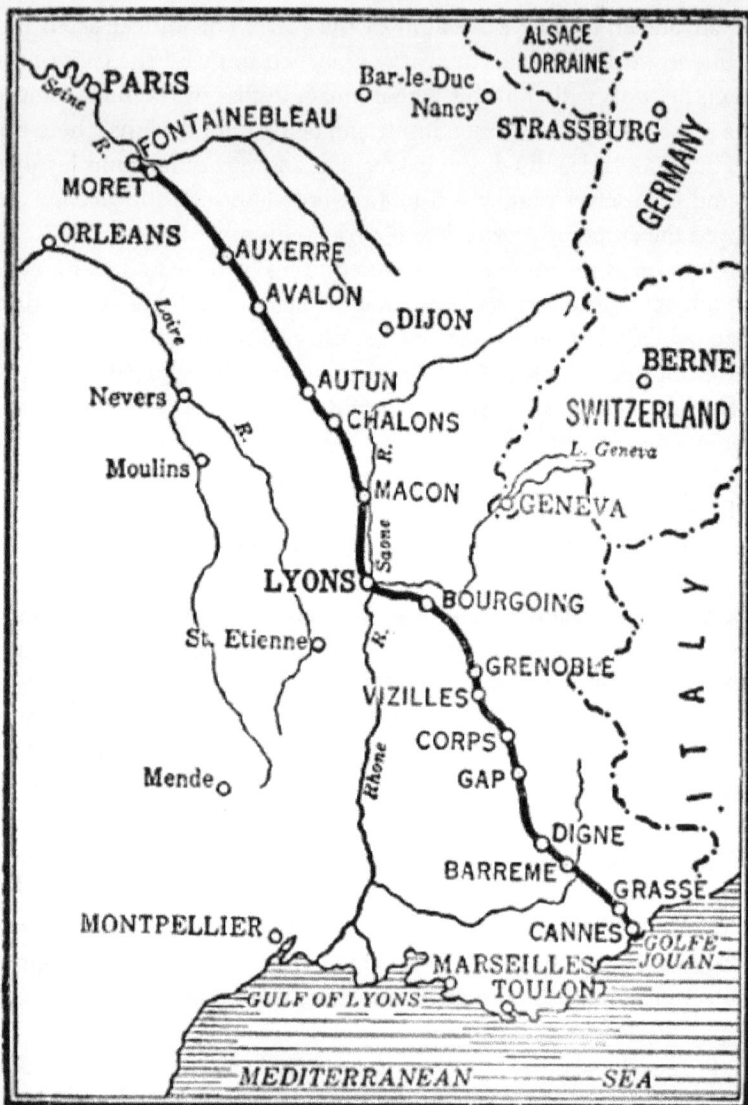

ROUTE OF NAPOLEON'S RETURN FROM ELBA

marched out. The few cavalrymen who had horses escorted the emperor, while the others, who were on foot, carried their saddles, their knapsacks and their arms on their backs. It was very uncomfortable and an extremely awkward load. We were going towards Grasse.

On our way the head of the column met the Prince of Monaco.[1] When the prince was informed of the emperor's presence he got out of his carriage and came to greet him. They went together to sit beside a bivouac fire which was on the right hand before one enters the village, and a little way from the road. Their conversation was still going on when the group with which I was marching was about to enter the village. This was the first village which we met with; it was probably Cannes. Half an hour later the emperor caught up with us and was soon ahead of us.

During the morning, fairly early, we arrived at Grasse. Like most of the members of the Household, I was on foot. The emperor got there long before us. We learned that he had gone on still farther. Before continuing on our way my companions and I wished to restore our strength by taking some food, so we went into a little inn and had a short meal. We ate it as rapidly as possible, being anxious not to be left behind.

The population of the little town was afoot. It appeared to us neither hostile nor sullen. In a little square where we stopped for a moment there was a fountain on which was carved a phrase in praise of the Bourbons, followed by the indispensable *"Vive le Roi."* On this same square I saw our two cannon and the emperor's carriage. The road over which we were to travel was impassable for carriages, in places, and as the country was very hilly they had wisely decided to leave them at Grasse, and they were perfectly right, for they would have delayed our march without being of the least use to us.

We set out again. As we left the town we had to climb a high mountain. When we reached the top we saw a circle formed by a considerable number of people, townsfolk and peasants, women and children, in the midst of whom were the emperor and his staff. His Majesty talked and chatted with most of the people who composed the circle, one after the other. In spite of all his efforts, these people remained almost cold. Probably the emperor had breakfasted at this spot, and all those about him had accompanied him from the town.

---

1. Honoré Gabriel Grimaldi, Prince of Monaco, was an equerry to Josephine, a position which he continued to hold after her divorce from Napoleon, when he refused a similar post in the household of Marie Louise.

We did not stop there. Being on foot, the best thing we could do was to get ahead and arrive at our camping ground as soon as possible. Consequently, we marched on with more zeal than ever.

Hardly anybody but the advanced guard marched in any order. The body of the little army was scattered along the road, forming a quantity of little squads, all more or less weak. Many of the soldiers marched alone. They were at home, and for that reason they had nothing to fear. We were in Provence, but those who wished us ill, taken by surprise, had not had time to do anything.

We bivouacked wherever the head of the column stopped. On the 2nd we slept at Séranon, on the 3rd at Barrème, on the 4th at Digne and the 5th at Gap. During these four days we suffered a good deal; we were not accustomed to fatigue. The first two days were the most painful. There were mountains whose tops we had to reach or narrow defiles through which we had to pass; sometimes snow, sometimes mud prevented us from marching as fast as we should have liked. I remember that in one extremely narrow and dangerous defile a mule rolled over a precipice. In spite of the fatigue of the long days of marching I do not think that anybody remained behind. We set out in the morning before day and it was always very late before we reached our halting place.

When once we had reached Gap we travelled more easily. In each city, town, or village through which we passed we bought all the horses able to carry a man, and it was in this way that the Poles, many officers, and all members of the Household were mounted. There were also some other means of transport for tired soldiers and the small amount of baggage which we had with us. All of us of the household had left our belongings at Porto Ferraio, bringing only what was necessary for the journey. It was at Gap that the emperor's first proclamation was printed; it was there, also, that we saw a little more enthusiasm on the part of the population, and a few soldiers who had retired to their homes came to augment our small army a little. It was something, anyhow. As we advanced the decisive moment approached.

When we landed we had no eagle; it was only on the second or third day that we got one. It was of wood and probably came from the rod of a bed or window curtain. It had been fastened on a pole, and with some pieces of stuff of the three colours they had made a flag of it.

On the 6th we slept at Corps, and it was on the 7th that we began to see daylight in our affairs. Thus far we had travelled, so to speak, like adventurers. On the 6th General Cambronne had marched with his advanced guard to La Mure and had slept there; he had met the advanced guard sent from Grenoble to stop the emperor's advance. The general had tried to parley, but they had replied that they were forbidden to communicate with us. On the 7th, as this advanced guard, which had fallen back several leagues, had left our way open, General Cambronne had been able to advance. The emperor, informed of what had happened, had collected all his forces, and they marched thereafter with order and prudence. As we advanced we caught up with the general, who had retarded his march by frequent halts.

In the middle of the day we saw the advanced guard which was opposed to us. The emperor brought up his Guard as close as possible, and put it in line of battle, with his little body of cavalry on the wings. I do not recollect seeing the Corsican battalion; I think it had not yet arrived. When the line was formed the emperor sent forward M. Roul, his first *aide-de-camp*, alone, to announce his presence to the troops which were before us. They told this officer that they had been forbidden to communicate with us. The emperor, seeing some uncertainty, decided to order his soldiers to put their muskets under their arms and to go forward on the double quick, which was immediately done. The emperor, on horseback, was a few steps before his Guard, which in a moment had come up to the opposing troops, who had their muskets ready.

At five or six yards apart they halted. The deepest silence reigned in the ranks on either side. The emperor, without losing any time, harangued the soldiers with the white cockades, and he had hardly pronounced the last words when cries of, "*Vive l'Empereur!*" were heard. These troops were a battalion of the 5th regiment of the line. At the same moment the soldiers of the Guard mingled with those of the line, they embraced, and again cries of "*Vive l'Empereur!*" rose from all sides. This scene, this spectacle, produced such an effect that there was not a single soldier who did not have tears in his eyes and enthusiasm in his heart. I think that the emperor got off his horse and embraced the commandant of the battalion. This poor man, stunned by all that he had seen about him, could hardly articulate a few words. I was told that he had served in the Guard. The white cockades were torn from the hats and trampled underfoot. A number of the soldiers who had come over to the emperor showed, by putting their ramrods into the barrels of their guns, that they were not loaded. "Here, see!" they said.

This first encounter increased the emperor's army. We marched on again. The procession was swelled at every step by the inhabitants who came to the road from all sides. Between Vizilles and Grenoble Colonel Labédoyere and his regiment came to take his place under the emperor's sword, and shortly afterward there appeared a group of soldiers escorted by many people. In the midst of them could be seen an eagle fixed on the end of a pole; it had belonged to a regimental flag. As soon as the group approached the emperor they presented him with the ensign which they had preserved, and cries of "*Vive l'Empereur!*" came at the same time from all their mouths. Peasants, townspeople, women, and children, they all marched pell-mell. The crowd was delirious. Refreshments were not lacking all along the way. It was a matchless triumph. It was already late when we reached the suburbs of Grenoble.

The emperor wished to complete the day by his entrance into the city, although he was tired. The night was very dark; the crowd was thick around him. General Marchand, who commanded the place, had caused his troops to go into the city and had closed the gates. The soldiers on the inside talked to those without, telling them that they had nothing to fear. Ours replied that they ought to open the gates. There was an exchange of jokes. We were in complete darkness. If any of the inhabitants of the place where we were showed a light several voices were heard calling out, "Put out the light!" While the soldiers continued to exchange pleasantries the group in which the emperor sat on his horse was silent and waited anxiously for the end of the scene. In spite of the good intentions manifested by those inside the fortifications the gates remained closed, at which they were astonished. Cries of, "*Vive l'Empereur!*" were heard from time to time. Finally several voices called out, "Break the gates!" "Yes, yes, axes, axes!" replied many others.

A few minutes later the blows of these tools could be heard, and in a few minutes the gate was broken down and thrown aside. At once the compact mass of the population which surrounded us rushed into the city with the cries of "*Vive l'Empereur!*" a thousand times repeated. The emperor and those who were with him, carried along by the current, found that they had passed through the gate without knowing it. The 4th Hussars, which was in the street which ended at the gate, served as an escort to the emperor and accompanied him to the inn, where His Majesty dismounted. The streets through which we had passed were so narrow as compared with the multitude which crowded through them, that we had only been able to advance very slowly.

Those who were on horseback had their knees so squeezed that it was a pain which we had to endure till we could get off our horses. It was not without difficulty that the emperor could dismount and get up the stairs to the apartment which was prepared for him. He was carried there. When he reached his sitting room he was exhausted; he had been almost stifled. I do not know how the staircase and the balusters could bear the heavy weight they had to carry for several minutes. What a day! What an extraordinary day! It was nearly ten o'clock, so far as I can remember.

When the emperor had received different people, civil and military, and had dined, all became orderly and calm, and of the multitude which had accompanied him there remained only a few individuals who stayed part of the night before the inn.

We learned that General Marchand, seeing that it was impossible to resist the emperor, had taken the wise course of going away rather than to break the oath which he had made to the Bourbons. He had, it was said, asked as a favour that they would not open the gates till he had left the city.

The next day the emperor remained in Grenoble. On the one hand his Guard needed rest, and on the other he had the authorities to receive and he had to review the five or six thousand men who composed the garrison. Early in the morning the whole population was afoot, the national colours floated on all sides, and all the soldiers and officials wore the tricolored cockade.

The review held by the emperor was very long. As I was not on duty that day I do not know what was said or done there. After the review several corps started to march to Lyons.

I recollect that during that day of the 8th the emperor received a visit from his former professor of mathematics. It was I who announced him. He was a tall, thin man, wearing a peruke. He appeared to be seventy or seventy-two years old, but was still erect. He was very modestly dressed. As soon as the emperor knew of his visit he went to meet him and they both, throwing their arms around each other, embraced warmly. As the door was closed, I could not hear the conversation of the two friends. They remained together for a long time. The emotion which the old professor had felt had been so deep during the interview that when he came out his face was radiant with joy and his eyes were full of tears. It was one of those circumstances in which I saw how much feeling the emperor had. The interview took place in the bedroom.

During the day of the 9th, rather late, the emperor set out again accompanied by the troops which were to serve him as an escort, and a good part of the population, which never ceased to cry out, "*Vive l'Empereur! À bas les Bourbons! À has les prêtres!*" When the inhabitants of the city had escorted him for a certain distance they were replaced successively by those of the country who had flocked to the road and who in their turn formed an escort, singing appropriate songs which they intermingled with cries of, "*Vive l'Empereur! À bas les Bourbons!*" It was like this all the way to Bourgoing, where the emperor arrived at dark and where he slept. I recollect that the peasants had lighted fires at intervals to light the road.

The emperor had made the journey from Grenoble to Bourgoing in a carriage, having the grand marshal with him. I do not know whether he had bought this carriage or whether it had been lent him, but I know that he used it all the way to Paris. It was all the more necessary because he had to rest and to cure a cold which he had caught the first or second day after he landed and which had left him very hoarse and almost with extinction of the voice. In the circumstances in which he was he needed to be able to speak, in order to reply to the authorities of all the places through which he passed, and to harangue the troops which had given themselves to him. Happily, the cold and the hoarseness diminished by degrees.

As Noverraz was on duty the day I entered Lyons, I could not see how matters went. I only arrived in the city rather late. I recollect that during the night there was a multitude of people who had taken their places before the archbishop's palace, where the emperor was lodged, and cried, "*Vive l'Empereur!*" from time to time.

The 11th and 12th we stopped there. These two days were employed in receiving the authorities, different deputations, and in holding reviews, without counting the office work for sending out orders. What delight must the emperor have felt! On every hand there was nothing but shouts of enthusiasm and public demonstrations in his favour. The common people were glad to see him again. I learned that one evening they had broken the windows of certain high royalist personages. Many of the troops received orders to march to Paris.

It was at Lyons that I first saw General Brayer.[2] The same day another general and a chief commissary dined at the table.

---

2. Count Michel Brayer served with distinction in the Republican and Imperial armies. After the second *Restauration* he went to South America, where the government of Buenos Aires entrusted him with the task of organising its army. Later he returned to France and entered the Chamber of Peers under Louis Philippe.

On the 13th the emperor went to and slept at Macon, where he arrived after nightfall. At every moment there were detachments of soldiers on foot or mounted, commanded by non-commissioned officers, who came to offer their services and to join the army, and the farther we advanced the greater the emperor's escort became. There were officers and soldiers of all arms who had left their corps to have the happiness of being with their father, and of accompanying him on his triumphal march. At a place which I do not recollect a sapper of dragoons with a long thick beard came to the emperor, put his arms around him, and kissed him repeatedly. This man never ceased to form part of the emperor's suite during the whole journey; he was conspicuous because of his large bearskin cap and his beard. There were two or three Mameluke officers among the escort.

On the 14th the emperor slept at Chalon. It was in the city that I first saw M. Fleury de Chaboulon.[3] Everywhere there was the same welcome, the same enthusiasm on the part of the people.

On the 15th he entered Autun. He received the mayor and the municipal council rather rudely. The emperor, having learned that these gentlemen allowed themselves to be directed by the nobles and the priests, all of whose suggestions they followed, said to them among other things that their business, in any case, was to keep order, tranquillity, and peace, and not to obey nobles and priests who strive to disturb people's minds and to stir up disorder, he continued:

> I have just taken back my throne. Well, can you prevent it? Can you resist for a moment those immense masses which accompany me, or even all those who have welcomed me to this city, etc.?

The mayor and some members of the council tried to get in a few words to defend themselves, but what they said was lost amid the vehement expressions which poured like a torrent from the emperor's mouth and permitted no reply. The emperor, in dismissing them, said a few more words to them, but a little more mildly, as if somewhat to soften the sharpness of the language which he had used to them. As everywhere, the house was surrounded by a crowd from which rose cries of "*Vive l'Empereur!* Down with the Bourbons! Down with the

---

3. Pierre Alexandre Edouard Fleury de Chaboulon filled various offices under the Empire. He joined Napoleon at Lyons and became his private secretary, and afterward filled a diplomatic mission to Basle during the Hundred Days He wrote a *Memorial pour servir à l'histoire de la vie privéc, du retour et du règne Napoléon en 1815.*

priests!"

On the 16th the emperor slept at Avallon, and on the 17th at Auxerre. In this city he was lodged in the hotels of the *prefecture*. Still enthusiasm, acclamations. From time to time detachments of *cuirassiers*, *chasseurs*, and dragoons had arrived to swell the army.

At Auxerre there was a scene like that which had taken place at Autun, but it was with the ecclesiastics, composed of a certain number of clergy, among whom there were one or two parish priests. It had been reported to the emperor that these clerical gentlemen mingled with their preaching political comments which bore on the events of the moment. As soon as they heard of his landing they had spoken of him in a manner far from reverential. He said, after giving them to understand that he had been informed about their un-Christian and ill-disposed behaviour toward him:

> What are you meddling with, pray? Why must you take a hand in politics? Preach peace and harmony, and confine yourselves to the moral teachings of the Bible. Spiritual things ought to be the sole object, the sole text of your preaching. Far from that, it is always worldly matters with which you are concerned. Why these furious declamations which you hurl from your pulpits, from which nothing ought to be heard except words of gentleness, sweetness, and peace, conciliation, justice, and submission to the laws?

It was at Auxerre that General Brayer, who dined with the emperor, proposed making a descent on Paris with a few hundred men to surprise the Bourbons in their beds. This proposal was not agreed to. In fact, what could the emperor have done with those princes? He would have been embarrassed with them; he much preferred to leave the door open for them. What had he to fear from them?

In order to expedite the march of the troops and to rest them, a certain number of boats had been collected on which the infantry were embarked. There was general joy and enthusiasm. It seemed to the soldiers as though they were going to a great *fête* to which they had been invited; songs, shouts, cries of "*Vive l'Empereur!* Down with this! Down with that!" resounded from the boats and on the banks of the Yonne, to the side of which rushed the people, who, in their turn, did not remain silent among all these demonstrations. There was delirium in every head. The electric spark had been communicated to everybody. The story of this marvellous journey can never be read in times to come without people's feeling the same emotions as did those who witnessed it. The disaster of the Pont sur Yonne is well known, where one of the boats struck against one of the piers of the bridge. Poor people! Poor soldiers! The emperor was profoundly affected by so sad an event, which took the lives of so many brave men.

During the morning of the 18th the emperor received Marshal Ney.[4] The marshal came up the back way. He remained for some minutes in the room next the bedroom. His eyes were full of tears. It has been said that he had some trouble in making up his mind to come and see the emperor. He was alone. The emperor did not keep him waiting long. I think it was the grand marshal who introduced him into the bedroom. As the door was immediately closed I could not see how the emperor received him, nor hear the conversation, at which no one was present, so far as I know, unless it was the Grand Marshal.

I think that the emperor started late from Auxerre, and I do not know where he slept the night of the 18th-19th, or even if he slept anywhere except in his carriage, but what I do recall is that in the night of the 19th-20th he arrived at Moret; it was perhaps ten, eleven o'clock, even midnight. The emperor took up his quarters in the inn, to await the result of the reconnaissance which was being made in the forest. It was half past one or two in the morning when he learned that the road was free. We took up our march for Fontainebleau, where we arrived about four. We could see, in the darkness, on the sides of the road, the *chasseurs* and grenadiers of the Guard, who were hurrying along at a trot like very tired men; they were like ghosts. If they did not arrive at the *château* at the same time as the emperor they came in a quarter of an hour afterward. The emperor entered by the Court of the White Horse and went to his apartments, where he took a few minutes' rest, after which he made his toilet, to freshen himself up. Although he had travelled a great part of the way from Grenoble in a carriage, he seemed fatigued. One might have been for less.

About six o'clock some regiments of lancers, *chasseurs*, or hussars came to form ranks in the Court of the White Horse. Each regiment was small in numbers, but its organisation was pleasant to see. They had new uniforms, and each company had horses of the same colour. I think that it was during the night that these corps had given themselves to the emperor. His Majesty went down, and when he appeared

---

4. Michel Ney, Duke d'Elchingen, Prince de la Moskowa, Marshal of France. He was shot in December, 1815, for returning to his allegiance to Napoleon and fighting for him during the Hundred Days.

cries of "*Vive l'Empereur!*" rose from all the ranks. The review was long. As soon as the troops had passed before him he gave the order (or these regiments to march to Paris.

The emperor went back to his apartments and breakfasted. Between eleven and twelve o'clock he gave orders to leave. The grenadiers and *chasseurs* of the Guards, although very tired, put their knapsacks back on their shoulders joyfully; it was the last march which they would have to make. When everything was ready the emperor got into his carriage with the grand marshal. Post horses had been used ever since Grenoble, and they continued to be used all the way to Paris. Part of the cavalry which had been reviewed in the morning served as an escort. The whole army preceded or followed the emperor's *cortège*. We went at a slow trot, in order that everybody might keep up. The cavalry of the escort marched in single file on the two sides of the road; a multitude of the inhabitants of the villages accompanied the emperor, some inside, some outside the hedge of horsemen. Every moment there came high officers and many other personages of distinction to welcome the emperor and to swell his staff, which was already of considerable size. At Essonnes we found carriages drawn by horses from the stables of Louis XVIII, driven by coachmen, outriders, and postilions dressed as civilians, many of whom had formed part of His Majesty's household.

What we had seen thus far was not at all comparable with the spectacle which was offered to our eyes when the emperor arrived at Essonnes; it was nothing but carriages, saddle horses, officers of every rank, of every age, peasants, townsfolk, children, soldiers of every corps, of all arms—it was, in a word, an immense rendezvous where everything was topsy-turvy. Never could one see a greater variety, and all this multitude, radiant with joy, with happiness and enthusiasm, made the air ring with their cries of "*Vive l'Empereur! Vive Napoleon!*"

All the greatest personages, both civil and military, came to greet the emperor, who received them in the most affectionate manner. The Duke of Vicenza, my dear protector, was there also. The emperor made him get into the carriage.

The emperor was asked whether he wished to get into the carriage which they had prepared for him, but he refused, preferring to remain in that in which he was. Four fresh post horses were hitched on.

They set out. In spite of the hubbub around me I could hear the emperor speak in praise of me to the grand equerry, and I was even for some time the object of the conversation. In the circumstances my little vanity experienced the liveliest satisfaction, and a few glances from the duke, which I caught as I turned about from time to time, made me understand all the pleasure which he himself felt.

Finally we reached the Villejuif entrance to the city; we followed the *boulevard* and we reached the Invalides; we crossed the bridge of Louis XVI and we entered the court of the Tuileries by the Pont Royale gate. An immense crowd of people which had grown at every step had preceded or followed the cortege from the entrance to the city. Part of the population of the quarters near the boulevard had collected as the emperor passed, and blocked all the outlets. Until we reached the gate, as there was plenty of space, we moved freely, but once we were in the court it was no longer possible for us to advance. All the part on the side of the Pavilion of Flora, near which is the ordinary entrance to the palace, was filled with so compact a mass of generals, of officers, of National Guards, and a great quantity of persons of distinction, that it was impossible for me to get the carriage up to the steps. The emperor, seeing that he could go no farther, got out in the midst of the immense crowd which pressed about him, and as soon as he had set foot on the ground they took possession of him; they carried him, so to speak, to his apartments, without his foot being able to touch the steps of the staircase. It was about nine o'clock.

When the emperor was out of his carriage I gave it into safe hands and tried to follow His Majesty, but I had to give up the attempt; it was not possible to force my way. Without losing any time I went up the staircase of the Pavilion of Flora and I arrived more easily in the *salon* of the underofficers and then went into that of the high officers, where the emperor was at table with some gentlemen, among whom were the Grand Marshal, the Duke of Vicenza, perhaps General Drouot. Around stood chamberlains, equerries, generals, colonels and many other people, both civil and military.

The dinner was served as though the emperor had not left the Tuileries. None of the persons whose duty it was to serve was absent; the controller, M. Colin, the *major-domo*, Dunant, the carrier, the ushers, the valets attached to the apartments, the footmen, all were at their posts; the only difference was that most of them were in civilian dress. During his repast the emperor talked with one or another of those who surrounded him, often talking with them all, telling them what had happened during his journey from the island of Elba, etc. When dinner was finished he rose from table, bowed to all those present, and passed into the *salon* accompanied by the grand marshal, the grand equerry, and some other persons with whom he was intimate. Soon afterward, as the crowd which had filled the *salons* and the staircase had dispersed, calm reigned in the interior of the palace as in the past.

I will not tell of the reception which the emperor met with in Paris on the part of the people; it was the same as those at Grenoble, at Lyons, and in all the cities and villages through which he had passed. The history of ancient and modern times offers nothing so extraordinary, so marvellous, as the events which unfolded themselves in so inconsiderable a space of time. It was one of the admirable parts of the great reign of Napoleon.

The emperor did not remain long in the Tuileries. He went to live in the Élysée; there he had more liberty and could walk. Exercise was necessary to take his mind off his heavy load of work.

He worked a great deal during the whole time that he occupied this residence. He rose habitually toward one or two o'clock in the morning and went into his study, which he did not leave till about seven or half past. Sometimes he would go back to bed and rest for half an hour, then he would dress and go to his levee, which was at nine o'clock. After that he would breakfast. I never saw him so active. This could not help being so, since he had to reorganise everything. He felt the necessity, the importance, of having everything pass through his hands and before his eyes. It was absolutely imperative that everything should be done quickly. He had no time to lose; the army especially needed all his attention, his watching, his care.

The disaster of 1814, the ease with which the Bourbons had yielded to the exactions of the Allies, all had impoverished the resources of France to such a point that nothing less than the prodigious genius of the emperor could produce favourable results with the scattered fragments which the *Restauration* had forgotten to destroy and to supply what was lacking. If the Hundred Days are conspicuous because of the unheard-of misfortunes which overwhelmed France, they are also remarkable for the marvellous and supernatural power which the emperor displayed in so critical a juncture. He was opposed by all parties and hindered in his progress at every step by the crowd of plotters of every sort, wrapped in Royalist or Republican cloaks, all directed by superannuated prejudices or personal interest. It was a difficult task, but the emperor would have accomplished it if it had not been for the many blunders which his generals committed in the Waterloo campaign.

CHAPTER 7

Waterloo

When the emperor had made all his arrangements for the campaign, and the Guard had started several days before, he left the Élysée on June 12th at two or three in the morning, to go to the army. The grand marshal was with him. It was I who rode on the box of his carriage. He breakfasted at Soissons, slept at Laon; the next day, the 13th, at Avesnes, the 14th at Beaumont and the 15th at Charleroi. He was received with enthusiasm everywhere. The 16th the Battle of Ligny took place.

During the entire afternoon the emperor remained near a mill situated on a little hill from which we could see the whole of the enemy's right. The telescopes were constantly turned in this direction; they thought every moment that they saw the arrival of Count d'Erlon's[1] corps, which was impatiently expected. It was learned afterward that it had lost its way.

Before the emperor had come to take his place by the mill there was a group of young staff officers a little way off, among them some orderly officers. They were laughing boisterously and jesting noisily about the different incidents which were happening a short distance before them in a fight between some Prussians and Frenchmen. The emperor, who heard the noise that these officers made, from time to time cast glances toward them which indicated disgust and irritation. Finally, annoyed and exasperated by so much gayety, he said, looking with severity at the one who was laughing and talking the loudest, "*Monsieur*, one ought not to laugh or jest when so many brave men are cutting one another's throats before our eyes."

At nightfall the emperor approached the village of Ligny. The artillery of the Guard had been and still was firing heavily at the other

1. Count Drouet d'Erlon. Marshal of France.

side of a ravine occupied by the Prussian Army when the head of the column of cuirassiers appeared. At the same moment this brave troop plunged unto the lane which divides the village in two, crossed the ravine, and fell upon the enemy. It had defiled before the emperor at a gallop. These gallant soldiers, whose squadrons followed one another rapidly, were so full of enthusiasm that they cried at the top of their lungs, "*Vive l'Empereur!*" which was heard far off. "Spare your horses! Spare your horses!" the emperor never stopped telling them. "You will need them later." But the *cuirassiers*, paying no attention to the words which they heard, although they were repeated by Marshal Soult,[2] still followed those who had preceded them. This march past the emperor, which took place to the light of cannon and accompanied. by their roar, was a magnificent spectacle. Brave *cuirassiers!* I still seem to see you brandishing your swords and rushing to the combat. How splendid you were!

During the whole day the enemy offered a strong resistance, but in the evening he was obliged to retreat, leaving many of his men on the field of battle. Glorious as the day had been for the French arms, people in general were not satisfied with it, as it did not afford the results which had been hoped for. There was nothing decisive. The loss of General Gérard was particularly to be regretted.

The night was far advanced when the enemy was in full retreat. Headquarters were quartered in a sort of *château*, or country house, not far from the field of battle.

The next morning the army moved against the English. The emperor went across the field of battle of the day before. When he reached a spot where two roads met he was greatly displeased at not finding Marshal Ney and his army corps there. His impatience showed itself in the highest degree. He had already waited a long time when the head of a column was seen; they were hussars or *chasseurs*. He said to the general who was at the head: "What have you been doing all the morning? The marshal's corps ought to have been here long ago! How much time you have made me lose!" He showed by reiterated expressions all the irritation which he felt at this delay, which stopped and suspended his operations. His horse, excited by the sound of the trumpets, kept turning to right and left, and would not keep still. He seemed to share his rider's annoyance.

The emperor could not comprehend this slowness on the marshal's part. It was only necessary for him to desire his lieutenants to show

2. Nicholas Jean de Dieu Soult, Duke of Dalmatia, Marshal of France.

activity and rapidity in their marches for them to be negligent in the execution of his orders; it seemed as though there was collusion among them. It might be said that in this short campaign everything conspired to go contrary to what the emperor wished. Two days before, General Vandamme,[3] instead of arriving at Charleroi at noon, did not reach there till three o'clock. All these delays had as their consequence the terrible catastrophe of June 18th. As soon as the emperor had finished speaking the column marched, and the soldiers, as they defiled before him, greeted him with cries of, "*Vive l'Empereur!*" a thousand times repeated.

The weather, which had been passable during the morning, turned to rain, and the water fell in such abundance that the plain became impassable. We were soaked to the bones. At a halt the emperor asked for his cloak.

At the entrance to a village on the main road the *chasseurs à cheval* were in pursuit of a body of English cavalry; they were so covered with mud that their faces were no longer human. In these circumstances they made prisoners of war of some English officers. The emperor was then on the right and close to the road; the spot was seven or eight feet above the causeway. One of the prisoners, who had the uniform of the hussars (grayish sky blue), passed by the emperor with a grave and disdainful air which seemed to say, "Today I am your prisoner, but tomorrow you and your army will be annihilated." He was on foot, free, and was making his way to the rear of the French Army.

A few minutes later, and in another spot equally close to the road, the emperor, seeing another officer of the same regiment as the preceding, had him brought to him. This one was wounded in the arm. The emperor questioned him through General Flahaut,[4] who knew English and served as interpreter. When the officer had answered the questions which were put him the emperor ordered his surgeon to dress his wound. This dressing was made a few steps behind His Majesty and close to the Guard. It was this same officer who sent the emperor at St. Helena, through his brother, who was in Canton, different articles of considerable value as a sign of his gratitude. This officer was

---

3. Dominique René Vandamme, made Count of Unebourg by Napoleon.

4. Auguste Charles Joseph, Comte de la Flahaut de la Billarderie, was generally believed to be the father of the Duke de Morny by Hortense after her separation from Louis, King of Holland. Morny helped his half-brother, Louis Napoleon, in the matter of the *coup d'état,* and held a prominent position in Parisian life for many years. Hortense seems to have regarded her relations with Flahaut in the light of a morganatic union.

named Mr. Elphinstone. The articles consisted of a set of ivory chessmen, of two open-work globes, also of ivory, and of a box containing counters of mother of pearl. Each piece had engraved on it a shield, on which was an N surmounted by a crown.

All the middle of the day the weather was very bad; it was only toward three or four o'clock that the rain ceased, but it remained foggy.

The emperor, who arrived by a road which joins the highroad to Brussels, went a quarter or half a league farther in advance, and we soon found ourselves on high ground which commands the large basin bounded on the north by the curtain of the Forest of Soignes. The horizon, which was gray, did not permit the naked eye to see distinctly; we only saw on our left an English rear guard followed by some French troops, where they fired from time to time cannon shots whose smoke we could see. It was near the end of the day. A little while after the emperor had finished examining the whole plain with his glass an immense line of fire shone in our eyes. It was the English artillery, which showed the immense front of its army in line of battle. There was only a single volley; then nothing more was heard but a few shots fired on the left, both by our advanced guard and by the enemy's rear guard, which was retiring.

It was night or nearly that when the emperor reached the Caillou Farm; he fixed his headquarters there. As his room was not yet ready, they made a bivouac fire near the buildings (these were to the right of the road), and there, lying on a bundle of straw, he waited while his room was being put in order to receive him. When he had taken possession of the little hovel in which he was to pass the night he had his boots taken off, and we had trouble in doing it, as they had been wet all day, and after undressing he went to bed, where he dined. That night he slept little, being disturbed every minute by people coming and going; one came to report, another to receive orders, etc.

The next day, the 18th, the emperor rose fairly early. He breakfasted with the Grand Marshal, the Duke of Dalmatia and some other persons, and then mounted his horse, followed by the Major General, the Duke of Dalmatia, the Grand Marshal, General Fouler, and all his suite. He went to the advanced posts to reconnoitre the positions occupied by the enemy and laid out the order of battle.

When all the corps had carried out their movements he passed through the ranks, where he was received with enthusiasm, after which he came and took his position back of Rosomme. The action began at the Park of Hougoumont. As this place was only a little way off, we could easily see the attack and defence. It was with great difficulty that we succeeded in dislodging the enemy from it. As the other parts of the line of battle were distant or concealed by inequalities in the ground, we could not see clearly with the naked eye the different movements which took place.

A good part of the day had passed, and it was but slowly that we gained any ground. In the afternoon General Bülow's[5] Prussian corps, which had been taken at first for Marshal Grouchy's,[6] commenced to make some progress and to give the enemy some chance of success. It was, I think, at three or four o'clock. At the moment when the first Prussian bullets came on our right I was sent to the Caillou Farm to tell Pierron, the *major-domo*, to bring something to eat, as the emperor and some of his suite needed to take some nourishment. As I went only a few bullets flew across the causeway, but on my way back there were a good many.

Not far away and behind the spot where the emperor was there was a hollow road in which a great number of the English Guards were killed (Horse Guards); we knew them by their height and by their large helmets with black crests.

When Bülow had been driven back the emperor sent forward the battalions of the Old Guard against the English. The cavalry had already been thrown in. Our wounded, who were very numerous, showed us the obstinacy with which the English resisted. Among the wounded I saw General Friant, who was still on horseback; a few minutes later Colonel Mallet, who was being carried by his soldiers. The latter, recognising me, made me a sign to give him a drop of brandy. I gave it to him at once. I was carrying the emperor's flask. The emperor, who half an hour before, perhaps longer, had left the greater part of his staff and his escort to direct the attack of the infantry of the Guard, came back to us half an hour later.

Night was beginning to cover the field of battle when Marshal Blücher came into action on our right and carried disorder into some French regiments, and this disorder, spreading from one to another, soon became general. The Guard was obliged to change front and then to form squares, in one of which the emperor and his suite took refuge, to escape from the Prussian cavalry, which was overrunning the field of battle. When the squall blew over the emperor gave the

5. Friedrich Wilhelm von Bülow, Count of Dannewitz.
6. Emmanuel, Marquis de Grouchy, Marshal of France.

NAPOLEON AT WATERLOO

order to retreat. Bülow's corps, which had resumed the offensive, and which was already cutting the main road, threatened to surround us entirely.

The emperor's carriage and the Household transport had remained at the Caillou Farm. The emperor's carriage was taken during the evening. The postilion, Horn, who drove it, not seeing room to extricate it from the carts and other vehicles which obstructed the road, seeing the Prussian cavalry on the point of cutting him off, and besides that seeing cannon balls and bullets falling around him, unhitched his horses, while the first footman, Archambault, took the portfolio and dressing case out of the carriage. This remained where it was, and almost immediately fell into the hands of the Prussians, who pillaged it, as well as Marchand's, which contained the emperor's clothes.

There was a sword which was forgotten by Archambault; it was in all respects like that which His Majesty was wearing, except that on this latter was written, on the broadest face of the blade, these words, inlaid in gold:

The sword which the emperor wore at the Battle of Austerlitz.

I have never heard anyone speak of the sword which was taken in the carriage. What has become of it? It seems to me that I have read somewhere that it fell into Wellington's hands. It is more probable that some Prussian soldier got it, broke off the blade, and kept the hilt as only being of real value to him. This hilt was of gold, as were the trimmings of the scabbard.

To come back to Horn—this poor fellow had his arm carried away by a ball during the confusion. The next day, as Blücher [7] was riding over the field of battle with some of his officers, he stopped before Horn, who was sitting on a stone, and asked him who he was. The postilion replied to him in German that he belonged to His Majesty's household and drove His Majesty's carriage. Blücher, who was a very violent and fiery man, and had a heart full of hatred and vengeance against him with whom he had had to do on the 16th, overwhelmed the unfortunate man with abuse and had the cruelty, one may say the barbarity, when Horn made some reply, to give him a blow. If the marshal had been a different sort of man, would he not have had the poor devil's wound dressed and have given him money, rather than to maltreat him as he did?

Later, when the carriage had been bought by an Englishman, Horn

7. Gebhardt Leberecht, Prince von Blücher, Field Marshal.

described it to the people to whom it was exhibited.[8]

In the long column of soldiers of all arms, of all corps, of all regiments who were retreating, each one going his own way, the very small group of which the Emperor was the centre marched with all the rest, going to Philippeville. It was a summer night without a moon; one could see, but not distinguish clearly. Bivouac fires were here and there on the road, and around them men were resting who were worn out and dying with hunger. We went on calmly and quietly, the horses at a walk.

During the 19th, in the middle of the day, we arrived at Philippeville. The emperor, extremely fatigued not only by the long journey but by the day of the 18th and the small quantity of sleep on the night before, went to a shabby inn and got a room. I half undressed him and he went to bed to try to get some rest. He was very sad, and, above all, very much absorbed in thought. It was in this town of Philippeville that the Duke of Bassano joined him again.

The emperor took a little food.

Toward evening they brought before the door of the inn two travelling carriages of a sort, I put in the box of that which was meant for the emperor fifteen or twenty packages of gold, each containing ten rolls of a thousand *francs*, which the Duke of Bassano had sent to me a moment before. The two field glasses belonging to the emperor were put in the carriage which was to follow, which was to be accompanied by the courier Daussin.

When the hour for departure arrived the post horses were hitched to the carriage, which could not hold more than two people and which had no box seat. As I was determined to accompany the Emperor at any cost, I was very much embarrassed. How was I to go? As there were iron points on the shelf behind the carriage I could not sit there. I saw no other way but to perch behind, after the manner of footmen, holding myself up by the aid of two straps which were on the top, and there was only just room for my two feet on the shelf. As the days were long, I hoped, as soon as daylight came, to find some other more agreeable way of travelling. The emperor and the grand marshal got into the carriage, I settled myself as well as I could, and we started.

The other carriage remained a good way behind, so that we should appear to be travelling separately and not attract the eyes of curious

---

8. This was probably the carriage which was long exhibited at Madame Tussaud's in London.

people whom we might meet. I suffered a great deal during the whole journey. I feared perpetually that the straps might break or come loose, and that I should fall over backward, with my feet caught on the iron points. The road was very rough and tired me terribly. It was a long time to spend in a most trying position. I kept up my courage, always hoping to relieve my pain at the first opportunity. Finally the emperor stopped at Laon, where he arrived on the 20th between three and four o'clock. I was worn out, as can well be imagined; it had not been possible for me to close my eyes in the position in which I had been obliged to remain so long.

I do not recollect where the emperor got out of his carriage, but I know that we found ourselves in the courtyard of an inn of good size, where the emperor remained for some hours, walking about and talking with the principal people of the town, such as the prefect, the mayor, officers of the National Guard, and some other people, sometimes with one, sometimes with another. I remember that the officers of the National Guard showed great devotion both by the warmth which they showed in their conversation and by the expressions which they used. There were a goodly number of townspeople and peasants in the courtyard who uttered cries of "*Vive l'Empereur!*" from time to time. Everybody was conscious of the great misfortune of him who had been at the head of a fine army, full of enthusiasm, a few days before, and who today had lost everything but honour. These cries of "*Vive l'Empereur!*" had something in them which saddened the soul.

It had at first been the emperor's intention to stop at Laon to await the remains of his army, to organise them and to unite with the corps of Marshal Grouchy, but, feeling that his presence might perhaps be useful in Paris, he decided to go to the capital.

The prefect, who had seen our pitiful equipage, offered his carriage to the emperor, who accepted it, and they went to fetch it. It was cleaner and more comfortable than that which had brought him from Laon. The horses were hitched to it and the emperor got into it with the grand marshal, and I was on the box. As we started, repeated cries of "*Vive l'Empereur!*" came to ring in our ears, but those who uttered them had sadness in their hearts and tears in their eyes.

Early on the 21st we arrived at the entrance to Paris, where the road ends which we had just come over, but the emperor, not wishing to go in by that entrance, made the carriage turn to the right to follow the outer wall to the entrance of the Barrière du Roule. We entered

Paris through that. We went down the rue du Faubourg. As the shops were closed, for the most part, we were able to reach the Élysée without anyone's knowing outside that the emperor had returned.

A single person was in the courtyard, where he was walking; it was the Duke of Vicenza. He ran to the steps to receive the emperor, and they both, followed by the grand marshal, entered the apartments. The silence of the place at the arrival of its master wrung my heart. As soon as the emperor and the grand marshal had got out I had the carriage driven into the small courtyard on the left, and I took out of it the packages of gold, which I carried into the little bedroom and put in the bottom of a wardrobe which was opposite the fireplace.

When the other carriage arrived Daussin gave me some of the things which I had given him to take care of, but he gave me only one of the two telescopes. The one which was missing had probably tempted some one who wanted to have a souvenir. It was silver mounted.

After talking for some time to the grand equerry the emperor came to his room, had himself undressed, and got into his bath. One would rather have seen him go to the Chamber of Deputies covered with the mud of the battlefield and the dust of the journey.

As soon as the emperor's arrival in Paris was known, a few people, some great, some small, came to resume their service, but there was no more that multitude of people coming and going as before. The emperor, for most people, was now only a ruined man, who consequently ought to be abandoned.

On the 22nd the emperor abdicated.

I do not recollect very clearly what I did after the emperor returned to the Élysée. Events succeeded one another so rapidly that of all that happened I remember only what I am going to tell.

I recollect that at the Élysée there were groups standing before the palace every day, as well as in the avenue Marigny, and that from time to time cries of "*Vive l'Empereur!*" were heard, and especially on the side by the terrace where the emperor occasionally walked. I also recollect that several bodies of troops shouted the same thing.

I do not know now what prevented my going to Malmaison with the emperor. Perhaps I was not on outside duty that day; perhaps I had been obliged to remain in Paris to get some clothes and replace the portmanteau and its contents which had remained at Waterloo in the emperor's carriage. It was only the following day that I went to Malmaison.

REVERY

A few minutes after I arrived at the *château* I was in the room next to the bedroom, when a door opened and I saw the emperor appear. "Where is Madame Walewska?" he asked.[9]

"Sire, I do not know. I have just arrived from Paris." He closed the door as soon as my reply was finished. Marchand, who was better informed than I, had just gone out.

I recollect that when the emperor wanted some sporting guns I was ordered to go to Versailles to ask for some at the kennels. I made the trip with the greatest speed. One of the head men gave me four—three single, silver mounted, and one with a revolving breech, double-barrelled. During my absence many carriages had been brought to Malmaison and a considerable number of saddle and carriage horses.

All the preparations for the emperor's departure had been made. A little travelling carriage of the most ordinary and most modest sort had been prepared for him, and carriages with coats of arms and other carriages were to receive the persons who composed the suite and carry the baggage of each of the travellers.

Among the different articles which the emperor took away there was a silver service, one of porcelain (the beautiful Paris one, from the Sèvres factory), toilet articles, a *lavabo* with pitcher and bowl of silver from the Élysée, two field beds with all the accessories, cards, books, etc., etc. The *calèche* was furnished with a little *cantine*, with some toilet articles, with a sum of money consisting of a good number of little rolls of gold and several pairs of pistols. There were also arms in most of the other carriages.

The *chef d'escadron*, Bellini, who had been equerry to Madame Mère at Elba, and his wife, who was a Spaniard, had come to Malmaison, hoping to be included among the people who were to accompany the emperor. But as the number of those who had been accepted was already too considerable, His Majesty caused them to be thanked by the grand marshal, who expressed to them the emperor's regrets at not being able to take them with him.

---

9. Countess Walewska's liaison with Napoleon was an example of the most disinterested patriotism. Napoleon met her, fell in love with her, and made advances to her which She sternly repelled, for she was of a very religious nature. But the greatest pressure was brought to bear upon her by the most prominent and respectable Poles, who insisted to her that she might be the saviour of her country by persuading Napoleon, through his love for her, to restore its liberty to Poland. She finally yielded. Although she did not love him, she remained faithful to him and was among the last who stood by him at Malmaison, as Saint-Denis shows.

CHAPTER 8

Malmaison to Rochefort

When the emperor had decided to start from Malmaison (June 29th) he sent for me. It was about half past three. I had been chosen to ride on the box. He asked me whether his carriage was furnished with everything that he could need. When I replied in the affirmative he commanded me to have it brought to a little door which he indicated. This door was in the right wing of the *château*, facing the walk which leads to the high road to Saint-Germain. I at once did what he had ordered, and a few minutes later he went to the door indicated, accompanied by the Duke of Rovigo,[1] the grand marshal, and General Beker. The latter was an agent of the provisional government furnished with powers to secure the emperor's safety, and probably to keep watch on his actions if there should be need.

Queen Hortense[2] and some other persons whom I had seen in the *salon*, and who accompanied the emperor to the foot of the staircase, remained inside without crossing the threshold of the door until the carriage had gone away.

In order to deceive those who were present at his departure the emperor had given orders to bring up the principal entrance to the *château* the diligence in which it was expected that he would ride, but this precaution was useless. He could not entirely escape the eyes of the spectators, who all knew him too well and were too eager to see him once more, to allow themselves to be deceived by appearances.

---

1. Anne Jean Marie René Savary, Duke of Rovigo. He was a general in the army, and the head of Napoleon's secret police in 1802. He returned to the army, and then, in 1810, became Minister of Police.

2. Both of Napoleon's stepchildren were intensely loyal to him. During the Hundred Days Hortense and her sons took their stand by his side, filling the place of Maria Louisa and the King of Rome.

Before setting foot in the carriage the emperor cast a rapid glance about him, as if to bid farewell to the spot which had been, so to speak, the cradle of his power, and where every one of his steps had left a memory.

The emperor and his companions were in civilian clothes with round hats on their heads. As soon as they had taken their places in the carriage, this, which had four horses hitched to it and was driven by two postilions, went out of Malmaison, turned to the right, and took the road which runs behind the park and ends at Versailles.

At the same time that the emperor's carriage started General Gourgaud, Messrs. de Las Cases (father and son),[3] Count and Countess de Montholon,[4] etc., got into those which were drawn up in the Court of Honour. At this moment the guard, which was composed of *chasseurs* of the Old Guard, got under arms and beat the assembly. The servants also got into the carriages which had been appointed for them. Several of these carriages had been ordered to follow the emperor, but to stay far enough behind not to make a procession with his. As for all the others, including that in which were General Gourgaud, etc., they were to leave the road which was to be taken by His Majesty

---

3. Emmanuel Auguste Dieudonné, Marquis de Las Cases, was in the French navy before the Revolution, but had to emigrate because of his noble connections, and he did not return to Paris till 1799, by which time he had gained some reputation as a writer. Napoleon appointed him a chamberlain in 1809, and in 1810 made him a count of the empire. He was employed in many diplomatic matters. He was made a councillor during the first Bourbon Restoration, but during the Hundred Days rejoined Napoleon. It is doubtful whether he meant from the first to accompany him in his exile, or whether circumstances made it impossible for him to withdraw, but the latter seems to be probable. He was transferred to the Cape of Good Hope in 1816 because of a letter which he wrote bitterly criticizing Sir Hudson Lowe, but there is evidence to show that he did this deliberately, in order to be sent away, because for various reasons his position had become intensely disagreeable. The atmosphere of the Longwood household was far from peaceful, and it is one of Saint-Denis's greatest merits that he never repeats any of the mean tittle-tattle in this connection. Las Cases published the *Mémorial de Saint Heléne*, which is an account of his conversations with Napoleon, giving the emperor's opinions on all sorts of subjects. He was confined at the Cape for a while, then at Frankfurt, and was finally allowed to return to France on Napoleon's death.

4. Count Charles Tristan de Montholon was first in the French navy, but later entered the army. He fought in all the campaigns of the Consulate and Empire, rose to the rank of general and went to St. Helena with Napoleon. After his return to France he published a book of memoirs of St. Helena. He remained a consistent Bonapartist, was involved in the abortive attempt of Louis Napoleon at Boulogne in 1840, and was imprisoned with him in the fortress of Ham.

and to go to Orleans and Tours.

Having left Malmaison and having reached the side road, we had to go up a hill which was somewhat long and steep. We were going at a walk. Amandru, who was acting as courier, was near the carriage. The emperor, seeing that he had a hunting knife with an eagle's head, and thinking that this might cause him to be recognized, ordered me to tell him to put it in the carriage. Amandru was irritated at the order and showed ill temper when he gave me the knife. As soon as we had reached the top of the hill he left us and went ahead as if to prepare the relays.

In order to reach Saint-Cyr we entered the large park of Versailles by the Saint-Antoine gate, and took the paved road which runs along the Trianon and passes before the Royal Gate. When we reached Coignières and stopped before the post we were surprised not to find the horses ready.

"Where is Amandru?" the emperor asked me.

"Sire, I do not know," I replied. "I do not see him."

I got off the box at once and went to find the master of the post, to find out if a courier had not preceded us. His reply was in the negative. The postilions immediately set about harnessing the four horses which we needed. After waiting about a quarter of an hour we went on. We thought that, instead of going to Coignières, Amandru had gone to Versailles, where he probably found that he needed to go, but that we should see him at the next relay.

The emperor, in order not to have it suspected who he was, had thought that he only ought to pay the postilions simply as a well-to-do private, person would do, but those who had been driving him knew him too well to be deceived, and it is to be presumed that at each relay, the first ones especially, the postilions did not fail to inform those who took their places who was the important person who was in the carriage.

When we arrived at the gate of the Park of Rambouillet the emperor had it opened and we went to the *château*. The sun had disappeared from the horizon. The porter or servant belonging to the *château* opened the gate of the *château* and then hastened to go and open the doors of the apartments. The emperor, who seemed somewhat indisposed, went to his bedchamber and told me to make his bed. I did not know anything about the room, never having entered it, and I should have been greatly embarrassed if Hébert, the porter, who had acted as valet indoors, had not come to my aid, happily, and had not given me everything that I needed. We made the bed and the emperor retired immediately. I think that Hébert's wife made him a cup of tea. He was very restless all night. The different situations in which he had found himself since the evening of the 18th of June, that in which he was at present, and those, shrouded in darkness, through which he was yet to go, must have been the object of all his thoughts and reflections. He seemed profoundly disheartened. With day, calmness came back to him. Feeling better, he had himself dressed and ate a bowl of soup which had been prepared for him.

The night before, in undressing the emperor, I noticed that a small bag was attached to the buckle of his suspenders, but on reflecting a little I suspected what it might contain, from the care which he took to have his suspenders always under his hand, so that he might not be obliged to look for them. I also perceived that he had around his waist a silken sash in which were a number of hard bodies having the feeling and form of apricot pits, somewhat elongated, which I thought rightly to be diamonds.

In the morning, when the carriage came up to the steps, I looked everywhere for Amandru, but, as I did not see him, there was no longer any doubt that he had abandoned the emperor. I never was able to understand what could have induced him to act in this way, for he had always served His Majesty well and had shown himself full of devotion. This behaviour of Amandru might have had very unpleasant consequences at Coignières, a place so near Versailles, and might have endangered the emperor's safety and even his life, since we had had to wait a good quarter of an hour while the horses were being hitched up. It seemed to me that when he left us his head was a little heated by certain glasses of wine or liqueur. Santini acted as courier, but I confess that I never saw him afoot or on horseback at any posting house from Rambouillet to Rochefort.

As the emperor had recovered, he set out about six o'clock in the morning (June 30th). Many of the inhabitants who were outside of the gates cried "*Vive l'Empereur!*" as the carriage started. We took the road through the park.

Toward the middle of the day we passed through a little town where there were a number of women selling fruit. The emperor stopped the carriage and told me to buy him some pounds of cherries. While I went to one of the dealers the carriage was surrounded by people who looked closely at the strangers, but the emperor, to escape their curiosity and not to be known, had his hand on the cheek which was visible and seemed to be asleep in his corner. As soon as we were outside of the town he and his companions took great pleasure in cooling their mouths, as I saw by the cherry stones which they threw out. It was a little distraction from the weariness of the journey.

The emperor stopped at Saint-Amand, or Chateau Renault, a village or little town eight or ten leagues before Tours. To tell the truth, I do not know whether it was in one of these towns or in another, but there was a relay. I recollect that the inn where the emperor stopped was situated on the right hand in a narrow street which was the principal one of the town. It might have been nine o'clock. The mistress of the house conducted the travellers into a room upstairs, where they settled themselves. They were waiting for their dinner to be served when some police officers came to ask for their passports.

One of the generals, the Duke of Rovigo, I think, went out of the room and showed them, but as they were not in very regular form there was a somewhat long discussion which ended after some explanations. The police officers being satisfied and having retired, the duke came back, the dinner was served, and the travellers began to eat. When the emperor had dined and rested a little he went down out of the room with his companions to get into his carriage again. The inn kitchen through which he had to pass was full of people; as he appeared everyone drew aside and made room for him to pass, and hardly was he in the carriage when cries of "*Vive l'Empereur!*" were heard both from the people who were inside and from groups which had been formed in the streets. Who had made the emperor's presence known? Perhaps the police officers themselves, perhaps some old soldiers. I saw some windows that were illuminated.

Between this place and Tours there are woods on both sides of the road. We were rolling along without any other noise than that of the carriage on the pavement when, about halfway, I heard the distant gallop of horses coming nearer and nearer. I informed the emperor. Shortly afterward I saw two *gendarmes*, who came up to the door and asked very politely if we had seen or heard anything; they explained to us that there were bandits in the neighbourhood who stopped and robbed travellers. When we replied that nothing had happened to us and that we had not heard anything they went away, saluting us and wishing us a pleasant journey.

We arrived at the post house in Tours in the middle of the night. It is on the right, on the road to Blois. The emperor sent the Duke of Rovigo to the prefect. When the horses were hitched up we passed the bridge. At an office which was in the first house on the right on entering the town they asked for our passports, which were *viséd* immediately, and then we reached the other end of the town. Outside of the gate the emperor had the carriage stopped and got out. We waited there nearly a quarter of an hour, and the Duke of Rovigo joined us with the prefect. Both went away with the emperor to a distance of twenty yards from the carriage and began a conversation. During this time the grand marshal and General Beker remained in the carriage, talking about indifferent matters. The emperor's interview with the prefect lasted nearly an hour. When the emperor came to get into the carriage the prefect said farewell to him and kissed his hand.

We continued our journey. During the morning, a short quarter of a league from Poitiers, the emperor stopped the carriage and went with the other gentlemen into the little house of a villager on the right, some twenty yards from the road. He asked for a glass of cool water, which I served to him after asking the woman of the house to give me a glass. He came back afterward to his carriage, which had remained on the road in the care of the postilions, got into it, and we reached the town, where the emperor lodged in an inn beyond and near the posthouse. He had breakfast served. We remained in this inn during all the great heat of the day. Toward two or three o'clock we set out again.

On leaving the town a sentry asked for the passports, which were returned to us almost immediately. We went toward Niort. During the journey, not far from Niort, there was rather a long hill to ascend. The sun had just set. The emperor and the other gentlemen had got out and were following a few yards behind the carriage. A man, who seemed to me a farmer, was walking on the right of the road. From time to time as he went he would glance at the emperor and look at him with a good deal of attention. Edging over in my direction, he came near me, who was close to the carriage, and said, "Who are these gentlemen?"

"They are officers of high rank who are going to Niort."

"I don't know," he replied at once, "but there is one of them whom I seem to recognise. Certainly I have seen him somewhere."

"*Monsieur*, that is very possible."

At every step we took the farmer turned his head in the direction of the one who excited his curiosity and examined him more attentively. I have no doubt that he had recognised the emperor. When we had got to the top of the hill the travellers got into their carriage again and we started on.

It was night when we entered Niort. The emperor had the carriage stop before the door of an inn situated on the right and got out. This inn was of rather poor appearance. The master or mistress of the house showed the travellers up to a room on the first floor, which the emperor took. It was a good-sized room with one bed. On the same landing were other rooms of which the other gentlemen took possession, and in one of them the table was laid for supper, which was served without delay. The emperor remained at table for a good while. It was late when he returned to his room. He was undressed and went to bed. He could not rest quietly, being disturbed by the chatter of the inn people, who were collected in the kitchen, which was separated from the emperor's room only by a partition of boards supported by joists. It was not until a late hour that this noise stopped.

All was in the most complete silence when an incident came to trouble our rest. I was lying in the room on a mattress which I had placed across the door. I was lying there peacefully when I heard the noise of men wearing boots coming up the stair. When these individuals reached the landing they came and knocked at the door behind which I was, and even tried to open it, raising the latch. I rose at once and, partly opening the door, asked them what they wanted. They were two officers of *gendarmerie* looking for the Duke of Rovigo. After I had shown them where the duke's room was and had closed the door, the emperor waked up and asked me what the matter was. I told him what had happened.

The next morning, pretty early, the emperor was dressed. The prefect, who had learned that he was at an inn in the town, sent him his carriage. He got into it and went to the *perfecture*. I could not go there at once, but as soon as I had collected the luggage and put it in the carriage, to which I had two horses hitched, I went to the hotel. I found the emperor in bed in the prefect's room, and Marchand with him. The baggage wagons had arrived during the night.

The whole day passed very well. After dinner the emperor held a reception. During the evening the city rang with "*Vive l'Empereur! Vive Napoléon!*" It was almost like the evening of a holiday.

The next day, July 3rd, about half past four in the morning, the emperor, rested by a good night, started again with the same companions, going to Rochefort. A detachment of twenty-five *chasseurs*, commanded by an officer, escorted him for a considerable distance. When they had reached the place where they had to turn back the emperor stopped the carriage, thanked the officer, and gave some napoleons to the soldiers. As he saluted them he signed to me to tell the postilion to go on. We arrived at Rochefort pretty early. The emperor stopped at the maritime prefect's hotel and took up his quarters there. All that I remember of Rochefort is that this hotel is preceded by a long court planted with trees where convicts, dragging their ball and chain, were moving about, busy with the work of the hotel, and I recollect that every night we heard the sentries calling out, "Sentinel, watch out!"

CHAPTER 9

Rochefort to St. Helena

All the members of the emperor's suite who had started from Malmaison found themselves reunited at Rochefort. Prince Joseph [1] often came to see the emperor. I saw General Lallemant, whom I did not know, nor did I know that he was one of His Majesty's suite. Every morning the maritime *prefect* came to report to the emperor what was the state of the sea and what had been seen upon it. On July 8th the emperor left Rochefort and went to sleep on the frigate *Saale*. That day Noverraz was on duty. When the emperor had gone they gave me a sailboat and I went to join him. The emperor was very uncomfortable on board the frigate.

The officers did not appear favourable to his cause; the captain was far from being satisfied at seeing on his ship the great misfortune which had come to take refuge there. Knowing the events which had just happened, and foreseeing all the results which might flow from them, he thought it well to walk warily. Consequently I think that when the emperor decided to live on the island of Aix Captain Philibert must have exclaimed, "Ah! now I can draw a long breath!" Moreover, the ship was extremely badly kept; it showed its commander's negligence.

The quarter-deck was divided into two parts by a sail; the larger served as a bedroom for the emperor and the smaller was a den into which General Beker retired. It was only there that I perceived that nobody spoke out freely, as the general had ears to hear and a tongue to speak. He was an agent of the provisional government, and particularly of Fouché. [2]

---

1. The oldest of Napoleon's brothers. He held many positions in public life through his own merits. In 1808 Napoleon made him King of Spain.
2. Saint-Denis seems to have been hardly fair to General Beker. The poor man was sent, much against his will, by the provisional government to see Napoleon safely out of France, but there is nothing to indicate that he ever spied on him.

On the 12th of July the emperor left the *Saale* and went to live on the island of Aix.

During the day the emperor seemed decided to embark on a lugger commanded by Captain Besson. He had given me orders to put all the arms in good condition; they consisted of several pairs of pistols and four fowling pieces, one double with a revolving breech. The sailors of the ship came to get them and the ammunition for them in the evening. They also carried away things for the emperor's use, and linen, clothes, etc., for the needs of the voyage. These sailors, who were three in number, were accompanied by M. Besson.

The persons who were to embark with His Majesty to go to America were the Duke of Rovigo, the grand marshal, and General Lallemant. I had been chosen to accompany the emperor, as being the one who could best endure seasickness and fatigue. All was prepared; I was waiting, fully equipped, when I learned, about midnight, that in a family council and after mature deliberation it had been decided that the emperor should surrender to the English.

On July 15th, early in the morning, the brig *Épervier* hoisted her sails and toward five or six o'clock, or perhaps a little later, the emperor went aboard with his principal officers and they sailed in the direction where the English vessel lay anchored. We had gone some distance when we saw a boat coming to meet us. It was a boat from the *Bellerophon*. The first lieutenant of that vessel was on board. The English officer came on deck and saluted the persons who were there. After a conversation which lasted less than a quarter of an hour the emperor and his generals got into the English boat, which immediately went away from the brig with great rapidity.

The sea was smooth; the sun, which was shining in all its brightness, allowed us to follow the boat, which was soon only a black spot on the horizon. Our brig continued slowly on its way; the wind was weak and it was with difficulty that we got up to the English ship, near which we anchored.

As soon as the captain of the *Épervier* had seen the English boat leave our ship he went down into the cabin, where I had remained to take care of the emperor's baggage, and threw himself into a chair. He seemed extremely moved; with his head on his hand and tears in his eyes he heaved deep sighs. After some moments of gloomy silence his grief burst forth. He said, with the accent of despair, "Ah! why did not the emperor come aboard my ship instead of the *Saale*? I would have taken him anywhere he wanted; we would have answered with our lives. Into what hands has he just put himself? If he had known the perfidy of the English as I and my crew do, he would never have taken so deadly a resolution. Who can have given him such deadly advice? Oh Napoleon," the officer went on, continuing to sob, "you are lost, lost forever; a frightful presentiment tells me so!" And turning toward me, he said:

How happy are you; how I envy you your place, your fate! But now all that I can say is useless. They have caused him to fall into the snare; his implacable enemies have him. I hope that he will be happy; it is all that my heart desires. O Napoleon, Napoleon! What fate is in store for you? You counted on the generosity of the English. I pray God that your confidence may not be misplaced. As for me, I cannot believe it.

I was weeping with him. Before and after the emperor's departure I had heard the different conversations of the sailors. Most of them, who had been prisoners of the English, wholly agreed with their captain; none of them could understand how the emperor had had such an evil inspiration.

The French brig, which was anchored near the *Bellerophon*, transhipped aboard her everything which she had belonging to the emperor, and the captain then went to salute His Majesty and to say farewell. During the day all the persons who composed the emperor's suite and household went on board the ship, and they put aboard all the baggage which was on the lugger.

During the afternoon the *Superb*, with Admiral Hotham, the commander of the station, came and anchored near us, and soon afterward the admiral came on the deck of the *Bellerophon*. He was received by the emperor and dined with His Majesty.

The next morning the emperor got into a boat to go on board of the *Superb*, where he was to breakfast. I accompanied him. The admiral received him with distinction; the marines were under arms and the sailors were on the yards and on the masts. His Majesty reviewed the marines, and the admiral, who spoke French very well, took him to all parts of the ship. The greatest order and cleanliness reigned everywhere. Everything above the water line was scrubbed with sand; it was marvellous. When he had inspected everything they went on deck again and the admiral conducted the emperor into the cabin, where a breakfast had been prepared with care and studied elegance, but with simplicity. The admiral, who had extremely good manners, did the honours of the table admirably. The meal lasted a good while. When it was finished the emperor took leave of the admiral and returned to the *Bellerophon*. The reception which had just been given him pleased him greatly; it seemed to presage well for the future. Shortly afterward we sailed for England.

In order to accommodate the emperor's suite at once Captain Maitland had had some carpentry done on board to make cabins. The deck, between the main and mizzen masts, was decorated with flags and covered with a tent.

The nearer we got to England the more ships we saw, furrowing the sea in every direction.

July 24th, in the morning, we cast anchor in the roadstead of Torbay. The emperor had risen early to see the coast of England. We were not a little surprised to see General Gourgaud come aboard; he had not been permitted to go ashore. From that moment we thought that we saw something in our position which was not very clear. During the day some boats came to sail about our ship, and the next day the number was greater. The public ashore had probably learned that the emperor was on the *Bellerophon*.

On the 26th, early, our ship got under sail and started for Portsmouth. It was four or five o'clock in the afternoon when we entered the harbour of that city. As soon as we had anchored, boats of all sorts came from every side, but armed launches did not permit them to come near us, and a little later two frigates came and placed themselves to starboard and port of the *Bellerophon*. "Why these arrangements? What does it mean?" It seemed as if the authorities feared lest the curious visitors, whose numbers increased every hour, might wish to carry the emperor off. All this seemed of evil augury to us; from that time we could not conceal from ourselves that the emperor was considered a prisoner.

We had among us the *major-domo*, or *valet de chambre*, of the Duke of Rovigo; this man, who was an Englishman, told us everything that he heard said, either by the servants on board or by the sailors, especially those who had been ashore. They spoke of all sorts of things, they spoke of St. Helena, but all that they brought back was very vague.

The next day, the 27th, nothing had changed in our position. The crowd of boats grew larger and larger. One would have said that the harbour of Portsmouth had become the rendezvous of all the curious people in England. No boat belonging to any private person could come near us; launches and boats manned by sailors were constantly prowling about the *Bellerophon* and driving away anyone who ventured to pass the circular line which had been drawn.

Every day, about five o'clock in the afternoon, the emperor walked on the deck. Then all the boats and an infinity of small craft collected and crowded in, trying to see him. The harbour was like a vast square where the curious populace crowds and presses to see something that it has never seen before.

At the moment when the emperor appeared there were acclamations from all sides; everybody moved about and stood on tiptoe to see him the better. At first it was simple curiosity, but later this curiosity was succeeded by interest and admiration. It was easy for us to judge. The greater part of the visitors had their hats off and those nearest saluted the emperor with respect; ladies waved their handkerchiefs. I saw a boat containing several officers come pretty near, and these officers took off their hats and made profound bows. At that moment if all those people had been masters of the emperor's person they would have taken him to London, drawing his car like that of a conqueror. One may say that by his presence alone the emperor had won the sympathy of the English people.

On the 28th it was the same spectacle as the day before.

29th and 30th. Lord Keith, accompanied by an undersecretary of state, came to notify the emperor of the ministerial decision which deported him to St. Helena.

On August 4th, early, the *Bellerophon* made sail and left Portsmouth Harbour and went and cruised in the Channel, awaiting the arrival of the *Northumberland*, the seventy-four-gun ship designated to take us to St. Helena.

On the 6th, about midday, we anchored at a place called Start Point. The *Northumberland* came and anchored near us, as well as two frigates and the *Le Tonnant*, with Admiral Keith on board. Lord Keith and the admiral. Sir George Cockburn, came on board the *Bellerophon* and were received by the emperor.

On the 7th Admiral Cockburn came on board and ordered a search made of all the emperor's effects and those of the members of his suite. They took a comfortable sum from the emperor; they seized all the arms that we had brought on board the *Bellerophon*. I do not recollect whether the other gentlemen were obliged to give up their swords, but they did not demand the emperor's.

When the operation was finished and the moment had come to leave the *Bellerophon* the emperor went down into the boat and went on board the *Northumberland*. He was accompanied by the grand marshal and three other persons who had been designated to accompany him. More than one tear flowed from the eyes of those of our people who had not been happy enough to obtain the favour of accompanying the emperor to St. Helena.

When M. Maingaud, a young doctor who had been given to the emperor by Dr. Corvisart,[3] had learned of His Majesty's deportation to a distant island, he had refused to go, probably influenced by the fear of losing his life on so long a voyage. Doctor O'Meara,[4] the surgeon of the *Bellerophon*, to whom it was proposed to take the place of M. Maingaud, had accepted the position after obtaining the assent and permission of his superiors.

When the emperor had arrived on the deck of the *Northumberland* Admiral Cockburn presented to him two Englishmen of distinction, Lord Lowther and Mr, Littleton; he talked to them for a long time near the first cannon on the port side, those nearest to the deck cabin.

When the embarkation was finished, sail was made; the two Englishmen took leave of the emperor and we sailed for St. Helena. It was three or four o'clock.

Admiral Cockburn called the emperor "General" and "Excellency," but his style of speaking was not followed by all the other Englishmen, for the next morning Sir George Bingham, colonel of the 53rd, asking me about the emperor, said, "How is His Majesty?"

At dinner, which was at five o'clock, I served the emperor. The admiral was attentive and offered all the dishes which were on the table. Shortly after dessert was served His Majesty rose from the table and went to walk on deck, where the grand marshal and M. de Las Cases followed him. The admiral and all the English rose and were astonished at this sudden disappearance of the emperor; but they sat down again when they were informed that it was His Majesty's habit to remain a short time at table. They continued to eat their dessert.

What happened at this dinner took place every day at this meal,

---

3. Jean Nicholas des Marets Corvisart, Napoleon's physician, had already become distinguished before the Revolution. He enjoyed Napoleon's high esteem and complete confidence.

4. Barry Edward O'Meara was Napoleon's personal physician until removed in 1818. He became "Napoleon's man," whether from interested or disinterested motives has been hotly disputed. On his return to England he published *A Voice from St. Helena*, which was a bitter attack on Sir Hudson Lowe. A tremendous storm raged about this book, and it was republished as late as 1888, renamed *Napoleon at St. Helena*.

only the admiral took care to hasten the first courses and to have the coffee ready as soon as the dessert was served.

The table was square; in the middle of the side which faced the *salon* were the emperor and the admiral. The latter was on the right side of His Majesty, who had Madame Bertrand on his left; Madame de Montholon was on the right of the admiral. The other persons occupied the other places. It is to be noticed that the middle of the side of the table facing the *salon* was between the emperor and the admiral; in this way there was equality of place.

· When the English had finished their dessert they went to take the air on deck, and before it was dark they went into the salon, either to play cards or to talk. The emperor retired to his room early. This first evening was the pattern of all those which followed it.

It is well to report here that the emperor, in order that a part of his little treasure might escape the eyes of the English, had, before the search, given belts containing a certain quantity of gold to those who were to accompany him. That which he entrusted to me contained at least 25,000 *francs* in gold in Spanish pieces. When the emperor was settled in his cabin each one returned the belt which he had received. In one of M. de Las Cases's atlases the emperor had glued to one of the leaves a receipt from M. Lafitte for a considerable sum.

When everyone had gone out of the *salon* I placed my bed, which was composed of a small hair mattress of an inch in thickness, along the door of the emperor's little room or cabin, with the head against the door of the *salon*. Marchand slept in His Majesty's room itself.

The next day the emperor took the habit of rising about seven or eight o'clock. He had breakfast in his room from nine to ten o'clock. He remained in his dressing gown or his shirt sleeves until three or four o'clock, the hour when he dressed. He then passed into the *salon*, where he played a game of chess with one of the generals till the admiral came to inform him that dinner was served.

During the morning he would send for one of the gentlemen to converse with and to learn the news of the ship. Most of the time he amused himself in reading. Nearly all the time he was seated in his armchair.

From the 22nd to the 26th of August. On the 22nd we arrived before Madeira. The wind became excessive, the heat very great, and the sea high. We passed these four days in beating to windward, in tacking or in lying to. Some ships of our squadron anchored in the bay of Funchal to get fresh provisions and water.

The 27th. In the morning we found ourselves passing the Canary Islands. The fog was so thick that we could not see the Peak of Teneriffe, though they showed us in which direction it lay.

On the 29th we passed the Tropic of Cancer. We saw some flying fish.

On the 31st, at a rather late hour in the evening, a man fell or threw himself into the sea. In a moment the ship came up in the wind, boats were put overboard, torches were lit; distant cries were heard from time to time. This scene, which was lighted only by the whitish light of the torches, carried fear into all hearts. The darkness was so great that they could not find the poor man.

September 9th. The emperor dictated some parts of the siege of Toulon to M. de Las Cases.

19th to the 22nd. His Majesty dictated on his campaigns of Italy.

23rd, crossing the line. Early in the morning the sailors made preparations for the ceremony. Everything being ready, a sailor, transformed into a grotesque Neptune, was rolled in on a sort of chariot (a gun carriage); he was escorted by savages. When he had arrived at the part of the deck which is between the mizzen and the mainmast Neptune addressed the commander of the ship and invited him to bring before him, god of the seas, all those who had not yet fulfilled the laws of his empire, etc. Then all the men who had not yet passed the line were pursued by the satellites of the god, who made them mount, one after another, on a sort of scaffolding on which was placed a seat, on which they seated the patient, whose chin and face the executioners of the god daubed with tar.

Another executioner approached, armed with a wooden razor two feet long with a blade indented like a saw, and scraped the cheeks and chin of the man being initiated pretty roughly. After this operation the latter was tumbled into a boat full of water which was behind him. Those who resisted were the least gently handled; nobody was spared, not even the officers, not even the captain of the ship. During all the time that this ceremony lasted everything on board was in the greatest confusion, but as soon as it had ended everything became orderly and discipline resumed its sway.

On the 14th of October, in the afternoon, toward the end of the day, the watch called out, "Land!" They thought that they could see St. Helena. They lay to all night.

The 15th, early, we could see the island and its steep sides. Toward midday they cast anchor. The admiral went ashore soon afterward; he only returned about six o'clock in the evening. Several ships of our squadron, which had taken the ordinary route, had arrived some days before.

The 16th, after dinner, the emperor disembarked, and the admiral lodged him in a furnished house situated at the left-hand corner of the street and the square. His room was on the first floor. It is there that the persons attached to the service of the private apartments joined him. The house was very clean, but supplied with very few articles of furniture; everything was extremely simple. The emperor passed the night there.

During the morning there had been a distribution of the belts for the landing; I had two for my share. I had put them around my waist and 50,000 *francs* was a considerable weight to carry during a large part of the day; consequently I felt greatly relieved when I could get rid of my burden. My hips were flayed.

Chapter 10

St. Helena

The 17th. Early in the morning the admiral came to the house occupied by the emperor. He had had his two horses landed and brought one with him for the emperor's use; two other horses were also before the door, one for the grand marshal and one for me.

The emperor was ready. Before mounting his horse he ordered me to try it so that I might know whether he could use it without danger. After circling about a little I dismounted, assuring him that the horse was easy and gentle. He mounted and, accompanied by the grand marshal and Sir George Cockburn, who acted as guide, took the road which leads to Longwood, the spot chosen by the admiral to be the prison of the illustrious captive of the Holy Alliance.

I followed a few steps behind. Immediately on leaving the town we went steadily up until we reached the spot where the road is on level ground. The road was very good, though narrow, but on either hand I saw very deep ravines, for the most part without vegetation. When we got to the top and went almost straight ahead we had on our left for a good while a large hollow which is known as the "Devil's Punchbowl."

This name paints perfectly the abyss which we had before our eyes, the depths of which are contorted in an extraordinary manner; they are a multitude of ravines which rtm into one another and unite in a few which are deeper and still more frightful. These last unite again to form a single one with which the former cannot compare. Imagine a narrow and winding gorge with high rocks, black and straight up and down, as though they had been hewn by repeated bolts of lightning. Nothing is more hideous than this last ravine, which runs in this way down to the sea. We reached a house called Hutt's Gate. The ground back of the house is an amphitheatre and is, so to speak, the place where the Punchbowl starts. This valley is covered with verdure and contrasts singularly with what we have just described, which has so wild a look because of its black colour. Before us was a road which had a mountain on the right which overhangs it and which rises and forms one of the *aretes*, or roots, of the high, conical mountain called Diana Peak. This latter is absolutely covered with verdure in all parts. Clouds almost always rest on its top.

On the left is a valley which runs from west to east; it is covered with verdure for the most part. But let us come back to Hutt's Gate. There, on the left, was the road which was to lead us to Longwood; it followed the curve of the Punchbowl and ran on a level at our right. We arrived at two little houses which served as an entrance to a large enclosure. We left the road, which turned to the left as it ran along the Bowl, and we passed between the two houses, which were like guardhouses, and we went straight forward toward a dwelling which was at the end of the road. We had seen this dwelling as soon as we had reached the place where the road begins to run along the Punchbowl. On the right, here and there, were trees which seemed stunted because of their short trunks and their dry and thin foliage. This vegetation is effective from a distance, but near it is ugly and arid. It was noticeable that all the trunks of these trees were inclined a little toward the south. We approached the dwelling by degrees; it seemed to us fairly extensive.

Everything was clean about it, and the different plantations, as well as the lawns, made an agreeable picture for the eye, but nevertheless one felt the aridity of the neighbourhood. The shade which the trees threw was not thick enough to protect one from the burning sun of the tropics. The master and mistress of the house received the emperor as he got off his horse. They walked about the gardens, after which they went into a room where breakfast was served in the English fashion. They sat down at table. The lady, who was a person of from thirty to thirty-six years old, tall, blonde, speaking French excellently (she had been brought up in Paris), did the honours of the house very well and gracefully.

During the whole of breakfast the emperor took great pleasure in talking to her. When breakfast was finished they took a few more turns about the garden, and the emperor took leave of Mr. and Mrs. Skelton (the master and mistress of the house, the husband being the lieutenant-governor of the island) and mounted his horse, with the two persons who accompanied him, and we went back by the same road. We had gone at a walk; we returned at a walk. As I was somewhat behind, I could hear them talking, but could not catch enough words to make out the subject of the conversation, which probably turned on what they saw on the way. When we reached the descent I could see the different sites much better, as they followed one another and changed their appearance from the different directions which were taken by the road, which was often winding.

When we reached the curve which goes down into the valley which opens upon the town the emperor saw a group of small buildings, behind which was a little waterfall. When we reached the road which led to them he took it. The principal building was occupied by the Balcombe family,[1] whose acquaintance he made. The spot pleased him and he asked to live in an isolated building which was on the right, thirty or forty yards from the principal building. As the admiral made no objection, the emperor took possession of this retreat, which consisted of only a single room with a little square at the rear, in which was a stairway at the top of which was a loft transformed into a little room.

Orders were given for the emperor's bed to be brought, and the few articles of furniture which he used on his campaigns. The emperor told M. de Las Cases and Marchand to come and join him. In less than two hours the baggage was transported to "The Briars," and Marchand, who had come with the things, went to work with me to arrange the room in the presence of the emperor. M. de Las Cases arrived soon afterward. The count was lodged in the little room or loft which was above the emperor. Dinner was brought from the town, where the *service de bouche* had been established.

After dinner the emperor walked about the neighbourhood of the Balcombe house, and in the evening, when he was tired and it grew late, he went to bed. M. de Las Cases went to his loft and Marchand and I stretched out on the thin mattresses which they had brought us and which were the same, I think, which we had had on board the *Northumberland*.

During the early part of our stay at "The Briars" Noverraz and I were obliged to go and find wood to feed the emperor's fire. We had to pick up dry wood, to knock down that which was in the trees, and even to cut down these same trees, then to carry our supply to the house and amuse ourselves in making it into kindling. In the serv-

---

1. *Recollections of Napoleon at St. Helena* by Mrs. Abell (late Miss Elizabeth Balcombe) is also published by Leonaur.

ice of the emperor's private apartments it was useless to be particular about what one did; it was a good deal like camp life. Later the government furnished what wood we needed and we had a Chinaman to do the heavy work. It was the emperor's habit not to want anyone in his apartments, especially the two little rooms, except his *valets de chambre*, and nothing was done except by their hands. [2]

After the emperor moved up to Longwood he was very curious to see everything which went on about his house, and it was for that purpose that he had a hole cut in one of the slats in the shutter of the first window, on the west side of the room called the reception room, so that he could apply the object glass of his telescope to it. He could already see everyone who came by the guardhouse very well. This was the way that Sir Hudson Lowe and Sir Thomas Reade usually came, as well as other members of the governor's suite and visitors. A similar hole was made in the shutter of one of the two little windows on the right and left of the veranda or trellised front porch, which enabled him to have a view over the whole camp, which was on the north. He also had one made in the shutter of the first window looking out on the east lawn and the wood. On this side he could see the arrival of the ships which put in to St. Helena.

Looking through his telescope was a pleasure which the emperor often gave himself during the course of the day, and he forgot nothing which could make him a spectator of what went on around him, so that he had the branches which might obstruct his view cut away. If the governor and his aids were at Longwood and they were outside of the space covered by his telescope, he would send one of his valets to find out what had become of them and what road they had taken.

One day when the emperor was in the reception room with Madame de Montholon he looked through his telescope and saw a number of people who had stopped outside of the boundary. They were M. and Mme. Sturmer, M. de Montchenu, and perhaps the Russian commissioner, M. Balmain.[3] Madame Bertrand, accompanied by

---

2. The emperor's household at St. Helena was composed, at the outset, of Count and Countess Bertrand, Count and Countess de Montholon, the two Las Cases (father and son), and General Gourgaud, besides the following servants: Marchand, first *valet de chambre*; Saint-Denis and Noverraz, *valets de chambre*; Santini, usher—these four being "servants of the chamber." Archambault senior and junior, grooms, and Gentilini, footman, were "servants in livery," and the "servants for the table" were Cypriani, *maître d'hôtel*; Pierron, butler; Lepage, cook; and Rousseau, steward.

3. Napoleon was considered by the Allies to be their joint prisoner, not the prisoner of England alone. They were determined that there should (cont over the nexr pages),

A. Sofa on which the Emperor was a great part of the day, turned toward the fireplace, B, over which were distributed three portraits of the Empress, five of the King of Rome, one with a background embroidered by the Empress, also a little marble bust of the King of Rome.

C. Small table on which the Emperor breakfasted; he often made my father come, especially at the time of his English lessons.

D. Little field bed in which the Emperor slept. It is of iron.

E. Another little bed like it. When he could not sleep at night he went from one to the other.

F. The Emperor's table: 1, the place which he occupied; 2, my father's place; 3, I, to whom he dictated. Each of us had his different hours and subjects.

G. Bathroom, which the Emperor frequently used when water was not lacking.

H. The dinner table: 1, the Emperor's place; 2, my father; 3, I; 4, Montholon; 5, Gourgaud; 6, Madame Montholon. The grand marshal and his wife only came to dine on Sunday. Our dinner hardly lasted eighteen or twenty minutes. Then the Emperor sent away his servants, practicing his English, "Go out; go to dinner." Then he would ask us whether we would go to a comedy or a tragedy; he would send me to get the piece which had been decided on and would read it to us himself. It was almost always Corneille, Racine, or Molière; he was happy when he could reach eleven o'clock in this way. He called it a victory over time.

I. Little table on which the Emperor very often played chess for half an hour before going to dinner: 1, the Emperor's place.

K. My father's and my bedroom. The room was only six feet by twelve.

L. Our little drawing- and work-room: 1, my father's table; 2, mine; 3, that of Ali (Saint-Denis), the Emperor's *valet de chambre*, who often transcribed for my father; 4, sofa on which my father lay a great part of the day. If the sun shone, we were stifled; if it rained, we were inundated. The roof, which was only a few feet high, was nothing but tarred paper. The sun caused the tar to melt and the rain passed through. How many times my father and I stayed there, walking, late at night, talking about things far off which filled our hearts!

PLAN OF LONGWOOD

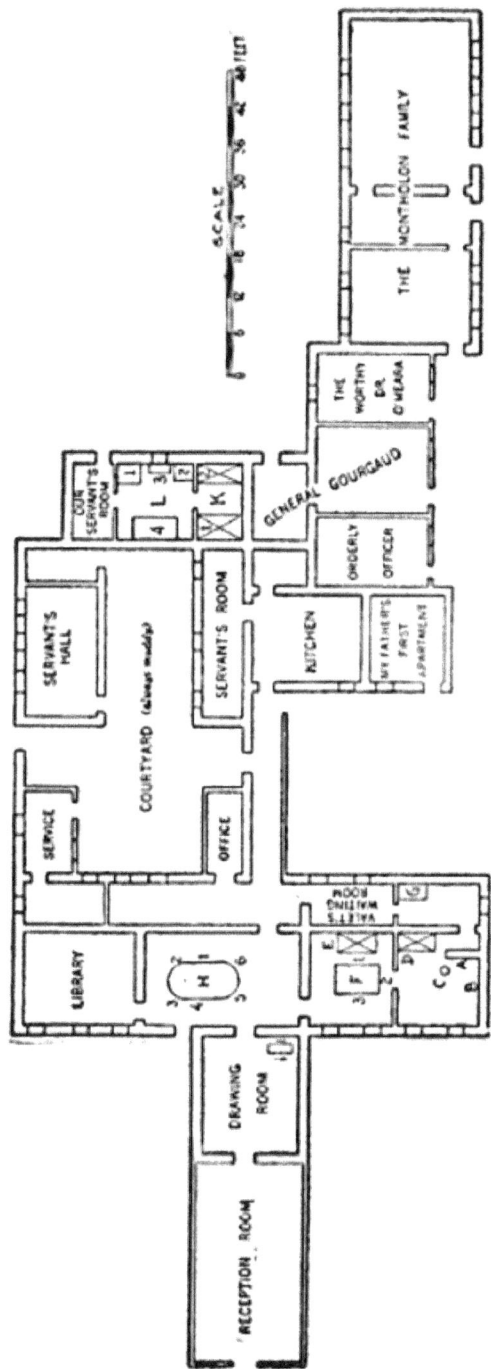

Reproduced from *L'Illustration* (France)

Drawn in 1816 by young Emmanuel de Las Cases for his mother, and described by him in the following manner:

SCALE

RECEPTION ROOM

DRAWING ROOM

LIBRARY

SERVICE

OFFICE

COURTYARD (always muddy)

SERVANT'S HALL

OUR SERVANT'S ROOM

SERVANT'S ROOM

L

K

VALET'S WAITING ROOM

KITCHEN

MY FATHER'S FIRST APARTMENT

ORDERLY OFFICER

GENERAL GOURGAUD

THE WORTHY DR O'MEARA

THE MONTHOLON FAMILY

M. de Montholon or the grand marshal, went to meet them. He said to Madame de Montholon, "Go and join them, *madame*."

"But, Sire, I must go and dress."

"You are all right," replied the emperor, impatiently. "Go!"

Madame de Montholon left the room, but instead of going toward the party she turned toward her quarters. The emperor, displeased at not seeing her, said to someone who stood by him at the moment, "Madame de Montholon is always well enough dressed to come and see me, but never handsome enough to see anyone else."

In a moment of irritation the emperor wished to dress or undress or needed something. He was angry with Marchand and me, I don't remember why, and said to Marchand, "Since you are not willing to wait on me, send me Gentilini; he will wait on me." I do not recollect what happened next, but it all ended like the others, whether on one side or the other. There were a few hours of sulkiness, after which the emperor came back to his habitual good humour and we went on with our service for him as if nothing had happened.

---

be no repetition of the failure at Elba to watch Napoleon and prevent him from escaping. For this purpose three of the powers sent commissioners to reside at St. Helena and keep an eye on both the emperor and on Sir Hudson Lowe. These gentlemen were Baron Sturmer for Austria, Count Balmain for Russia, and the Marquis de Montchenu for France.

CHAPTER 11

The Emperor's Day

As I did not keep a journal at St. Helena any more than I had done previously, I shall confine myself to describing things as I have done heretofore and as my memory has retained them. Having no work or date which can serve me as a guide, I shall place the separate articles almost at random.

When the emperor lived at "The Briars" he dressed in the uniform of the mounted *chasseurs* of the Guard. He had worn that costume on board of the *Bellerophon* and the *Northumberland*, with, of course, the three-cornered hat and the tricolored cockade. He stopped wearing this cockade later. Shortly after he moved into Longwood he wore a shooting coat at first, and when this, after having been turned, became really too bad, he wore in its place a civilian's coat, green or brown, I do not recollect which. These three coats were cut on the same pattern. When he dressed he always wore the Grand Ribbon of the Legion of Honour (this ribbon was without a cross and was worn under the coat), and the star on the coat.

Whether in military or civilian dress, he wore a waistcoat of pique or white kerseymere, with little figured pockets, and short breeches of kerseymere with flap and pockets. He never wore anything but silk stockings having a crown in the comer, and gold buckles on his shoes; these were round, and ornamented with little roses. The knee buckles were also of gold with little designs and were somewhat longer than broad. He always wore a muslin cravat and a collar of black silk folded, which was buckled behind by a square, narrow gold buckle. In *incognito* he wore a green frock coat and a round hat.

When the emperor superintended the work in his gardens he wore a hunting waistcoat and nankeen pantaloons with feet, a broad-brimmed straw hat with a narrow black ribbon, and red or green slippers on his feet. He usually had in his hand a little rosewood billiard cue which served him both for a stick and a measure. In his room he wore a frock coat of pique as a dressing gown, pantaloons of white fustian or swanskin with feet, and a madras handkerchief on his head. Except when he went into the gardens he dressed in this way part of the day; he was comfortable in it. If he went to walk in the gardens during the morning, which happened, to tell the truth, every day, he wore nothing else. For the first four years he dressed every day, unless he felt indisposed. It was usually about three that he dressed. He only shaved every two or three days.

When he was dressed, before leaving his room, he put in the pockets of his coat a handkerchief, a snuff box, a little opera glass, and a tortoise-shell *bonbonnière* in which were liquorice and sometimes, if he had a cold, jujube paste, but never anything else. He never wore gloves unless he were going out on horseback, and then he was more likely to put them in his pocket than on his hands.

The emperor never wore any jewellery except a watch with which there was a chain of the Empress Marie Louise's hair. On this was a gold key and a little seal of the same metal on which was engraved an N with a crown. In the centre of the under side of the watch was engraved a small B. During the last year of his exile the emperor exchanged this watch for the grand marshal's; when he placed it in his hands he said, "This one marked the hour of my battles."

The emperor had several snuff boxes which he used habitually; they were of tortoise shell lined with gold, and on the cover of each was an antique medal, Greek or Roman, of silver, set in a circle of gold. One of these snuff boxes had on the lower part of the opening a little gold medal of Timoleon. The form of some of these snuff boxes was oval, others were square; these last were longer than broad, with the corners cut off. There were also two others of tortoise shell, lined with gold. On one was the portrait of the empress, and on the other a naked child, who was the King of Rome. At first he used these snuff boxes like the others, but afterward he had them put aside.

In a box which was called the snuff-box case the emperor had still other snuff boxes with medals, paintings, and cameos. The handsomest was square and ornamented with an antique cameo of Alexander the Great. There was another one, round, and rather large, but of ordinary workmanship, ornamented with two large medals of gold; above was Francis I and beneath Charles V.

The emperor was of exemplary sobriety. Brought up in this ordinary classes of society, he had preserved in his greatness the habits of his youth. The simplest dishes were those which suited him the best. He was, indeed, extremely particular; the slightest breach of cleanliness or a badly set table aroused his disgust. He preferred a good soup (he liked it very hot) and a good piece of boiled beef to all the complicated and succulent dishes which his cooks could make for him. Boiled or poached eggs, an omelette, a small leg of mutton, a cutlet, a filet of beef, broiled breast of lamb, or a chicken wing, lentils, beans in a salad were the dishes which they habitually served at his breakfasts. There were never more than two dishes on the table for this meal— one of vegetables, preceded by a soup.

The dinner was more elaborate, the table more abundantly served, but he never ate any but the most simply cooked things, whether meat or vegetables. A piece of Parmesan or Roquefort cheese closed his meals. If there happened to be any fruit it was served to him, but if he ate any of it, it was but very little. For instance, he would only take a quarter of a pear or an apple, or a very small bunch of grapes. What he especially liked were fresh almonds. He was so fond of them that he would eat almost the whole plate. He also liked rolled waffles in which a little cream had been put. Two or three lozenges were all the candy that he ate. After his meals, whether breakfast or dinner, they gave him a little coffee, of which he often left a good part. Never any liqueurs. When he was on board the *Northumberland*, at the admiral's table, they offered him a small glass of some liqueur every day; he rarely raised it to his lips; he only enjoyed inhaling the perfume.

His food in Paris had been what it was at St. Helena, but here it lacked the quality, the variety of the food and its delicacy. He often complained of not getting tender meat. When he ate salad or fish he used his fingers more than his fork. When he found any bones in the fish he had his plate changed at once. "I don't like thorns," he would say. That was the name which he gave to the little bones; he was afraid that one might stick in his throat and make him sick at his stomach. His drink at St. Helena was claret; in France it had been Chambertin. He rarely drank his half bottle, and always with the addition of as much water as there was wine. There were hardly ever any fine wines. Sometimes, in the daytime, he would drink a glass of champagne, but never without adding at least as much water; it was a lemonade. The time occupied at his meals was scarcely more than fifteen or twenty minutes, but at St. Helena, if the weather was bad, he would prolong the dessert for a good while, amusing himself reading aloud an act of a comedy, a tragedy, or some piece of verse, or something else.

After the departure of M. de Las Cases and General Gourgaud the emperor liked to breakfast in the open air in one of his gardens, sometimes on one side, sometimes on the other, in the company of General Montholon, and sometimes also of the grand marshal, when the latter was summoned or came to see the emperor.

When the emperor did not feel well he took tea and hot lemonade or chicken broth. He thought that dieting was a sovereign remedy for any disease. If he felt better after he had fasted he would send to find out what there was for him to eat. If there was nothing that he liked he would order a mutton chop or a couple of poached eggs. When he had not been hungry during the day he would order something to be ready for the night in case he should wake up and his body need nourishment. If the night passed and he had not asked for anything he would have them bring him some soup with rice or paste early in the morning and he would also take a small glass of Constance wine. His manner of life agreed in all respects with the state of his health, his humour, his caprices, his needs, and his work.

Ordinarily, towards five, half past five, or six in the morning the emperor would ring for the *valet de chambre* on duty, have his curtains drawn and his windows and shutters opened.

"What sort of weather is it?"

"Sire, it is clear."

"Give me my dressing gown and my pantaloons." The valet would put these on, as well as his slippers. "Open the doors and windows," he would say, "let in the air which God made." This was a phrase which he used when he was in a good humour. "Call Montholon." He would go into the garden, singing some old opera air that he remembered. If the weather was bad, if it rained or was foggy, he would say: "Cursed country! It is always bad weather." After being dressed he would sit down at his desk and write, or he would lie on the sofa and amuse himself with reading. Otherwise he would go and walk in the *salon* and the reception room and would look with his glass through the little openings in the slats of his shutters. If he had sent for M. de Montholon they would walk together till breakfast time. When breakfast was over the emperor and M. de Montholon would continue to walk together about an hour longer, and then the emperor would go in again and go to his sofa or desk or to bed. Whether the emperor had worked or rested, he dressed about three o'clock.

When the emperor was dressed he went out of his private apartments and had M. de Montholon called again, going with him to walk in the garden, and toward four or five o'clock they came in for dinner. If the weather was damp or rainy the emperor would go into the salon, where M. de Montholon joined him, and with the chess table placed before the sofa they would play a few games before dinner. Sometimes they would walk in the *salon* and reception room. When the dinner hour had come the table would be set on a small table which was in the middle of the salon, if the emperor did not order otherwise.

The first part of the dinner was soon over, but often when the dessert was on the table the emperor would ask for such and such a book, of verse or prose, and would send away the two men who were waiting on the table, the *major-domo* and the *valet de chambre*, saying to them: "Go and dine, you two. Come back in half an hour and give me my coffee." When the half hour was over they would sometimes find him at table, sometimes walking about the reception room, or in the gardens if the weather permitted him to set foot out of doors. As soon as he had taken his coffee he would send for the grand marshal, and all three would walk in the alley in the garden, which was the habitual evening walk.

During the first two years of the life at Longwood—that is to say, until the successive departures of M. de Las Cases and General Gourgaud—the emperor dined with all the members of his suite with the exception of the Grand Marshal and Madame Bertrand, and then, until the departure of Madame Montholon, he invited the grand marshal, sometimes alone, sometimes with the countess; another day it would be M. and Mme. de Montholon, and still another time everybody together. It also often happened that he dined alone. After the departure of his wife, General de Montholon almost always took his meals with the emperor, unless the latter was indisposed or wanted to eat but little. The emperor felt that the state of a man left by himself was very sad, above all for one who, like M. de Montholon, had just seen his family depart. The grand marshal, not being in the same circumstances as M. de Montholon, was not so often invited. Surrounded by a numerous family, the grand marshal had a well-furnished house, and everything, or nearly everything, could be done there. It would have been too great an inconvenience for him and his family always to be obliged to take their meals at Longwood, particularly in bad weather, as his house was three or four hundred paces away from the emperor's.

The walk continued till eight or nine o'clock. At that hour the cordon of sentries about Longwood was drawn nearer the house. Then the emperor went into his own apartments and the other gentlemen went home. Sometimes, however, one of them, would be kept. The emperor would call Marchand to finish undressing him, for he would no sooner be in his room that he would throw his hat on the carpet, remove his coat, take off his ribbon, his waistcoat, his collar, his cravat, his suspenders; everything was scattered about him. If he wished to work the valet put on his dressing gown and pantaloons. If he did not feel like sleeping when he went to bed he would keep that one of the gentlemen whom he had brought with him or Marchand.

When he was in a good humour he talked; in a bad one he said nothing, unless a word here and there. Whoever was with him stayed till he was dismissed or till His Majesty went to sleep. When the emperor went to bed late the valet on duty was almost sure to pass a good night, but if he went to bed early one might expect him to ring toward one or two o'clock, ask for a light, and begin to work. Sometimes at that hour he would order a bath, which he would take or not, or might not take till daybreak. When he wanted to go to bed again after working he was often obliging enough to put out the light himself in order not to disturb the *valet de chambre*.

If some nights passed well, how many, a great number, passed badly! When he came in from his walk, somewhat late, and had caught a little cold, it was generally in his head. One was almost sure to pass a sleepless night if he got up after his first sleep. Then he would sneeze, and after the sneezing would come a little cough which grew stronger and which he had difficulty in stopping. To calm it he would take a tea made of the leaves of orange flowers, with a spoonful of maidenhair syrup or some other, and would drink the tea till the fits of coughing had ceased in a measure. He would cough so hard that he could be heard all over the house.

For the hour or two that the attack lasted he would not stop coughing. Finally his chest would be so tired by the efforts which he made that he would be obliged to go back to bed again, and spend the time till day half awake and half asleep. If the cold was sometimes a passing one, it would sometimes last for several days, but in that case he would not leave his room and would eat very little: a *soupe à la reine*, a little tea, and an egg or two were enough for him. When he was in this state of weakness he hardly permitted the door to be opened for people to go in or come out of his room; he could not bear the least draught.

During these nights of coughing the *valet de chambre* on duty was very uncomfortable. As there was no fire anywhere it was necessary that one should be made in the emperor's room with wood that was almost green, so that one had to have taken care to provide a certain quantity of brushwood or chips, to help combustion, and it was on this fire that the water was warmed for the tea which the emperor was asking for. The emperor preferred to have all this fuss made in his own room, before his eyes, rather than to have it made in the kitchen, in order not to disturb anyone belonging to the outside service.

How many times has it happened to me to pass long hours near the emperor's bed, and in the most complete darkness, waiting till he should tell me to go to bed. In order not to have to remain on my feet too long I would take the precaution to bring a pillow and lie at the foot of his bed in order to rest. I was careful to have my ears open, in order to be on my feet at the slightest movement and at the slightest word which I might hear.

The emperor did not at all know how to take care of his health. He knew that dampness gave him colds; well, it often happened that he went to walk and allowed himself to be caught in the rain. Instead of coming back into the house at the first drops, he would continue his walk and his conversation and let himself get wet. Wearing only knee breeches, silk stockings, and very thin shoes, he became chilled easily, and when he came in his shoes and stockings would be as wet as if they had been dipped in water. He was absolutely like a child. But when he felt that he had taken cold he took a great many remedies, which he gave up very quickly as soon as he felt a little better.

The emperor had a really kind heart and was capable of a strong attachment. In his household at St. Helena he was an excellent father of a family in the midst of his children. His bad humour never lasted long; it disappeared a short time after it had shown itself. If he was in the wrong, he would soon come and pull the ear of the one on whom his anger had fallen, or give him a slap on the back. After saying a few words relating to his irritation he would lavish the most agreeable expressions on him—"My son—My boy—My child." What would not one do for such a man, for such a master?

If anyone had not obeyed his orders or had acted contrary to his intentions he got angry easily; he would overwhelm the person with the bitterest words and even threaten to have him punished. But when the moment of heat had passed he would return by degrees to moderation. In his moments of anger he never permitted one to say anything; that was the way to irritate him in the highest degree. If one was in the right he would quickly recognise it. In fact, he was no sooner alone than he would study the case, not as an offending or an offended party, but as an upright judge. He would weigh the evidence on both sides as if the two parties were face to face. One was sure to win his case before him with the greatest ease if he had any good arguments to advance, and the next day, or a few days later, he would send for the one whom he had scolded.

At the outset he would receive him with a severe countenance, but when the first explanations had been made the severity disappeared and gave place to good will and kindness. One must have offended him deeply for the ill humour to last. In that case one was, so to speak, put aside, and even forgotten; yet still opportunities might present themselves for one to present himself before his eyes, and a moment sufficed for the past to be forgotten. Faults injurious to the public good were never forgiven, if they were committed intentionally, but those which were not he forgave willingly if the honesty and honor of the person remained untouched. Indulgence for others naturally inclined him to pardon; he knew that man is not infallible.

The emperor had a great and generous soul, and had all the virtues of the great men of antiquity, without having their faults. He was great on the throne, at the pinnacle of human power, and still greater in the chains of his mortal and implacable enemies. Those who in prosperity had flattered and fawned upon him, those who had bowed down the lowest, who had wiped the dust from his feet with their foreheads, those whom he had raised to the highest offices, the most exalted dignities, those whom he had enriched—these, for the most part, loaded him with insults as soon as they saw him in adversity.

They forgot the good which he had done to remember only a few errors scattered here and there in the course of his reign, which served as a pretext for them to tear him to pieces. He was a wild beast, a blood-thirsty tiger, a being vomited on earth by a spirit from hell; in short, the emperor was everything most abominable that malice could invent to befoul a man and make him an object of execration in the eyes of all nations. In spite of what they have done, of what they have wished to do, he has remained, for the mass of the people, the ideal man, the good father of a family, the honest man, the great citizen, the great man, the man of France, and the man of whom Europe still preserves an eternal memory.

If he is to be reproached with some acts of severity when he was on the throne, it is because men with turbulent passions and bad intentions, and the old royalist party which was hostile to him, needed to be repressed. He never did anything without mature reflection and without weighing the chances for and against, so that he never reproached himself with what he had done. I have heard him say that if he had to run his career over again and the same circumstances occurred he would again do what he had done before.

CHAPTER 12

Literary Work

The emperor had an extraordinary imagination and a remarkable memory. The mobility of his tongue was, so to speak, insufficient to convey all that his mind furnished him with, and his pen was still more so. He could dictate for several hours together without stopping. His memory furnished him with everything that he needed. He compared it to a piece of furniture composed of a great number of drawers; he would pull out that one which he needed in order to take from it the materials which belonged to his subject. The classification of everything was done as if automatically, and then nothing remained for him to do but to speak the words. He often said that he was equal to killing six secretaries. Those who wrote from his dictation, although they wrote in the most abbreviated way, were always one or two, or even three, sentences behind. Only stenographers were able to keep up with him. Therefore, as soon as he learned of this method of writing as fast as speech (it was when he returned from the Russian campaign), he never failed to have a secretary (M. Joanne) who was very skilful at it, which greatly relieved his other secretaries. It was to this stenographer that he dictated the Concordat at Fontainebleau.

The emperor wrote fast enough, but he had not the patience to write. The first lines were passably written, but those that followed were illegible. [1] One had to be very much accustomed to the form of his letters, of his words, and the way they were run together, in order to be able to decipher them, and even the ablest would seek for a long time before divining the meaning of this sort of hieroglyphics. To read the emperor's writing one had to have good eyes and a good memory,

---

1. Josephine wrote to the Marquise de la Tour du Pin, "I cannot make out his letters; he writes like a cat." *Napoleon's Letters to Josephine* by Henry Foljambe Hall is also published by Leonaur.

because sometimes he wrote very small, and on the other hand certain words were written differently in different places.

What made the difficulty greater was that the emperor, who usually wrote in a very abbreviated manner, often omitted necessary letters or put in others which did not belong there. Finally, it almost always happened that he could not read his own writing; he knew what ought to be there, but did not know what he had put down. Many a time when I went to ask him what he had written I would get, by way of answer, "What, imbecile, don't you know how to read?"

"No, Sire."

"Yet it is written as clearly as though it were printed. Look!"

"Sire, I have looked with all my eyes. I can't make out the word which Your Majesty has written."

The emperor would look, too, but he would not prove more skilful than I. After trying in vain for a minute or two he would say to me, "Sit down there and write," and he would go to work to dictate to me a few phrases of a paragraph to take the place of the part where there were illegible words. He ended by giving up pens and ink and substituting pencils. He had a number of them ready on his writing table, which enabled him to write more rapidly and saved the time which it took him to dip his pen in the ink. If he thought that what he had to write would need more pencils than he had he would keep someone with him to sharpen them as they were used up, and with that it often happened that he wrote on the wood. For that matter, whether he wrote with a pen or a pencil, he did not write his words any better, and very often when I had something written by him I would substitute another word for that which I could not read, and when he read over what I had written he would either put in another word or leave mine.

The emperor corrected everything that he had done endlessly; he never stopped scratching out words, phrases, whole lines, and even quarter pages. He was constantly adding, changing, cutting out; there were corrections of corrections, even in what he considered a clean copy. He would say in connection with this, "*Hé!* Rousseau copied his *Nouvelle Héloise* seven times!"

In making corrections, if it was to add, he would write them in pencil between the lines, between which he would put as many as two or three other lines, and what he wrote was so fine that generally I was obliged to resort to a magnifying glass in order to enlarge the letters and ease my eyes. If he cut out, he drew lines from left to right across words and phrases.

The emperor was infinitely fond of reading. The Greek and Roman historians were often in his hands, especially Plutarch. He could appreciate this excellent author more than anyone else. Therefore *The Lives of Illustrious Men* always appeared on the shelves of his campaign libraries. He often read Rollin. The history of the middle ages, modern history, and particular histories occupied him only casually. The only religious book which he had was the Bible. He liked to read over in it the chapters which he had heard read in the ruins of the ancient cities of Syria. They painted for him the customs of those countries and the patriarchal life of the desert. It was, he said, a faithful picture of what he had seen with his own eyes. Every time that he read Homer it was with a new admiration. No one, in his view, had known what was truly beautiful and great better than this author; consequently he often took him up again and read him from the first page to the last.

The drama had great charms for the emperor. Corneille, Racine, Voltaire, often had one or two acts of their pieces read aloud. He preferred Corneille to the others, in spite of his imperfections; he always chose what was as lofty as he himself. Napoleon. Sometimes he would ask for some comedy which he had seen played, and from time to time a piece of poetry, for instance, *Vert-Vert*.[2] He also took pleasure in reading some parts of Voltaire's *Essai sur les moeurs et l'esprit des nations*, as well as some articles from the *Dictionnaire Philosophique* of the same author. Novels helped him to relax and broke the seriousness of his habitual occupations. *Gil Blas, Don Quixote* and a small number of others would be reread by him.

Those of Mesdames de Staël, Genlis, Cottin, Souza, etc., he read over sometimes, but the novels which he could not bear were those of Pigault Lebrun. He could not endure this author, although he had almost all his works; he never thought of asking for a volume of them, and would have refused one if it had been offered to him. He had nearly always under his eyes all the works relative to the military art and the campaigns of the great captains. One author, Polybius, which he had desired for a long time, he received only during his last days, when he had almost given up work. It was only by chance that he took up a scientific work; books of this sort were only occasional.

If the emperor had in his hands a book which interested him he

---

2. *Vert-Vert* is a humorous poem by Gresset. It is the story of a parrot which belonged to a convent and it paints the absurdities and weakness of convent life with delicate and inoffensive railery.

would never lay it down till he knew it thoroughly. He read with his thumb, as the Abbé de Pradt said, yet nothing of its contents escaped him, and he knew it so well that long afterward he could make a detailed analysis of it, and even cite textually, so to speak, the passages which had struck him the most. If he heard anything spoken of with which he was not familiar, or of which he knew nothing, he would have all the books in his library in which it might possibly be treated of brought to him at once. He was not satisfied with a superficial knowledge; he went into the matter as deeply as possible. This was the way in which he proceeded to enlighten himself and to furnish his mind.

When boxes of books were received the emperor never rested until they had been opened. The volumes were handed to him one after another; he would turn over the pages rapidly and lay on a table those which he suspected of containing something. As for the others, he would throw them in a pile beside him, intending to examine them later. He had the books which he had chosen taken into his study and placed on a table near his sofa. The reading of these novelties would make him pass several mornings agreeably.

When he received newspapers he did not lay them down until he had seen everything in them which could interest him. At these moments he was not the same man as before; his bearing, his voice, his gestures, all showed that fire was circulating in his veins; his imagination became excited to such a point that he became a supernatural man. He seemed still to command Europe. This state of vigour, of animation, would last for several days; after that the emperor would resume his habitual condition and his usual occupations. This heat, this power were revealed also when he dictated the events of his life, as, for example, the story of a battle; it was like one of those bulletins to the Grand Army after a victory.

Sometimes, when he read the English papers, I would stand near him with an English-French dictionary, and when he found a word which he did not understand I would look it up for him. He would go on with his reading until he found himself stopped again by another word.

The emperor was very orderly in everything. He could not bear those who were not. In the matter of finance he wanted the bills made out and paid every month. He carefully examined all the expenditures, one after the other. When he saw that too much had been paid for something he called attention to it, in order that they might take care in future. He placed as much importance on an account of some hundreds of *francs* as he would have on one of some millions. He had a good memory and knew too much about figures to be misled, which was not at all agreeable to knaves. He quoted on this subject those too famous contractors for the armies of the Republic, who made the government pay twice or three times the value of what they furnished by means of frauds which they practiced during those times of disorder. He did not like to pay more than a thing was worth, although he knew that as a great personage he would have to pay more than a simple private citizen. He did not like to be robbed, and thought it a very bad thing that in a country like France dealers should have several prices for the same thing. He would have liked the merchant to be forbidden to raise or lower the price at will when once it was fixed; in this way the buyer could take the goods or leave them. He could not endure this system of bargaining. He added:

If things were as I wish, a great confidence would result; anyone, even a child, could buy without being afraid of being cheated. If I had remained in France I should have established this method in commercial affairs, and I am convinced that everybody would have gained by it. The English charge high, it is true, but they do not have two prices, and consequently they are not subject to the quantity of small disputes which make them lose so much time. If I had not had this idea myself I should have been grateful to anyone who had suggested it to me. They are not concerned in France with simplifying this part of commerce, yet it is very necessary.

He reprimanded severely those of his attendants, great or small, who incurred debts. All current expenses ought to be paid, according to him, at the end of a month or the beginning of the next. "How many times," he would say, "have I paid the debts of several of my generals in order not to hear them complained of!"

In his apartments, his room, his study, his *salon*, he liked to see everything in order. He could not bear to have anything which he used habitually moved from its place. Consequently, those who served him were so accustomed to his habits that it was very rare that they had to look for anything that the Emperor asked for. What had happened at Paris was the case equally at St. Helena.

Order reigned in his papers not less than in everything else. Those belonging to a piece of work that was finished were carefully locked up in a small closet in his desk, and those belonging to an unfinished piece were arranged to right and left of the place which he occupied at this same desk.

When the emperor had given his confidence to anyone it was hard to take it from him. But as soon as he saw that he had been deceived or imposed upon he could not bear to have the guilty man near him. He sent him away, never to see him again; he forgot him entirely.

At the time of Marchand's intestinal disease he was cared for by Doctor Verling, surgeon of the English artillery, who had been at Longwood by order of the governor since the departure of Messrs. O'Meara and Stokoe.[3] The emperor, knowing how the mansards, or, more truly, the garrets, over his apartments were exposed to the heat, particularly the sick man's, which was the hottest, had the kindness to have a bed set up for him in the dining room, that Marchand might be cooler and more comfortable.

Every morning the emperor did not fail to ask how he was, as well as during the day. When he went to walk in his gardens, if he happened to pass through the dining room, he would come up to the sick man's bed and say to him, "Well, Mam'zelle Marchand, is the princess coming to see you? Has she sent to know how you are? Look out, she may be unfaithful to you." (Marchand had a mistress named Esther who lived in Jamestown. She came to Longwood habitually every week with her little boy, who was named Jimmy.) When the emperor had left the house he would ask whoever was with him what Verling thought and what medicine he had ordered. When he learned that the doctor was giving mercury to Marchand he said: "These devils of English doctors treat their patients as they treat horses. Well, if Verling cures him, that is all that I ask." Marchand was confined to his bed for twenty days and then got well promptly.

It was on board the *Northumberland* that I first saw Doctor Verling. This doctor, who was a man of distinction, spoke French very easily and purely. He was received by Madame Bertrand, of whom, I think, he took care. He left the island a short time after Antommarchi arrived and I have never heard of him since.

Doctor O'Meara's departure had preceded that of General Gourgaud, and was followed, after a certain number of months, by that of Madame de Montholon and her children. Of the members of the

---

3. John Stokoe was presented to Napoleon by O'Meara and in 1819 paid some professional visits to him. He was mixed up in a matter of clandestine correspondence, court-martialled and dismissed from the service, apparently unjustly.

suite, Cypriani had died in February, 1818, and after that Lepage and Gentilini had returned, the one to France and the other to Elba. The former's place was taken by a French cook who had, I think, been attached to the household of Lord Amherst,[4] and had remained at Longwood after his departure for Europe. Of all those who had formed the colony at Longwood, there remained with the emperor only the grand marshal and his family. General de Montholon and five servants.

What a sad future presented itself to the emperor's eyes! A number of those who had accompanied him into exile had left, and he saw the years flowing by without his gaolers thinking of loosening his chains. Had he not been unhappy enough? Would he have to drink the chalice to the dregs? What mortal could experience greater vicissitudes of fortune than he had? Once he had seen all the princes and all the nations of Europe at his feet, and today he was reduced almost to himself, abandoned on a rock which was separated from the rest of the universe. He would say in his sad moments:

"The time will come when everybody, friends and enemies, will all be satisfied. The first will have nothing to fear from a power which oppresses them and the latter will find themselves free from all obstacles to their designs. The gray frock coat will never frighten them any more, and they will march ahead without looking behind them."

The emperor seemed to rise superior to all his sorrows. His moral courage had been put to the proof long ago; nothing which went on in his soul could be seen on his features. He looked with a calm air on everything about him. Apparently he had nothing more to fear from this earth which saw him still standing erect; but all his woes were concentrated at the bottom of his heart, and it was not in his power to drive them away, do what he might. So, when he was plunged in reflections he was swamped by them; hope alone held him up. At times he liked to think that in time the hatred of his enemies would cease to pursue him and persecute him and that at last he would enjoy the inexpressible benefit of liberty on some hospitable shore.

Since the departure of Madame de Montholon and her children Longwood had become more lonely; one needed all his courage to divert his thoughts from this increase in monotony. If one can im-

---

4. Lord Amherst touched at St. Helena in 1817 on his return from an embassy to China. Admiral Malcolm, in command of the squadron on the station, hoped to make him a mediator between Napoleon and Sir Hudson Lowe, but nothing came of it.

agine a small number of people constantly in one another's society, for an unlimited time and separated from all other human beings, he can form a just idea of their existence. If the life appeared gloomy for those about the emperor, what must it have been for him, Napoleon? Movement, activity was necessary for the colony at Longwood; the emperor himself gave the example of it in opposing active work to idleness. One was the remedy for all ills, while the other was the source of them, by leaving too much time for the reflections to which one was naturally led when he had no distraction to break the monotony of the daily life.

The emperor went to work again on his memoirs, which he had neglected for a long time; he made corrections, additions, and changes in them. The campaigns of Italy and Egypt were almost finished, the provisional consulate also. Other parts received a first dictation. What stopped the emperor in his work was that he had not yet got the numbers of the *Moniteur* which he needed. While waiting for them to be sent he occupied himself with summaries of the campaigns of Caesar, Turenne, and Frederick the Great. If he had had all the books that he wanted and if his health had permitted he would have carried out his design of making summaries of the campaigns of all the great captains, ancient as well as modern.

When the three summaries which he had planned were finished he designed a work on field fortifications. The models that he intended to use in this new work were constructed on the spot, and when he had tried them he had a fair copy made of the profiles and then dictated instructions as to the manner and time of using them. This work gave him great pleasure. It recalled to him his first years in the military profession. At almost the same time he made a plan for the composition of an army and on the subject of staffs. He did not have time to perfect these different works.

He only worked spasmodically. He did not like to do dry work for several months on the same subject. His imagination led him to change them ceaselessly, and consequently most of what he did remained imperfect. His ideas were, so to speak, only thrown on paper, and he awaited materials to complete and develop them.

All the writings which the emperor caused to be made employed only the Grand Marshal, M. de Montholon, Marchand and myself— that is, of course, after the departure of M. de Las Cases and General Gourgaud. The first two wrote from his dictation and the two others made clean copies.

About the middle of the year 1819, I think, all of us who were in the emperor's household service had the idea of cleaning up our rooms as well as the corridor which led to them. Everything had remained as Admiral Cockburn's sailors had made it, but damp, dryness, and wind had caused the paper to peel off the partitions and had torn it, and these partitions were only of slats sawn by a pit saw. The corridor had no ceiling but the black roof beams, which were hidden by an immense quantity of spider webs which hung down on our heads. The whole place was hideous. After making our preparations we went to work. To make a ceiling for the corridor we stretched cloth from one end of it to the other and glued blue paper on it. The partitions were also covered with paper. So much for the exterior.

When this first thing had been done it gave a little air of neatness to the place. There was somewhat more style in our rooms. We used a lighter paper for the ceilings than for that of the corridor, and the walls of each room were covered with a figured paper, each one having chosen a colour and design different from his neighbour's. When this was finished we still needed something to cover the floor, which was composed of badly joined boards. One of us, Noverraz, discovered the way for us to procure what we needed. He recollected that the floor of the emperor's reception room had originally been covered with a painted cloth and that a carpet had been laid down later over it. He thought that this cloth, which was perfectly useless, would be doing much better by concealing our planks. When he had given us the example we followed it. Our rooms, which had become quite passable, became still more so, thanks to this new decoration.

One day the emperor, who wished to see what we had done, honoured our garrets with his presence. He examined and inspected scrupulously everything there, and complimented each of us on the manner in which his room was arranged. He began with Marchand's room, in which was a mahogany wardrobe which contained all the visitor's clothes, his linen, and many other articles belonging to him. He examined everything that belonged to him carefully and in detail, turning everything over, but without taking the trouble to put it back in its place.

The emperor had passed from Marchand's room to the next one, and finally he arrived at Noverraz's, which was at the end of the left wing of the house. He thought the view from it admirable; he could look down from the window on the wood of Longwood; the black rock was on his left, and on the right there were the numerous ravines in which the valley ended. Above and directly facing one were the sea and its vast horizon.

The emperor saw an engraving in Noverraz's room which displeased him; it was the inauguration of Waterloo Bridge in London. It was a handsome coloured engraving, but the subject, or rather the name, Waterloo, brought a frown to his face. He rebuked Noverraz for having such an engraving in his room.

When the emperor had finished his visit he wanted to go down again, but our staircase was only a ladder, very straight up and down, so that he had to have the help of some one's arm in order to get down. He said:

"What a vile staircase! A ship's ladder is not so dangerous. One is likely to break his neck here."

As a matter of fact, the staircase was so bad that several of us had more than once gone down on our heels or had struck our heads against a piece of wood which ran across the opening and which one did not always take care to avoid.

It was toward the middle of the year 1820 that the emperor put a number of his manuscripts in order and had them copied, among them being that of the campaign of Egypt. He had worked pretty regularly on this campaign during the two preceding years. After a first dictation, made partly to the grand marshal and partly to General Gourgaud, Marchand had made a clean copy of it; but this had become in time so full of corrections, changes, and transpositions that the emperor gave it to me to do over. My work was finished, except one or two chapters concerning the administration of Egypt, when the first symptoms of his illness appeared. He had not time to review this chapter or chapters, which were entirely in the writing of the grand marshal.

I wish to point out that all the Longwood manuscripts are in my hand except a few of little importance, or which were from a first dictation.

THE LONGWOOD GARDENS

If the different occupations of his study distracted the emperor's mind, his body did not take enough exercise. The short turns which he took in the long walk in the enclosure were not enough to keep up his strength. He had refrained for a long time from any excursion beyond the grounds of Longwood, in order not to give the governor a chance to subject him to new vexations. He thought that gardening was what best suited his state of seclusion, to compensate a little for this lack of outside exercise. From that time nothing but gardens was talked of; the building in which he lived was surrounded by them. It was the models of fortifications which gave him the idea, and then he wished to have fruits and vegetables under his hand; he wanted to have some shady alleys; he wanted to hide the sentinels from his windows, etc.

On the side of the camp (the north), Longwood House had a building in front with two wings behind, and up to the line of the *façade* there were two squares of turf. The windows of the study and the bedroom on one side, and those of the reception room and *salon* on the other, opened on the western square; the glass door of the dining room, the windows of the library, and those of the reception room and *salon* opened on the square on the east side. These squares were each about thirty feet by forty. The long side was that next the *salon* and reception room.

In the centre of the first square, that on the west, they drew a lozenge; a little path two feet wide ran around it, and another, three feet wide, ran around the triangles, leaving a flower bed between. The beds were filled with a great quantity of rose trees; there were strawberry plants in front of them, with grass for a border. The interior of the lozenge was turfed, and in the centre the emperor had planted a coffee tree which had been presented to him. He called this little garden his *parterre*.

The other garden, laid out in the centre of the square on the east side, became so thick that while the leaves lasted the sunlight hardly penetrated it at all. The emperor called it his grove, or the Garden of Ali. The other was Marchand's garden.

When all the planting was finished the emperor had fences made to enclose his little gardens, at the foot of which climbing plants called the passion flower were put; in less than three months the fences became thick hedges. This plant makes an extraordinary growth in the island; it will throw out shoots half a foot long in twenty-four hours. The leaf is a deep green and the stalk is furnished with corkscrew growths; the flower, which is composed of different colours, is large, and somewhat resembles the plaque of a large decoration.

As three or four months had passed without the emperor's carrying out the plan which he had conceived, it was thought that he intended to limit himself to the two little gardens, but this was a mistake. He caused the work to be taken up again when we least expected it. In the first place, he complained that the southeast wind annoyed him when he was in his grove. The governor had a semicircular turf wall built eight or nine feet high, according to a wish expressed to him by M. de Montholon. Six months before his death the emperor had a mound of turf built at the end of it five or six feet high, with a platform six feet square, and on it he built a summerhouse of light framework, the walls and roof of which were of sail cloth. It was lighted by diamond-shaped glass windows. This summerhouse was intended to serve the emperor as an observatory in which he could sit comfortably and see the arrival of ships at Jamestown. When it was finished and the soldiers had gone away the emperor ordered M. de Montholon to make him a plan of a garden to fill all the space between the wall which they had just built and the gardener's cabin.

When the ground had been enclosed they levelled it off in several places and marked out all that had been designed on the plan. The emperor had a basin dug near the turf wall, leaving a walk between them. Masons belonging to the engineers were brought and the basin was lined with stone which was plastered with cement on the inside, and this cement was covered with several layers of oil paint. It was thought that by this arrangement it could hold water. They set in a little pipe which brought water from the reservoir of the house to the basin. When the work was finished and the workmen had gone, the emperor, eager to enjoy it, had the water turned on and when the basin was full caused a hundred little red fish to be thrown into it which he had had brought from the town. The next day the basin was half empty and the bodies of some of the fish were lying on their sides on the surface of the water. Probably these fish had been poisoned by the paint, which was not yet entirely dry.

The basin was filled again; the next day it was as it had been the day before, and it went on in this way for a number of days; every day some of the fish were dead. The emperor, seeing that his basin could not hold water, decided to have it lined with lead. The fish which had survived were taken out and put in a hogshead, waiting till the new work was finished. The plumber was sent for at once, and immediately went to work. In a few days the basin was in a condition to hold water and the fish were thrown in again; they played about more comfortably than in the hogshead in which they had been. In spite of all the care and the precautions which were taken to keep these fish, four or five months later not one was left alive.

The work on the new garden went forward. In front of and around the basin there was a circular walk which was furnished with benches of turf. The wall and the basin were separated by a walk four feet broad; this walk ran around the garden beside the fence and the arbour. All the part around the basin was planted with peach trees, acacias, willows, and other trees, among which were shrubs, sweet-smelling plants, and many strawberry plants. From one end of the turf wall to the other they made, in a diametrical line, a bank of turf which served to support the earth contained in the semicircle. A walk four feet broad which ran beside it was divided by a stream of water two feet broad, over which a bridge was built, also two feet long. This canal was filled with water by a trench through which ran the overflow of the basin.

The emperor wished to have some shade in this walk at once, and had some oaks transplanted there, of fairly good size, which he had planted at intervals along the bank. But these trees died at the end of a fortnight, in spite of the precaution which had been taken to leave a large lump of earth at their feet, which was liberally watered every day. It was necessary to replace them with peach trees; these did not suffer from transplanting.

Near this walk, between the canal and the walk which ran along the fence on the east, there was a pretty little oak which had not been transplanted. At the foot of this the emperor had a place arranged on the north side large enough to hold a table and several chairs. He often took breakfast at this spot, which he liked.

As soon as the small hydraulic operations were ended, every day about sunset the emperor, who would be in his gardens at that time, would say to one of his valets, "Come, let us make the fountains play!" The valet would go and turn the principal stopcock as well as the secondary ones, and the water would run from the basins into the trenches. In order to enjoy this pleasure, which one might call infantile, the emperor would stand between the basin at the fence and the grotto and would watch the water run down and reach there. The noise and movement would amuse him for a few moments. He would laugh at himself for being amused by so little. The sport ended when there was no more water in the reservoir.

Unfortunately, it happened quite often, especially in the dry season, that there was only just enough water in the reservoir for the needs of the house.

There always was water at Longwood, but in the dry season, the summer in that part of the world, it had to be sparingly used. Diana

Peak was less covered with clouds, the springs were low, and that one which gave us drinking water also supplied the camp. It sometimes happened that when the stopcock at the camp was open Longwood could not have any water, especially when there was any unusual expenditure of it. The emperor often emptied his basins, but always wanted to see them full.

When the garden was finished the emperor wished to have a second on the opposite side—that is to say, on the west, beside March-and's garden, as the other was alongside the grove. Outside of the fences on the west and north a border four feet wide was marked out and a little wall of turf was made, such as I have spoken of above. In the circular border, up to the western end of the turf wall, they planted peach trees in sufficient quantities to form a curtain, so as to shut off the guardhouse from being seen from Longwood.

When they had dug the large basin in Noverraz's garden, that in which the fish had been put, they had injured and even cut through the principal roots of a pine tree; this tree had dried up, being deprived of the sources of life. To fill its place the emperor had a Chinaman make a large cage or aviary of bamboo, with a sort of bird on top which the Chinaman said was an eagle, and the emperor had several canaries bought to people it. These birds stayed for a month or two in their little cages hung in the arbour, waiting for the aviary to be finished. They were given everything every day that they needed to live, but they were taken with a disease from which they nearly all died by degrees. The few that remained became the prey of the cats. Ultimately, when the aviary was finished and in place, the first in-habitants were a lame pheasant and some chickens. In order not to lose the latter, they had to be taken out of the cage after a few days. As for the unfortunate pheasant, he ended his days in prison. Then it occurred to the emperor to put some pigeons in the cage. They kept the new inhabitants shut up for a few days, but as soon as their door was opened they all went back to their old home. The cage remained without birds as the basin did without fish.

All this work which the emperor made us do was extremely trying to us who had never before handled a pickaxe, a shovel or a spade, or pushed a wheelbarrow. When we came in from work our breeches, our stockings, our shirts, our waistcoats were all wringing wet, and our faces were covered with sweat and dirt. We often said that the emperor would kill us if he had the idea of making another garden. When he was present we all worked as hard as we could, we did not

163

spare ourselves, we went at it soul and body; there were no laggards. We never stopped from five or six in the morning. But as soon as the emperor had given the signal to stop work each of us made haste to wash his face and hands and to go and sit down at the table. As we were people with good appetites, we were as active in masticating our food as we had been in digging up the earth. It was after restoring our strength that we went to make a complete toilet, of which we all stood in great need.

Never had Longwood been so animated as it was while we were working in these gardens; the activity seemed to have revived us. Before, we had lived in a sort of torpor. Never since we had been at St. Helena had the emperor been better; consequently he was always in a good humour. He rose at five or half past, and waited very impatiently till the sentries had been withdrawn, to go into the garden. He had the windows of his apartments opened and went to walk in the grove, talking with the valet on duty. As soon as the sun appeared on the horizon he would have everybody waked up. When I was not on duty he would call me by throwing little lumps of earth against the windows of my room, which opened on the grove. "Ali! Ali! you sleep!" and singing, "You will sleep more comfortably When you have gone in again," he would go on with the song. At the same moment I would open the window. "Come, lazybones," he would cry when he saw me, "don't you see the sun?"

Another time he would say, more simply, "Ali! Ali! ah! ah! *Allah!* it is day!" Marchand would have his turn, but less often, because the emperor was less frequently on the side where Marchand lived. "Marchand! Mam'zelle Marchand!" he would say, as he called him, "It is day! Get up!" When Marchand arrived he would look at him, laughing, and say, "Did you sleep enough last night? Were your slumbers broken? You will be ill all day because you got up so early." Then, taking his usual tone, "Come, take that pickaxe, that spade; make me a hole to put such and such a tree in."

While Marchand was making the hole the emperor would go a little further and, seeing a newly planted tree, "Marchand, bring a little water here and water this tree," and, a moment afterward, "Go and get me my foot-rule, my yardstick." To another, as he came up to him, "Go and tell Archambault to bring me some manure, and tell the Chinese to cut some turf; there is no more, etc., etc."

Then, coming to me, who was holding a shovel to load a wheelbarrow with, "What, you have not finished removing that earth?"

"No, Sire, and yet I have not been playing."

"By the way, rascal, have you finished the chapter which I gave you?"

"But, Sire, Your Majesty only gave it to me last night."

"Try to finish it today. I have another to give you."

Then the emperor would pass on to Pierron, who was laying a piece of turf. "What, you haven't finished that wall? Have you enough turf to finish it with?"

"Yes, Sire."

Then, coming back to me, "What time was it that I waked you last night?"

"Two o'clock, Sire."

"Ah!" and a little later he asked me, "Is Montholon awake?"

"I don't know, Sire."

"Go and see; above everything, do not wake him, let him sleep."

Then, going to Noverraz, who was digging with his pickaxe, "Come, work hard! Ah, lazybones, what have you been doing all the morning?"

"Yesterday Your Majesty told me to have the bath tarred; as I could not find anyone willing to do it, I did the job myself. Sire, there is M. de Montholon."

"Ah! Good morning, Montholon."

M. de Montholon, bowing respectfully, "How is Your Majesty?"

"Fairly well. Did they disturb you?"

"No, Sire. I was up when they came to my room."

"Has Your Excellency anything to tell me? They say there is a ship in sight."

"I do not know, Sire. I have not seen anybody."

"Take a telescope and go and see if it is in sight."

M. de Montholon came back a few minutes later and told the emperor what he had seen. The emperor would go here and there as he walked, and would come back to his workers from time to time. In this way he would await the hour of breakfast. When he felt hungry he would ask what time it was, and if he was told that it was near ten o'clock he would order it served. It was usually served in his bedroom. Then the emperor would leave his workmen and go and sit down at table. Those who were to wait on him would leave their tools, go and wash their faces and hands, and go to him.

When breakfast was over, the emperor would come back to his workmen and remain till midday, or only till eleven o'clock if the sun was too hot, and when he left them he would say: "Go and get your breakfasts; it is enough for today. It is too hot." When the emperor had gone back to his room, where he was followed by one of his valets, he would take off his dressing gown or his jacket and his pantaloons, and get into bed. If he remained dressed he would sit down on his sofa or at his desk. If he did not feel like going to sleep when he lay down he would send for Marchand, for him to read aloud, but he directed him not to come till he had had his breakfast and had dressed. In the other case he would have the shutters closed and the curtains drawn, and would sleep for some hours. Also, it often happened that he took a bath some hours after his meal. During the work on the gardens he almost always had a bath ready. The rest of the day he passed as I have told elsewhere.

The work on the gardens had gone on for several months. For a long time great activity had been shown in them, but little by little this activity decreased. The emperor himself also slowed up.

The result of making the gardens was, for the emperor, that he kept his people busy, that he amused himself, that he got gardens and walks about his house where he felt at home, and that he removed the guards to a distance, for previously they had been under his very windows. As for the product, it was nil, except that once in a while he had a little bowl of salad, a little dish of beans or peas and a bunch of radishes on his table. As for fruit, there were only peaches, and the emperor did not eat them. When the emperor saw something on his table which came from his garden he would say: "After all, our trouble has not been wholly lost. Our gardens are feeding us." We could not help smiling. "What, rascal, are you smiling?" the emperor would say, looking at one of those who were waiting on him, and he would smile himself.

Sometimes the emperor would amuse himself watering the first wall which the English had built in Noverraz's garden. This wall was less exposed to the sun than that which we had built in the west garden and had preserved its first freshness. The emperor had bought a pump with a cistern attachment in order to enjoy this pleasure, and it was precisely about three o'clock, when he had just finished dressing, that he would think of sprinkling the turf of his wall, and that which was around the stone basins. All that he had to do was to hold the nozzle and aim it while one of us pumped. As he never took any care, he never let go the pipe without having his shoes and stockings wet and covered with mud, and it was only when those about him pointed out to him that if he remained in this condition he might catch cold that he consented to change his things.

CHAPTER 13

Religion

Some months after Madame de Montholon's departure (that lady had left the island in July, 1819) it had been learned at Longwood that several persons had started from Rome for England, where they were to embark for St. Helena. Word of it had been received, and every day, for a month or two, their arrival had been expected. Finally they landed at Jamestown on September 18th or 19th, in the morning, and were sent on to Longwood about six o'clock in the evening. These men had been sent by the imperial family in response to the request which had been made for them. There were five of them—two priests, a doctor, a cook and a servant. The first three were Corsicans, the two others French.

The emperor received the two priests and the physician one after the other. He expressed to all of them his surprise that they had not been furnished with some lines of introduction. He attributed the blame for this to the cardinal, and could not conceive how, in the position in which he. Napoleon, found himself, they should have omitted something which was in his eyes of the greatest importance, and which the members of his family had passed over so easily and lightly. In spite of so great an irregularity he accepted the newcomers. He talked to them for a long time and entered into the greatest detail.

It was a great pleasure for the emperor to learn, from the account which they gave of their journey, that from Rome to London his name was venerated among the people through whom they had passed. He secretly enjoyed having left impressions strong enough to merit the affection and the regrets of these same people, although they had had to suffer much during the unhappy times of 1813 and 1814. The supremacy of France was still dear to them, and they prayed that he whose memory they held in such affection might be restored to liberty. The Holy Father also, forgetting his past ills, showed that he felt the hard treatment to which one of his sons was being subjected. Such were the feelings of the people, from the banks of the Tiber to those of the Rhine. And you, Frenchmen, what were yours? The travellers had not set foot on the soil of France.

The emperor sent for all the trunks which had been entrusted to the newcomers, either at Rome or at London. As soon as they were open he inspected all that they contained, piece by piece. The principal articles were, first, an oil painting representing the King of Rome in the costume of a prince (a court costume of white satin). He was descending a broad double staircase and had reached a landing. The staircase was in a park. This picture, which was in a gilt frame, was about a foot and a half high by a foot broad. It was hung between the two windows in the *salon*, over the marble bust of the prince, which is spoken of in Doctor O'Meara's book. Second, a green morocco case which held two miniatures joined together. They were about five inches high by four wide.

One was of the King of Rome and the other was, I think, of King Jerôme's son. This case remained for a long time on the emperor's bureau, and he used often to open it to look at his son's face. Third, a small medallion portrait of Madame Mere surrounded by little pearls. It was fastened over the study mantelpiece. There were also some toilet articles sent by Princess Pauline and some things with which to amuse himself sent by Lady Holland. There were two boxes filled with books and newspapers which had been sent from London. The emperor examined the books one after another, as was his custom; there was a good quantity of them, but half were only old books which the priests had bought. The emperor examined the vases and ornaments which Cardinal Fesch had given the priests for their ministry.

The chasubles were magnificent, the albs very handsome; the chalice and the paten were of silver gilt, as was the boat and the oil stock. The ciborium was of silver. There was a little silver crucifix on an ebony cross. The doctor's trunk was also opened. The emperor found some orange-flower water, among a great many bottles, something which pleased him very much, as he used it frequently. As the rest were only drugs, he did not want them.

Abbé Buonavita was a man of some sixty years of age, already very much bent, and one could not understand how he resolved to undertake so long a journey, and how and why the imperial family had chosen a man who was so far from strong. But whether from real attachment to the emperor or some other motive, the *abbé* had determined to start.

Abbé Vignaly might have been thirty years old. He had studied medicine for some time. He was a little man, dark and thickset. It had been considered wise to send him, to take the place of the Abbé Buonavita, who might break down, and to help the doctor, if it should be necessary.

M. Antommarchi was the physician; he was from thirty to thirty-two years of age. He had practiced his profession at Florence and was a pupil of a famous anatomist named Mascagni, who had, it was said, designated him as his successor.

The man named Coursot had been valet of Grand Marshal Duroc; he was with the duke and cared for him when he was mortally wounded in 1813. In 1815 he had gone into the service of Madame Mère, and had gone with her to Rome. Chandelier, employed in the emperor's *service de bouche* in 1813, had since passed into the service of the Princess Pauline.

As soon as these men had learned that they were designated to go to St. Helena they had made their preparations with joy, feeling happy that they were to go and share the exile of him who had been, and still was, the admiration of all Europe. The emperor appeared satisfied with their devotion. Two or three times the priests had the honour of being admitted to his table at breakfast. As soon as the two priests and the doctor were settled in their quarters Chinamen were given to them, to serve them.

At last the emperor had a doctor of his own. He had been deprived of one since the departure of Doctors O'Meara and Stokoe. It is true that he could command the services of Doctor Verling, of whom I have written, but the emperor had never admitted him to his private apartments. It was enough that the doctor had been stationed at Longwood by the governor for the emperor to refuse to receive him or to see him. Yet Dr. Verling was a serious man, who seemed very capable. The care which he had taken of the Grand Marshal's family and some other people at Longwood, among them Marchand, whom he had cured of a very serious illness, had gained for him the confidence of all of us, and I have no doubt that if the emperor had found himself seriously ill he would not have hesitated to call in the doctor, whom he knew perfectly well, having seen him on board the Northumberland.

On the two Sundays which followed the arrival of the priests the emperor heard mass in the *salon*, where the altar had been set up; but he wanted it to be said in the dining room in the future, as this room suited him and the priests better. Consequently, he ordered that all expenses necessary to render the place fit for divine service should be paid, so that the dining room was converted into a chapel on Sundays and *fête* days for the hour of mass.

The priests had indeed brought the sacred vessels, the sacred stone, their vestments and ornaments, but all the rest was lacking. First, the room was put in order. White paper was pasted on the ceiling and Chinese paper, a red ground having golden flowers and a border, covered the walls. A large quantity of white satin was brought to hang the back and sides of the spot where the altar was to be placed, and green satin for the hangings, which were festooned like drapery. Two rods of gilded wood, placed end to end and having hangings of green silk with a fringe of yellow silk ornamented with bells, divided the room into two parts. A new carpet covered the floor. The handsome mahogany dessert table was transformed into an altar. The front was made of white satin, framed by a border of green velvet; at the lower comers there were two crowned N's, and in the centre there was a cross of gold lace.

The altar was covered with two cloths of cambric, with broad lace borders. A little tabernacle in the shape of an antique temple, ornamented with columns and surmounted by a cross, was made of cardboard by Pierron. Four candlesticks with candles and vases of flowers composed the ornaments of the altar. As the emperor heard that the Grand Marshal had a picture (a life-sized head of Christ, the "*Ecce Homo!*") he asked him for it and placed it above the tabernacle. The two pier tables in the *salon* were placed to right and left of the altar, and on each was a five-branched candlestick of silver. A large rug of green velvet covered the steps of the altar. It was edged with a yellow silk cord and embroideries; on the front was a large N with a crown, and two other crowns at the comers, all in gold lace.

The emperor's armchair was four or five feet from the steps of the altar, with a small chair before it. The chairs of the Grand Marshal, Madame Bertrand, and M. de Montholon were placed on either side of the emperor and a little behind him. The members of the household remained standing near the screens. Abbé Buonavita said mass, Abbé Vignaly and Napoleon Bertrand acting as servers. It was Vignaly who gave the Bible to be kissed.

The chapel was lighted only by the candles in the candelabra and chandeliers, as the glass door into the garden was concealed by the hangings.

Mass was said every Sunday. The emperor was present at it unless he was indisposed or in bed, but in that case they opened the door of his room in order that the priest's words might reach him.

When mass was finished and the emperor had gone into the garden, the chapel had become the dining room again in less than a quarter of an hour and everything was restored to its previous condition.

One of the first Sundays, as the emperor was coming out of mass, he said, with a smile, to those who were with him, "I hope the Holy Father will not find fault with us; we have become Christians again. If he could see our chapel he would grant us indulgences."

And he went on, "If any of you has a conscience overburdened with sins, Buonavita is there to take them and give you absolution."

One day (I don't know how it came about) the priests came up into our corridor armed with a holy-water basin and sprinkler, and went through it, sprinkling it and stopping at every door, where they said a prayer or two. This ceremony might be good for Italy or in Corsica for Italians, but at St. Helena, and for Frenchmen who were far from devout, it was treated as a joke by those who lived in the corridor.

A few weeks after the chapel was arranged the emperor permitted Abbé Vignaly to say mass every Sunday at the grand marshal's house, first in order that Madame Bertrand might not be obliged to come to Longwood, especially when the weather was bad, and then that people whom she knew who lived at the camp might be present at it. Many good Catholics were grateful to the emperor for this attention.

THE EMPEROR'S RELIGION

Was the emperor religious in the sense which devotees give to the word? I never saw any proof of it. But he was religious in the meaning which philosophers give to it. Although the emperor went to mass, was present at religious ceremonies, and had heard some sermons during his life, that was no reason why he should attach importance to religious observances or set much store by them. His mind rose higher, and consequently his belief was different from the common run of men who go to church. But it will be said that he went to mass. Yes, but how did he understand it? He stood up when he had to stand up, he sat down when everybody did, knelt with them and kissed the Bible when it was handed to him. During divine service his bearing was serious, his hat was under his left arm when he did not put it on the chair in front of him, and his right hand was generally in his trousers pocket (and rattling some small change in it, at the Island of Elba). But he never made any other outward demonstration after the fashion of devotees. It sometimes happened at St. Helena that he would ask for a volume of the Bible during mass.

At St. Helena once (it was Holy Thursday) the chapel was set up, as was usual on Sundays and feast days, in the dining room, which was separated from the bedroom by a simple partition, with a door opening through it. The emperor was ill and in bed that day. He had ordered the door to be left open during mass, and when it was over one of the priests had remained on his knees before the altar, as it is customary to do on Holy Thursday before the tomb. The emperor was annoyed to know that the altar was still set up and the priest there, and he said to Marchand, with a frown, "Have they finished?"

"No, Sire."

"Tell them to stop it."

M. Méneval, [1] following M. Beauterne's example, speaks of bells. The sound of a church bell proclaims a prayer, a mass, a death, etc. Consequently, when one hears a bell he remembers having heard in his youth the bell of his village or his parish, and that it called to such and such a religious exercise. At Brienne the scholars were called to their studies, to the services or to the refectory by a bell, and the emperor must naturally have remembered it. One notices the ringing of a village bell, but not the carillon of the church bells of a large city. But are religious ideas always awakened by the sound of a bell? The effect which it makes generally depends on the state of mind in which one is. One notices it if one is thoughtful or alone, but when the mind is occupied the ear is deaf to it.

At Elba the church was close to the palace, or the emperor's dwelling; there were large and small bells in it. They were rung very early. They so deafened the new neighbours that the order was given that they should be rung with greater moderation.

No one ever knew or knows whether the emperor, during the last days of his life, had recourse to the consolations and help of religion. No one ever saw anything—what can be called seeing. Abbé Vignaly is the only person who knew whether or not the emperor indulged in the practices of religion. What I myself know, what I remember

1. Méneval, who was Napoleon's private secretary, notes that the emperor crossed himself involuntarily when in great danger.

very distinctly, is that when the emperor came out of his room in the morning he would often say to the *valet de chambre* on duty, "Open the doors and windows, and let in the air which God has made." He often said these words at St. Helena.

CHAPTER 14

The Emperor's Rooms

The emperor was satisfied with the manner in which his servants had decorated the chapel, and he wished to exercise their talents still further in decorating his bedroom and his study. These two rooms were so dirty that he was disgusted with living in them. They had the same hangings which Admiral Cockburn had put in when we took possession of Longwood; they were of yellow nankeen with borders of paper with flowers which had been cut out. The dampness and the dust had made the stuff frightful.

When the emperor had decided to go out of his rooms he himself tore off some pieces of the hangings, and with as little difficulty as one tears burnt paper. We went to work. To begin with, we pasted white paper on the ceilings and then on the walls, to hide their dirty condition. When that was done M. de Montholon bought a quantity of striped muslin for the bedroom and of cambric for the study. In these two rooms, by means of strings at top and bottom, the hangings formed rolls from the angle of the ceiling to the plinth. In the study a little valance decorated the top, and in the bedroom there was a little drapery of the same muslin as the hangings, supported at intervals by small pegs of gilded brass from which tassels hung. The windows were provided with large and small curtains. There were new carpets, and the furniture was somewhat changed and added to. The field beds were repaired and the curtains and mosquito nettings were replaced by new ones. A little later a complete change was made in the hangings of each room. Everything was arranged as follows:

The Study.—There were four openings—two doors and two windows. All the windows of the emperor's apartments at Longwood were à *guillotine*—guillotine fashion—that is to say that the upper half of the window was fixed and the bottom one movable, so that it could be raised or lowered at will by means of weights and pulleys concealed in the frame. At the right, as one came into the room from the bedroom, was an iron camp bed in the corner, with the head against the partition on the side of the door. There was a little carpet before the bed and a campaign wardrobe near the head. There was a large sofa covered with white cambric and furnished with one or two pillows. It was placed near and alongside of the fireplace, in the same direction as the bed, that is to say, at right angles to the fireplace. It was surrounded with a screen; behind it there was room to open the door which was there.

Between the foot of the bed and one of the arms of the sofa there was only a narrow passage, wide enough for one person to get through. The screen, which was five feet and a half high, was covered with light-blue silk having roses and green leaves on it. It protected the sofa from the wind from the door. One leaf lay between the wall and the arm of the sofa. Above this leaf was a framed painting by Isabey representing the King of Rome in the arms of the empress; the young prince, who seemed to be three or four years old, was dressed in sky-blue velvet. A small mahogany table was near the sofa. The chimney piece was of mahogany, ornamented with gilt bronzes. This chimney piece took the place of another, which, like the ordinary English chimney pieces, had only a narrow mantelpiece of painted wood.

Before the fireplace were a screen and a fender. The fireplace had a grate made to burn coal. On the mantelpiece was a glass which came from a dressing table which had been used by Madame de Montholon. Before that time there had been a mirror which the emperor gave to the general. On the mantelpiece, in the middle, there was a little white marble bust of the King of Rome [1] on a yellow marble pedestal. Two bottles of Cologne water and two silver candelabra were on each side of the bust.

A silver-gilt cup with a porcelain saucer was at the extreme right of the mantelpiece. These five articles came from the dressing case, and, with the bust, made up all the ornaments of the mantelpiece.

---

1. Napoleon Francis Joseph Charles, Duke of Reichstadt, King of Rome, was born in 1811 and died in 1832. He was removed to Vienna in 1814, and brought up with as little knowledge of his fatherland—France—as possible. He always regarded himself, however, as a French prince, and was preparing to take his place on the French throne if the people should call him. He inherited many of Napoleon's characteristics. He was described as "hot headed, vehement, possessed of quenchless thirst for action, and an extraordinary ambition."

On the left of the glass was a little oval portrait, surrounded by pearls, of the Empress Josephine. This painting had belonged to Madame Bertrand; the emperor had given her in exchange for it a copy made by Marchand. Above was a little miniature of the King of Rome; the little prince was putting on his shoe upside down. On the right of the glass was a little medallion, surrounded by pearls, of Madame Mère. This portrait was the one brought by the priests. Above it there was a miniature painted by Mademoiselle Aimée Thibaut representing the little king sitting on a sheep in a grove; different playthings were scattered here and there on the turf. To the right of the glass was hung Frederick the Great's watch.

There was a recess to the right of the fireplace where there was a mahogany table with a folding top on which was the dressing case. This dressing case, the principal articles in which were of silver, was open, and on it was a folded handkerchief on which was a mahogany snuff jar. In the middle of the recess and somewhat high up was a picture of the Empress Marie Louise embroidered in chenille; it represented a little girl holding a cat in her arms. She was in a grove decorated with an antique vase. The head, the hands, and the feet were, I believe, painted by Isabey.

The emperor had two or three other paintings, one a miniature a few inches high representing the little king on his knees praying to God for France, and the other, which was of the same size as that which was at the foot of the sofa, was of the little king, very young and naked, with his head in a helmet. A light linen cloth was partly around his body; he was lying on the ground, which was covered with laurel leaves, and was reposing in the shadow of French flags. This picture, which is now Marchand's property, is eight or nine inches high by twelve wide. I cannot now recollect where these two paintings were placed in the emperor's study; perhaps the latter was in Marchand's room.

Between the two windows was a large desk of mahogany root, decorated with black wooden mouldings. The two sides of the table were higher than the middle. In the front, to right and left of the place where one sits, were two little doors of closets for memorandum books. This desk was covered with books and papers arranged in an orderly manner. On the left there were two pasteboard boxes, a silver salver on which there were an inkstand, a sand box, and a box containing a sponge, besides several pens, a great many pencils and a compass. These pieces, except the sponge box, belonged to the dressing case. A large writing case of wood, inlaid with brass ornaments, was on the right, on the high part of the table. It was used by the person who was writing from the emperor's dictation.

On the right of the door which led into the bedroom (as one looked toward this door) there was a little Chinese table, and in the corner near the fireplace was the emperor's sword. A light armchair, painted green, with its seat and back of reed, and two mahogany chairs, also with reed seats and having cushions over these, completed the furniture of the room called the study, the floor of which was covered with a *moquette* carpet.

The Bedroom.—Four openings—two doors and two windows. One of these had been changed into a glass door; it was near the corner of the partition which separated this room from the dining room. On the right as one came in by the door from the study, on the side opposite the windows was a brass bedstead with green silk curtains. It had been bought by Madame de Montholon, and the count, hoping that the emperor would be more comfortable in it than in his little beds, had given it to him. It was covered with a coverlet of the same muslin as the hangings of the room, and the bolster was also of the same stuff, and both were trimmed with a broad lace.

At the foot and the head of the bed were two Chinese screens, of a very high polish, with figures in gold and silver. They were alike; that on the right hid a chair and a little Chinese table on which were the emperor's clothes. The screen on the left hid a little mahogany table on which were a carafe of water, two glasses, with a small spoon and a sugar bowl on a plate covered with a folded napkin. Beside this were ranged several bottles of syrup, orange-flower water and, I think, one of Constance wine. Between the screen and the door of the dining room was placed a broad, deep armchair, covered with silk, with large flowers and leaves on a red ground; there was a white pillow before it for the feet. Between the screen and the armchair was a small table like that in the study.

Between the two windows, the first of which was the glass door which opened on the garden, was a little commode of mahogany, pretty common, and having drawers which contained different articles belonging to the emperor. It had a wooden top over which was a rather handsome glass. This glass and six chairs had been secured from the governor after reiterated requests by M. de Montholon. On the middle of the commode was a little travelling clock of gilt brass which Madame Bertrand had given to the emperor. On the right and left were two porcelain vases called *glacières*; they formed part of the handsome Sevres service which the emperor had at Longwood. At the front of the top of the commode there were three folded handkerchiefs on which were snuff boxes, *bonbonnières*, opera glasses, small scissors, and one or two small knives, all arranged symmetrically with the handkerchiefs.

Near the left-hand window was a washstand of the root of yew, decorated with gilt bronzes, the ewer and basin of which were of silver. It was that which the emperor had at the Élysée. Between the washstand and the door into the study there were two little Chinese tables, one inside the other. The other little Chinese tables which I have mentioned above formed part of it; the largest held the three others, which grew smaller by degrees. Four mahogany chairs, with reed bottoms, having cushions, stood here and there in the room, which had a *moquette* carpet. Before the bed there was a little rug.

It was an agreeable surprise for the emperor to find himself so neatly lodged. He had never been so comfortable since he had been at St. Helena. "Whoever sees my room will think it belongs to a dainty lady." Formerly little things had not attracted his attention, but at Longwood the simplest, most ordinary things were objects of curiosity for him.

Sometime before Madame de Montholon left, the governor had begun to build the new house, which was situated some sixty yards from that of the grand marshal. Since then the work had been pushed forward very actively under the supervision and direction of the engineer officers. All the men available had been requisitioned—soldiers, workmen, Chinese, slaves, each one according to what he knew how to do. Every day the road to Longwood had been covered with trains of men and carts, carrying stone, wood, iron, lead, etc.—in short, everything necessary for a good-sized building. All these things had come from England, as the island could hardly furnish anything more than rubble stone, and in order to obtain this more cheaply they had pulled down most of the dry stone walls about Longwood. At the time the priests arrived the house was already well advanced—in fact, almost completed. Indeed, there was nothing to do but to finish the interior.

Before the work was begun the governor had sent the plan of the house and all its outbuildings to General de Montholon, that he might submit them to the emperor, who would make any changes and corrections in them which he should consider necessary. But the emperor would not hear of these plans spoken of and even had the governor told that he earnestly begged him to let him alone; that he. Napoleon, did not need any house other than that in which he lived, which was all that he needed for the time which was left him to live; that when the building was ready he would need nothing but a coffin. It was a sort of prediction which was unhappily only too well fulfilled.

CHAPTER 15

Sir Hudson Lowe

During the whole time that the emperor had been occupied with his gardens, the arrival of the priests, and the decoration of his rooms he seemed to have forgotten his position. In fact, for that length of time activity had driven away that anxious and thoughtful air which had marked him previously. But the English Ministry and the governor, its faithful agent, were not satisfied, one may say, unless they were rattling their prisoner's chains; it was necessary to make him feel them, and even to make them heavier. A Colossus, a Hercules like General Bonaparte ought to be loaded down till he bent under the burden; consequently annoyances of every sort and ill treatment of all kinds were frequently repeated. The victim only asked for quiet, and this quiet he could not have. Here is one among many of the amiable proceedings of this executioner of the Britannic oligarchy.

If two or three days passed without the spies seeing the emperor, Sir Hudson Lowe would arrive at Longwood escorted by several officers of his staff, and would order the orderly officer to go and walk under the prisoner's windows and to go near enough to see inside. So indelicate and dishonourable an order did not fail to fill the officer with disgust, but he had to obey under pain of dismissal. It was useless for the officer to approach the windows, for he could not see anything; the curtains were drawn. He would return to the governor and report on his walk.

Sir Hudson, not satisfied, would order this same officer to put on his uniform and to present himself at the principal door of the house, which was that of the reception room, and to knock at it repeatedly if he was not answered at first. No one would reply, this not being a room where anyone remained on duty. After knocking again and again the officer would go away as he had come. The governor, vexed and humiliated, would order one of his officers to accompany the orderly officer, to present himself at the door of the private apartments, and to knock there. The door opened at the first stroke. We had our orders; everything was arranged in advance. "What do the gentlemen want?" asked the valet, who had opened the door and who remained outside with the officers.

"Where is General Bonaparte?"

"The emperor is in his bedroom, ill."

"What is the matter with him?"

"The governor must have been informed about it from the bulletins which are furnished him every day."

"Is he very ill?"

"Gentlemen, there is nobody but his first *valet de chambre* who can tell you. He is the only person who goes into His Majesty's bedroom."

"Tell Marchand that we would like to speak to him."

"He is with the emperor now."

"When he leaves the general's room be good enough to tell him to report at the guardhouse." Then the officers offered a package addressed to General Bonaparte, and said to the servant, "Will you hand this letter to the general?"

"No, gentlemen; I cannot take it; it is not my duty to take letters which are addressed to His Majesty. If you want it to reach him give it to M. de Montholon or to Count Bertrand." The officers withdrew and went to join the governor, who remained a short distance from the house or at the guard house, and who finally decided to go to see M. de Montholon or the Grand Marshal. As soon as the officers were away from the house the *valet de chambre*, who had seen in what direction they had gone, immediately went to give an account of what had happened to the emperor.

As soon as the letter reached the emperor, either through M. de Montholon or the grand marshal, he sent it back or threw it unopened out of the window. "What does he want? Let him leave me in peace. I have no need to have a correspondence with a man who takes every opportunity to insult me." Whether from indisposition or ill humour or some other cause, the emperor would stay in his apartment for several days at a time and would not set foot out of doors until he was tired of his seclusion. Bad weather sometimes prevented him from going out, but he sometimes stayed in deliberately, in order to see how far the governor would go.

One of these scenes had irritated him so much in August, 1819, before the priests arrived, that he had had his doors closed and bolted and had had bars placed behind the shutters of his windows; he had his guns and pistols near his bed, loaded, as well as his sword, his sabre, and his dagger. He had sworn to stretch on the sill of his door the first person who should be bold enough to pass it. He added that no one should come into his private apartments until he, Napoleon, was a corpse. The emperor, believing that the governor was capable of anything, had thought it necessary to take all possible precautions to prevent his last asylum from being violated.[1]

Sir Hudson Lowe was the most timid and suspicious man among the English. Night and day he dreamed of nothing but the escape of his prisoner. Yet he must have been very silly to think that escape was possible to a man shut up by day in an enclosure a few thousand yards square, looked down on every side by mountains on which a number of points were occupied by military posts, with all the avenues which communicated with the sea watched, while at night the house was surrounded with sentries so close to one another that not a cat could have passed through without being seen. Were not all these obstacles sufficient to take away from the prisoner all idea of escaping?

Independent of a very active watch, did Sir Hudson Lowe count for nothing the difficulties which would have to be overcome in order to reach the sea? The paths, if there were any, were almost impracticable by day for a young and active man. What would they have been at night for one who had not the slightest acquaintance with those hills which are furrowed with ravines, each one deeper than the other? Would the emperor have been able, heavy as he was and unaccustomed to mountain climbing, to undertake so dangerous an enterprise, the success of which could only have been imaginary? Did the governor forget that the shores of the island are very steep or perpendicular except in a few places? Did he further forget that brigs were always cruising around the island, day and night, and that signals kept him informed of what was happening at sea? What means, then, had Napoleon of escaping from the island? Could he swim on a plank to a continent four hundred leagues away? The governor had nothing to fear but a fleet, and even that fleet would have had difficulty in making

---

1. Sir Hudson Lowe was a shocking misfit, taking the kindest view of him. He was undoubtedly controlled by very strict orders from his superiors, and he carried them out in a tactless way, but Saint-Denis here shows that Napoleon himself was not above petty tricks which made Lowe's job more difficult.

itself master of an island which was impregnable on all sides.

I do not doubt that the governor was the slave of the orders or instructions which he received from the British Ministry, but in executing them, even literally, he should have shown more kindness and gentlemanlike conduct, and, if these instructions were too severe and dishonourable, he should have resigned. Such conduct on his part would have been a very honourable action, which the English nation would certainly not have disapproved.

CHAPTER 16

The Emperor's Sayings

During the early part of the year 1819 Madame Bertrand had sent her by her aunt, Lady Jerningham, a young woman to be the governess of the grand marshal's children. Several years had passed since we reached Longwood, and how many more might we spend there? In this uncertainty for the future, and living, so to speak, in a sort of continual seclusion, having no other distraction but work which demanded a great deal of assiduity and which was broken only by a few minutes for a walk, I thought I ought to marry in order to lead the life of a husband and father. I saw a great deal of the young woman and I learned to know her and to appreciate her good qualities, which everybody praised. She had been very well brought up. After some months of attentions I decided to carry out my plan, being certain that I was not displeasing to Miss Hall (this was the young woman's name).

Noverraz had been married for a few months and the priests had arrived not long before. Having made my declaration, I continued to pay court to her whom my heart had chosen, while awaiting a favourable moment to speak to the emperor about it. I hesitated, fearing a refusal; finally one day I made up my mind and I seized my opportunity. He was in a good humour, and passed into his *salon*, where I followed him. I told him that I intended to get married, but that I wished to have his assent, or, to speak more accurately, his consent. I do not recollect what objections he made or what I replied. In short, I obtained his approval. As soon as I had a moment's liberty I went to see Madame Bertrand, to whom I told my good news, and I hastened to tell it to my intended, who received it with great pleasure.

I thought that I needed the ceremony of the English Church, although my *fiancée* was a Catholic; but she was English and we were in a Protestant country. It was a civil marriage for me. Wishing to avoid all ceremony at Longwood, I arranged with Abbé Buonavita to have the marriage take place in his apartments, which presented no difficulty. The next day or the day after my wife and I went on horseback to Plantation House, where there was a Protestant chapel. Pierron, Noverraz and his wife, and perhaps some one else accompanied us. When we got to the chapel we found the clergyman there, Mr. Vernon, who proceeded at once with the customary service. When this ceremony, which was very simple, was finished, we got on horses again and went to ride about on different estates to use up the time which we had to ourselves.

When we had finished our ride we went back to Longwood, where we arrived in time for the emperor's dinner. Ours was a sort of little wedding feast; there were more dishes on the table than usual. During the evening Madame Bertrand sent my wife a box filled with different articles of dress. The next day I resumed my service with the emperor and my wife went on with hers at the countess's.

Before my marriage I had been lodged like the rest, in one of the attics which were above the emperor's rooms. The place was good enough for one person, but it was much too small for two. When I was staying with my wife the emperor said to M. de Montholon, "It would be well to enlarge All's lodging so that he could come back there. Give him Cypriani's room," he went on; "have it arranged for him. It would not be human to leave him in such a hole." M. de Montholon had a window made which had a view on the emperor's garden, and had a rafter cut away so as to reach it. Partitions covered with paper transformed a wretched garret into a very pretty and most agreeable apartment. We had a view of part of the emperor's garden, the lawn, the wood of Longwood, the black rocks, and the sea on the horizon.

One day, as he was walking in his gardens, the emperor, seeing some cows pasturing in one of the spots which he had had surrounded by little walls of turf, sent to me to ask for his guns, to drive them away. He was very angry because these animals had been permitted to get into a place which was reserved for him and where they spoiled everything. I went to find him and tell him that I was not bringing his guns because, having just cleaned them thoroughly, I had not put them together again. He got angry, and when I replied to him hurriedly, having made use of the pronoun *you* instead of the customary expression *Your Majesty*, he gave me a kick to punish me for my lack of respect or for my impertinence, apostrophising me with the sharpest and most humiliating expressions which could be suggested by great anger.

I was far, very far, from having deserved such treatment, for I had had no idea of offending him. I was too much attached and too devoted to him for that. It was a momentary forgetfulness of the proprieties, at most. I went out from his presence with sadness in my soul. I told Noverraz to take care of his arms. The emperor's ill humour was never durable. The first time that I had to take the night service we were both a little embarrassed, each one a little reserved; but after the first few minutes the emperor resumed his usual attitude toward me, which was one of kindliness, and I forgot the unhappiness which had been caused by the kick and the abusive words which had sounded in my ears. A short time was enough to cause all trace of the unfortunate scene which had so deeply affected me to disappear. I was directed to take charge of the arms again.

One evening, when I was on duty, I was lying on the sofa in our antechamber, with my wife sitting near me. We had left the table half an hour before. Marchand and the other members of the household were still in the dining room. The emperor was in his room. At the moment when I least expected it I saw him appear in his shirt, coming out of the door of his dining room. Ill humour showed in his face. He passed before me, going toward his bathroom, saying that he was badly served. I did not know what he meant. The moment I saw him I had risen and was watching him go. At first he did not seem to see me, but afterward, turning his eyes in my direction, he said to me, "You go up to your room to see your wife and leave me alone."

I replied, begging his pardon, that I had not gone away and that I was there on the sofa, and I added, with a somewhat serious air, "Sire, when I am on duty I never absent myself." But he continued to repeat that he was badly served, as though I had not said anything. Before going back to his room through the bathroom he ordered me to call Marchand. The latter came at once, and had to catch the tail end of the squall. The cause of the emperor's irritation was that he had pulled the rope of his bell, and the bell had not rung because something was out of order in the mechanism. When the weather was fine the emperor was accustomed to go and walk in his gardens immediately after he rose and before and after his dinner. If he saw the grand marshal's children he would call them.

The children, who were accustomed to receive something from him, would remain at a little distance, and as soon as they heard him call they quickly covered the distance which separated them from him. It amused him to question them as to what they were doing and what they were going to do. "Do you know your lessons well?" he would say to one; and to another, "Say your multiplication table to me." If he was pleased with their replies he would send for *bonbons* and give them some. He would make them breakfast with him once in a while; he was pleased when he got a chance to play tricks on them and their little quarrels amused him. He was very fond of seeing them about him.

He was charmed by their innocence and by the frankness with which they expressed their thoughts and desires. "There is no beating about the bush with them," he would say. "They say naturally whatever comes into their heads. If they are greedy, they ask without hesitation. Ah! the little belly always rules. What a happy age is childhood!" he would go on. "It is the golden age of man's life." His misfortunes would have been greatly softened, he would have borne them with still more resignation, if he had had his son with him. This consolation had been refused him; consequently he would often say: "How much happier is a cobbler than I am! He at least has his wife and children with him!"

In spite of the trials which he had to suffer in so many ways the memory of his power was always a very agreeable dream to him. He said:

> I placed all my glory in making the French the first people of the universe; all my desire, all my ambition, was that they should surpass the Persians, the Greeks and the Romans, as much in arms as in the sciences and arts. France was already the most beautiful, the most fertile country; manners had there arrived at a degree of civilization unknown till then. In a word, it was already as worthy to command the world as was ancient Rome. I should have accomplished my end if marplots, conspirators, men of party, immoral men had not raised up obstacle after obstacle and stopped me in my march. I know very well that such a project was gigantic, but what can one not do with Frenchmen? It was no small accomplishment to have succeeded in governing the principal part of Europe and to have subjected it to a unity of laws. Nations directed by a just, wise, enlightened government would, in time, have drawn in other nations, and all would have made one family.

When once everything had been settled I should have established a government in which the people would have nothing to dread from arbitrary authority; every man would have been a man, and simply subject to the common law; there would be nothing privileged but merit. But to make such a project succeed one would have to be fortunate and to have twenty years ahead of him. Religion was a slight obstacle to my system, but there was a way in which it could be used; that was to close my eyes and favour all sects which presented themselves and had healthy and true morals as a base. Men divided in this way as respects all matters of conscience would have been only the more submissive to law. That being so, one would have the advantage of being able to diminish the abuses and reach the perfectibility possible to men.

A just and wise toleration in religion is a benefit to governments. A religion is only a law which directs the conscience. So long as it undertakes to follow the impulse of nature in all that is good and social, when it purifies morals and rejects everything which can injure the propagation of the human race, order, liberty, it ought to be adopted, protected, and supported. Have we not seen, during the centuries which preceded us, how dangerous it was to be intolerant, exclusive? God protect us from having to endure such a calamity, which is the destruction of the nations. Let us be wiser than our ancestors; let us look only for the public welfare and happiness. It is too much, undoubtedly, to have involved questions in public affairs. The simpler things are, the less trouble they give us. Alas! yesterday we came into this world; today we possess it, and tomorrow we disappear under its surface. Let us try, then, to be happy in this world, where we stay only a few minutes.

Some months after the assassination of the Duc de Berry[1] the emperor received news from Europe. As his custom was, he eagerly ran over all the books, pamphlets, and newspapers which they sent him from England. He read in these an account of the prince's assassination. The following night he talked a long time to me, I being on duty. He said:

---

1. Son of Charles X. He was assassinated at the door of the Opéra in Paris by Louvel, a fanatical hater of the Bourbons, who designed to kill off the principal members of the family, one after the other. The Duc de Berry was father of the Count de Chambord, the Legitimist pretender to the throne of France.

What thoughtlessness on the part of the Duc de Berry, a prince of the blood, who could and would be called to ascend the throne, and who could have had children, to go and take his pleasure in great public assemblies and at a moment when all opinions are so strongly irritated! Was he not a great enough noble to have balls and performances in his own palace, rather than to show himself at the opera? And when one mingles with the crowds he ought at least to take the necessary precautions and not trust to appearances, which are often deceitful. What a heart-rending picture for a family, and especially for a young wife! All the circumstances of this assassination are frightful.

Ah! If I had acted so inconsiderately, so imprudently, how many times should I have fallen beneath the poniards of assassins! But I always took care to be where I was least expected.

The affair of the rue St. Nicaise [2] came near being fatal to me because I was going to a place where I was expected. It was only owing to the solicitations of the Empress Josephine that I decided to go in a carriage, and if it had not been for the drunkenness of my coachman, and the uncertainty as to which carriage I was in, and the kick which one of my grenadiers gave the man who was to explode the cask, I should infallibly have perished with all my suite. From that time everyone about me always took care not to allow me to be approached too closely, and caused the police to take the proper measures, especially when I had to go in public. That is the way in which I protected myself against the surprises of my enemies.

Of all assassins, fanatics are the most dangerous; it is very difficult to protect oneself from the ferocity of these men. A man who has the intention, the will, to sacrifice himself, is always

---

2. On December 24, 1800, when Napoleon was First Consul, the supporters of the royalist cause placed an infernal machine before his carriage as he and Josephine were driving to the *Opéra* through the rue St. Nicaise. The explosion, which occurred just after Napoleon's carriage had passed, killed outright several innocent persons, wounded over sixty, and destroyed about forty houses. It was known as the Plot of Nivose, from *Nivose* (snowy), the fourth Republican month, which ran from December 21st to January 19th. This occurrence ultimately furnished the pretext for the execution of the Duc d'Enghien. It is said that Hortense was slightly wounded by this explosion. There were many reported attempts to kill or abduct Napoleon. Some of these stories may have been started by the police, in order to make themselves indispensable, others by Napoleon himself. Constant tells of one of which he himself was cognisant—*viz.*, to assassinate Napoleon by means of poisoned snuff at Malmaison.

master of the life of another man, and when he is a fanatic, and above all a religious fanatic, he delivers his blows with more certainty. History swarms with such acts: Caesar, Henry III, Henry IV, Gustavus, Kleber, etc., etc., were among the number of their victims. Religious fanatics, political fanatics, all are to be feared. The accomplices of these great criminals, if they have any (for these great criminals often have no accomplices but themselves), are always wrapped in an impenetrable veil which conceals them from the most active, the strictest search. It is well to appear popular, but one must act circumspectly; misfortunes come soon enough without going to look for them.

When the emperor heard that Prince Eugene had placed the museum at Malmaison on sale, he was exasperated:

Is it possible that Eugene, (see note following), my adopted son, should dirty himself by making money out of the precious things which this *château* holds? Have I not made him rich enough to get along without performing such a piece of meanness? Wretched greed! Should all those beautiful things, which for the most part were acquired at the cost of French blood, have such a fate? It would have been dignified, it would have been noble of Eugene to present them to France, and the Paris Museum would have been indemnified in a small measure for the losses of 1815. From this action the world would have recognised a French heart, and one of my family. There is nothing left for him now but to sell Malmaison. This dwelling ought to be sacred and dear to him for more than one reason; he ought to transmit it to his descendants. But no! it seems as though those who belong to me and those who surrounded me have conspired together to sink to the lowest dregs. One would say that they deliberately undertake to show themselves incapable of lofty sentiments. O man! Shall you always be so mad?

★★★★★★

Note:—Eugene was the son of Gen. Vicomte de Beauharnais, who died on the scaffold during the Terror, and of Josephine de la Pagerie. His mother, fearing that his noble birth might cause his prosecution, apprenticed him to a carpenter. Owing to the constant uprisings against the Republic, the inhabitants of Paris were obliged to give up all their weapons, and in this way General de Beauharnais's sword got into the hands of the government. In 1794 or 1795 Eugene, being then thirteen or fourteen years old, called on General Bonaparte and asked him for his help in recovering his father's sword. Napoleon was charmed with his face, his manner, and his frank request, with which he complied at once. Madame de Beauharnais thought it her duty to call and thank him, and he, being greatly pleased with her, returned her visit, thus beginning the acquaintance which ended in their marriage.

Josephine bought Malmaison at the end of September, 1798. Constant says that the property comprised a *château* which General Bonaparte found in a rather poor condition on his return from Egypt, a park which was already very pretty, and a farm the yearly income from which certainly did not exceed 12,000 *francs*.

The pictures and other works of art in Malmaison had been taken by Napoleon from the different towns through which his troops had marched and had been given by him to Josephine, who left them to Eugene and Hortense. Napoleon also enriched the collection with a number of examples of Egyptian and Etruscan art. Eugene had in his palace in Munich a collection of works of art by Rubens, Canova, Van Dyck, Murillo, Teniers, and Rembrandt which were probably acquired in the same way. Many French generals had such collections, made up of the loot of Europe, and some of them were of great value.

Napoleon was unjust to Eugene when he said that he had made him rich, though he undoubtedly believed it. But of the dotation of 40,000,000 *francs* which he says in his will that he gave his stepson, only half ever reached him, and this was confiscated by the Pope.

★★★★★★

For a long time the emperor had announced and had often repeated that an end would be put to his misfortunes sooner than was believed, and neither he nor anyone else believed this sort of prediction, which nevertheless was to be accomplished a few years later. What prevented our having such an idea was that his physique showed no signs which could make us suspect that he was ill. He kept his stoutness, he had a good appetite and was often in a good humour. Of all the indispositions which he had at St. Helena, the only remarkable one was a sort of catarrh, and he had been known to have that before 1814. Aside from this indisposition, which, for that matter, was merely transient, he had another which was only discomfort, which he said he felt in his body, and which sometimes caused him dull pains; he thought that he had a disease of the liver.

We thought that his object in saying that he was ill was to deceive the governor and the English Ministry and to induce the latter to give orders to have him transferred to another country or set at liberty. But the emperor had to do with men who felt but little for the ills of others and were incapable of generous sentiments. It was only in the last months of 1820 that those about him perceived some change in his health and realized, in the first months of 1821, that he was really ill. He had not deceived them. Sometimes he said to those who smiled at his internal pains: "Eh! gentlemen, you think I am jesting? It is none the less true that I feel something unusual here" (putting his hand on his side, where his ribs end).

Chapter 17

The Illness

It was toward the end of September and October that the emperor perceived that a disease which might be said to be unknown seemed to be trying to show itself in him. The incredulity of those about him diminished with the almost insensible progress of the illness. All hope of a better future had vanished. The five years which it had been pretended that his exile was to last had expired and no amelioration had come to soften his unhappy existence. As he no longer saw any hope of an end to his sufferings, he looked upon death as a boon; he prayed that it might come to deliver him from the persecution of the Holy Alliance.

At the end of the year the emperor began to feel that his health was really failing and he had less ability to work. His walks, no matter how short he made them, became more fatiguing, and insensibly his features came to bear more the impress of suffering. He felt, he said, a dull internal pain from which he suffered more particularly at night. He thought that he had liver disease. His remedies consisted only of warm napkins applied to his side, to baths, which he took frequently, and to a diet which he observed from time to time. Long before, it had been thought that his disease was only imaginary and that what he said was designed to impose on the governor, in order to bring the English Government to more humane sentiments towards him, and to decide it to allow him to go to America.

What had also created the belief that his illness was not real was that at times he seemed to be very ill and at others he was extremely gay. The emperor's life, since he had been at St. Helena, had been pretty irregular, but it was much more so from the time when his pains became more perceptible, more positive, and more frequent. He became as uncertain in his temper as in his manner of life or his work, sometimes gay, sometimes thoughtful and absorbed. One day he would be out of the house all the time, another shut up in his rooms. For a week or two he would devote himself to work, after which he would stay for whole days on his sofa with a book in his hand, trying to sleep. Sometimes he would dress very early, sometimes he would stay in his dressing gown. He would often turn night into day and day into night. In a word, he acted like a man who is overcome with weariness and makes use of every means to shorten the time.

It was rarely that he allowed the *valet de chambre* on duty to sleep quietly through the whole night; it was a bath which must be prepared for him, hot napkins to give him, tea to be made for him, books or cards which must be brought him. Sometimes M. de Montholon also was disturbed at night; it was to converse, to write from dictation. Since the countess had gone away M. de Montholon had become the man necessary to the emperor. He was always at his orders, entirely at his service, night as well as day. The grand marshal also had his turn at being disturbed, but it was usually only by day, and sometimes in the evening. As he lived a good gunshot from the emperor's dwelling and the space between was obstructed by sentinels at night, he did not have him under his hand.

I have very often seen the grand marshal remain for hours in the emperor's room with the shutters closed—that is, in the most complete darkness—before the bed or the sofa, without a word coming out of the mouth of one or the other. What happened with the grand marshal was the case also with M. de Montholon and Marchand. At night it was very often the turn of the *valet de chambre* on duty to find himself in that situation with the emperor. So I, in order to save myself from the fatigue of remaining on my feet almost without moving, took the precaution to have a pillow and to lie down on the carpet at the foot of the bed, having an ear open to the smallest noise or to the first movement which the emperor might make. In these circumstances the emperor would never permit a light.

During the last fortnight of December the emperor learned of the death of the Princess Eliza. He said:—

There is the first member of my family who has set out on the great journey; in a few months I shall go to join her. I shall be the second, certainly, since I am not the first. The end of my sufferings is only postponed.

It was at night that he spoke in this way. I replied to him:

Ah, Sire, we must hope that Providence will re-establish Your Majesty's health, and that your friends will not have to weep for your loss so soon; it is too much for them now to know that you are in chains. And we, Sire, what would become of us if we were to lose Your Majesty, we who are so happy at having accompanied you, at being with you and at serving you?

He uttered some consolatory words, to which he added, "You will have the happiness of seeing your family again, your friends, your country, beautiful France." Tears rolled from my eyes, and if I had dared they would have moistened the hands of my master.

In the month of January, 1821, the emperor was no longer what he had been two months before. He grew weaker every day. His face changed perceptibly. The work on his memoirs had ceased almost entirely, and if it went on at all it was without courage. He never dressed any more; he remained in his dressing gown when he was not in bed. His only occupation, in fact, was reading, and at that he most often had Marchand do it for him. Sometimes, in order to divert his mind from serious reading, he would amuse himself by turning over the leaves of a novel.

As the emperor did not care to go out to walk, he caused to be placed in the reception room a machine called a seesaw, which consisted of a long piece of wood supported in the middle by a notched post. He hoped that the movement of going up and down would keep up his strength. The two ends of the piece of wood were arranged with saddles comfortably stuffed, with an iron T in front for the rider to hold on by. As the emperor was rather a heavy weight, the end opposite his was loaded with enough lead for the ends to be of equal weight. It was M. de Montholon who rode habitually. This exercise suited the emperor for about a fortnight, and then he gave it up. Before he was seriously ill the machine was taken down and the floor put in its original condition.

About the same time as the above, the new house was finished inside and out, except for some small amount of terracing. It remained to complete the furnishing. The governor, to force the emperor, in a way, to take possession of this dwelling, had prevented any repairs on the old buildings at Longwood, which were in a very bad condition, and for a long time he had refused linen, dishes, and other articles indispensable for the service; he wished, he said, to keep all that for the time when General Bonaparte should be in his new home.

Finally the emperor, in spite of the disgust which he felt at the idea of changing his residence, decided to go and become acquainted with the place which was destined for him. He took Marchand with him. He examined everything in the greatest detail, praised the good arrangement of the apartments, their size and their character as a whole, but found that his quarters were not well fitted for his use; he found that he was too far from his *valets de chambre*, whom he liked to have under his hand. According to the English custom, everything had been sacrificed to the master. Except for some garrets, which were over his rooms, there was not a spot near him where Marchand could be lodged.

After going over and examining everything, the emperor went home and told M. de Montholon what he desired to have done in order to have two members of his household service near him, Marchand and me. The details of what His Majesty wished were transmitted to the governor. The workmen had hardly finished the changes which His Majesty had ordered when the illness which was to take him from us assumed a very serious character.

The emperor felt his strength diminishing every day, but he thought that he ought to attribute this prolonged weakness, this incessant torpor, to lack of exercise. Although his condition was already very serious, he decided to take a ride in a carriage every day, to revive his strength. This lasted for a fortnight. He drove around the wood two or three times with the horses at a gallop, but this speed fatigued him so much that he only wanted to go at a walk. At the last he did not want the carriage to come for him; he went himself to get it at the stables. He strove in this way to keep up the little strength which he had left. When he felt too weak to walk alone he took M. de Montholon's arm, who generally accompanied him, or Marchand's, if the count had not yet arrived, and he would get to the stables in this way. His walk lasted about an hour and he took it before dinner, which was then at about three or four o'clock.

When he came back from his walk he would go into the *salon* and lie down on the sofa, which had been moved back against the pier table, and there he would lie for some minutes, like a man completely exhausted, to recover his breath and rest. During this time his table was being laid. "Let me alone, let me breathe," he said to Pierron and me and, looking alternately at M. de Montholon and us, he added, "I don't know what is the matter with my stomach; the pain that I feel there is like that which I would feel if some one were to enjoy driving a knife into it and turning it around." When he was a little rested he would have the table moved up and would begin to eat.

The hunger which had tormented him during his walk still tormented him when he stretched his napkin over his knees, but he had no sooner raised the first spoonful of soup to his lips than the appetite disappeared all of a sudden. He would continue to eat, nevertheless, but without pleasure or without feeling the need of it. He found nothing good; everything disgusted him except some thin slices of bread dipped in the juice of a leg of mutton and potatoes cut very thin and fried. He never took anything to drink but half a glass of wine mixed with the same amount of water. A drop of coffee ended the meal. He would lie down again on his sofa, where he would remain for an hour or so and then go to bed.

Since the emperor had been living in this state of suffering he had no longer felt the courage to dress. When he wanted to go out in the carriage he kept on his pantaloons and slippers, and would put on a green frock coat instead of his dressing gown, and a round hat instead of his madras handkerchief.

Every morning he would go and enjoy the fresh air under his arbour, to which he took a little walk, every day, and he would sit down on his folding camp-chair when he felt his legs bending under him. He would often repeat, "Ah, me! Poor me!" and, turning his eyes on whoever was with him, he would say those lines which Voltaire places in the mouth of Lusignan:

> *Mais à revoir Paris je ne dois plus prétendre.*
> *Vous voyez qu' au tombeau je suis prêt à descendre.*
> *Je vais au Roi des rois demander aujoiord' hui*
> *Le prix de tous les mavix que j'ai soufferts pour lui!* [1]

And he would pronounce them with the accent of a man who has lost all hope, and in a manner to imprint on those present what he felt himself. He could perceive on the face and in the eyes of each what effect was produced by these words which had come from his mouth.

At a happier time, but still at a very critical moment, he had been heard to say this on the field of battle:

> *Et dans les factions comme dans les combats*

---

1. *I can never hope to see Paris again. You see that I am ready to descend into the tomb. I am going to the King of kings to ask of him today The price of all the ills which I have suffered for him.*

Du triomphe à la chute il n'est souvent qu'un pas.
J'ai servi, commandé, vaincu quarante années;
Du monde, entre mes mains, j'ai vu les destinées,
Et j'ai toujours connu qu'en chaque événement
Le destin des états dépendait d'un moment. [2]

The condition of languor and weakness in which the emperor saw himself, and the cause of which he could not explain, induced him to have blisters put on his arms. He thought that in this way he could ward off an illness which seemed to promise to be very serious. But these blisters produced no effect, and dried up. Some days afterward he had them replaced by a cautery which, in turn, did no good. In spite of the uselessness of this, he kept at it, hoping that in time this remedy, which he regarded as sovereign, would have favourable results, in accordance with the experience which he had had with it in different circumstances. But, although the disease was not really clear and defined, it was unchangeably established, and all that was done to restore the emperor to health could have no effect against the will of Heaven.

Abbé Buonavita, the elder of the two priests, had been for some months crippled in his members, and to the point where he was really not able to leave his room. It was feared every morning that he would be found dead. One day the emperor sent for him and explained that it would be better and more prudent for him to return to Europe than to remain at St. Helena, whose climate must be injurious to his health, while that of Italy would probably prolong his days. Then he had a letter written to the imperial family, directing it to pay him a pension of three thousand *francs*. When the *abbé* thanked the emperor for his goodness he expressed his regret at not ending his days with him to whom he had meant to devote his life. The poor old man was then far from dreaming that shortly after his arrival in Europe he would hear of the death of his benefactor. Before he left for Jamestown, M. Buonavita made a last visit to the emperor, who gave him various instructions to be transmitted to the family, and probably charged him with a mission to the Pope.

The more time went on the more the emperor's face changed, and his strength diminished. It was visible, and very visible, that the spark

---

2. *And in factions as in battles From triumph to fall is often only a step. I have served, commanded, conquered forty years; I have seen the destinies of the world in my hands And I have always known that in every event The fate of states depended on a moment.*

of life in him was growing dimmer by degrees and that the end of his existence was not far off. M. de Montholon was with him more frequently, and the grand marshal came every day to spend some hours in the morning and during the day.

One day, about two months before his death, the emperor was in the reception room, and M. de Montholon was with him. He asked for his dinner, which was served a few minutes later. Pierron and I were serving him. He ate his soup, which, I think I recollect, was vermicelli. He had hardly finished it when he had an attack of nausea. M. Antommarchi was called. He did not come till a quarter or half an hour later, and saw nothing but the result of a transient indisposition. The next day there was the same vomiting as the day before, and at almost the same hour. Antommarchi was called again, but he made no other explanation than that which he had given the day before. The days which followed were the same with this difference, that the vomiting became more frequent. Each time they examined the contents of the basin, and, as before, saw nothing extraordinary. But later filaments of blood were noticed, the quantity of which increased every day.

In order not to load his stomach the emperor ate very little at a time, and only things which were very light and easily digested, such as clear soups, meat juice and jelly, sliced potatoes fried, boiled eggs, etc. He ate very little bread with these different dishes. He took several light meals during the day and he sometimes had something brought to him at night. In spite of all his precautions, the vomiting did not diminish.

One day Antommarchi was sent for when the emperor was at dinner. I do not remember whether he came immediately, for sometimes he would go for a walk to the camp. Perhaps he had been there that day. The emperor asked him whether, in the conversations which he had had with the army surgeons, he had spoken of him. Napoleon, of his illness and had consulted with them. Antommarchi, instead of accepting what the emperor had said as a suggestion, made an answer which I do not remember, but which might be translated, "They cannot teach me anything; I know more than they do." The emperor was so exasperated by the doctor's words and laughter that he said the hardest things to him that a tongue could utter. He added, "The camp doctors have travelled a great deal and must be men full of experience," and that it was to presumptuous to despise their knowledge. That was the most violent scene that I ever saw, and in it Antommarchi was most abused by the emperor.

When the doctor had placed his blisters on the emperor's arm he had forgotten or had not taken the trouble to shave the place where he was to put them, and consequently every time that it was necessary to dress them the emperor complained of the pain which it gave him. The hair which got attached to the plaster caused him some of those small sufferings which annoyed and irritated him, and which the doctor might so easily have spared him.

When the doctor was sent for in the morning the emperor would hold out his wrist for him to feel his pulse. Antommarchi's hands were often cold, and the emperor, feeling the icy fingers, would draw back his hand, saying: "You are freezing me; go and warm your hands before you touch me."

During the first phase of his illness the emperor frequently sent for Antommarchi. When one of us went to his quarters to tell him that the emperor wanted him, he was most often away from Longwood or at Madame Bertrand's. When it was reported to the emperor that Antommarchi was out, he would show his dissatisfaction. As soon as the doctor was informed that they had been looking for him he would hurry back and the emperor would not fail to give him a dressing down. He would very often go to Madame Bertrand's in the evening, and that was precisely the time the emperor would send for him. Once the emperor, very irritated at having to wait for him a long time, said to him, "You come to me as though you were paying a thirty-*sous* visit. You are here in my service and at my orders. If Larrey[3] were here he would not leave the head of my bed; he would sleep there, on the carpet. When I send for you it is because I need you. You ought to be at home, and not somewhere else," etc. Antommarchi, after such a scolding, ought to have paid attention to it, but, whether he was bored by remaining in his room or for some other reason, he still continued to go away, which was the case during the whole time the emperor's illness lasted, and so this conduct, which was wholly unreasonable, increased the emperor's ill humour more and more.

A good number of days had passed since the first vomiting without the emperor's feeling any change in his condition. Finally, forty-odd days before he died, as he was walking in his *salon*, he felt a chill which ran all over him. As he could no longer sit up, he took to his bed, which had been carefully warmed. Hot napkins were put at his feet and at his

---

3. Baron Jean Dominique Larrey was surgeon-in-chief of the French Army. Napoleon left him 100,000 *francs* in his will, describing him as "the most virtuous man that I have known."

stomach, and by degrees he got a slight fever, which continued almost without interruption to the end. In this condition of perspiration he would have his flannel waistcoat, his shirt, and his bandanna changed every time that he felt damp, which happened five or six times during the day and the same number of times during the night.

It was reported that when the governor was informed that the emperor was ill he appeared very much disturbed. He wished his *aide-de-camp* or a doctor to be permitted to see the patient, and he insisted on it so much that it was necessary to allow the orderly officer to get a look at the emperor. As the bedroom and the study were very narrow and on a level with the ground, and the windows were very low, it was easy for anyone outside to see the people who were inside. In consequence of this situation of the localities the following plan was pitched upon to spare the emperor a most disagreeable scene. M. de Montholon, having probably arranged the matter with ————, told the orderly officer, or caused him to be told, that he would be notified when the moment arrived when he could see the emperor. What had been agreed upon took place. The emperor habitually took an enema. When he passed it that day the seat was arranged in such a way that it was easy to see him from outside. The officer, who had been notified, went to a window from which the curtain had been removed and there he could see the emperor, and, consequently, testify to his presence.

It was on this occasion, I believe, that Captain Nichols, who was orderly officer at that time, was replaced in his duties by a Captain Crokat. Captain Nichols, it must be believed, felt a repugnance for playing the part of a low-caste police officer.

The governor, still unsatisfied with the means which he had employed, again insisted on an officer's entering the emperor's room. The grand marshal and M. de Montholon were greatly embarrassed when they knew of this almost imperative desire of the governor's. They finally decided, after long reflection and consultation, to explain to the emperor, with infinite precautions, that in his present condition they thought it necessary to have a doctor who would assist Doctor Antommarchi with his advice. "Two opinions are better than one," said the grand marshal. Contrary to their expectation, the emperor decided to allow an English doctor to come into his apartments. They spoke of Doctor Arnott, surgeon of the 20th regiment, who was at the camp, and of whom the emperor had heard before he was seriously ill. As soon as he had given his permission these gentlemen sent for the doctor through an *aide-de-camp*, and he came at once, and was brought in to the emperor, who received him with pleasure.

Doctor Arnott was a tall man, dressed in a blue frock coat; he was already advanced in years and had a grave manner. He had travelled a great deal and seemed very well informed and full of experience. He inspired confidence in the emperor. The first interview passed off very well. After a consultation the two doctors ordered diluent remedies. The English doctor came to see the emperor every day. But in spite of all that they could do, the invalid's condition did not improve; the vomiting continued. A good deal of bile, mingled with little filaments of blood, was observed in what the emperor threw up.

Sometime before the emperor was obliged to take to his bed Noverraz was confined to his (with heart trouble, so far as I can recollect), and remained there all through the emperor's illness. From that time night duty was performed by Marchand and me.

During the day the emperor slept in his little bedroom and at night in his study. In the course of the night, during which he almost always had a fever and consequently was in a perspiration, he frequently had his flannel waistcoat and bandanna changed. Whoever was on duty remained in the same room as the emperor, seated on a chair, waiting till he should be asked to change the waistcoat and bandanna or for a drink. A light was not allowed; the covered light, in which only a single candle was burning, was hidden in the next room (the bedroom), so that one was lighted only by a very feeble light which did not always permit him to see what he was doing. He groped, so to speak.

One night, after having taken off the emperor's flannel waistcoat and wiped his back and sides with it, I got confused in putting on the other waistcoat, cramped as I was by the pillow and not seeing clearly enough. The waistcoat was not put on so fast or so well as he wished; he got impatient, then angry, said some things to me which I do not remember, and sent me to bring Marchand, which I did at once, and Marchand, having arrived, finished what there was to do. I was sometimes awkward, being afraid of doing wrong, and the emperor was very quick tempered. Yet the preceding nights all had gone perfectly well and I had gone about it that night as I had before.

The next day my work was changed. I was replaced by M. de Montholon and he and Marchand shared the night duty. The former sat up till midnight or one o'clock, and the second from that time till morning. As for me, I had no longer anything to do but prepare what the emperor needed and to aid these gentlemen; it was only accidentally that I happened to do anything about his person. However, I took care of him when one or other of them was absent.

After Doctor Arnott had visited him several times, the emperor, seeing that he did not get any relief, asked him one day, after many questions on his campaigns, his travels, his family, his fortune, whether he would die from the illness which was keeping him in bed, and how many chances there were for and against his recovering his health. The doctor replied that the favourable chances were the more numerous, but the emperor, who felt his position, thinking that if Doctor Arnott spoke in this way it was one of the precautions customary with physicians in order not to destroy all hope in the patient, said to him: "Don't be afraid to speak, doctor; you have to do with an old soldier who likes frankness. Tell me, what do you think of me?" The doctor continued to speak in the same way as at first, trying to remove from his patient's mind every foreboding of his approaching end. As Doctor Arnott did not speak French, the grand marshal usually acted as interpreter.

During the day, whoever was taking care of the emperor stood before his bed with a handkerchief in his hand and drove away the flies in order that they might not trouble the very light doze in which he remained almost continually.

When the emperor had gone fifteen or twenty days unshaven he wished to shave. It was the first time since he had been ill in bed. Although he was not very well placed in bed to do such a thing, he succeeded with some trouble. In order to give him the necessary light his bed had to be rolled into the middle of the room so that he might shave himself as he was accustomed to do. As soon as he had shaved I observed that the emperor's face was no longer what it had been a fortnight or three weeks before; it was greatly changed and much thinner. A short time had been enough to make a considerable alteration in him. He was not the same man. His limbs had lost their roundness; his thighs had diminished by a good third, his calves had melted away, and his fingers were more slender.

He always rose during the heat of the day to get a little air, got into his large garden chair, which had been placed near the glass door of the garden, and remained there for several hours. As soon as he felt tired he would go to bed again. He drank orgeat, barley water, currant syrup, and some other things which were refreshing.

In order to divert himself a little when he was in bed he would have Marchand read to him. One day it was General Dumouriez's

Memoirs, and I think it was the last thing of the sort which was read to him.

Towards the beginning of the last fortnight of his life the emperor would not sleep in his study; he thought that there was not enough air there. He gave orders to have his bed placed in the *salon* between two windows. That in the bedroom was placed in the same manner; he found it much more comfortable. He would get from one room to the other at night with the help of his arms passed over M. de Montholon's and Marchand's shoulders, holding them by the neck, and the next morning he would come back to go to bed in his room. In order that he might not catch cold in passing from one room to another they used to unfold the screens to cover the door of his room and that of his salon.

It was a little before the first days of this last fortnight that the emperor worked on his will and the codicils which follow it. It was in his little bedroom that he wrote these last expressions of his will. M. de Montholon had made me prepare pens and paper. As the emperor did not wish to be disturbed during his work, he gave me orders, through the count, with whom he was to work, that I should remain in the antechamber and that I should not allow anyone to come into his apartments. Marchand, who was to remain in the study, had the same orders. The door between the study and the bathroom was bolted, I think. When these precautions had been taken the emperor dictated all the articles of his will to M. de Montholon. When the day's dictation was finished M. de Montholon would make a clean copy of what he had written, and it was from this copy that the emperor wrote.

This work lasted from eight to ten days, and every day the same orders were given. It was very laborious work for the emperor, whose strength was visibly failing. From time to time he would take a few drops of Constance wine to revive it. He only stopped writing when he felt exhausted, and the next day he would go to work again. He went on in this way till he had done all that he had to do.

When the will and codicils were signed and sealed they were placed in envelopes, after which the emperor sent for the Grand Marshal and Abbé Vignaly and ordered them, as well as M. de Montholon and Marchand, to place their seals on the openings of the principal envelopes. The whole was entrusted to Marchand's care, and the emperor told him into whose hands it was to be given when he, Napoleon, had drawn his last breath. Marchand had all the valuables in his possession—that is to say, the snuff boxes and other things which the emperor used, and, I believe, the diamond necklace which Queen Hortense gave the emperor when he left Malmaison. This last the emperor himself placed in Marchand's hands, and gave it to him as his own property, in order that he might be protected against all eventualities. He was afraid that the execution of his last will might encounter some obstacle, on the part either of the French government or of some other. The grand marshal had charge of the arms and M. de Montholon had the papers, the silverware, the porcelain and, I think, all the money at Longwood.

Toward the middle of the last fortnight a little comet was seen in the west, almost imperceptible; it was said that it had a very long tail (as for me, I saw nothing of the comet or its tail). It was visible about seven or eight o'clock and appeared upon the horizon. When the emperor heard of this apparition he said, "It comes to mark the end of my career." This comet, after appearing for several evenings in succession, was seen no more. Some days afterward there was a frightful storm at sea which lasted two or three days, overthrowing the embankments and carrying away some people who were on the quay. Several ships lost their anchors and had to put to sea in order to avoid the danger of going on the rocks. The naval officers who were ashore were obliged to wait till the gale had passed, as they could not put a boat in the water to join their ships. [4] It seemed as though heaven and earth wished to mark the end of a great life by something extraordinary.

Five or six days before his death the emperor, who was then in the *salon*, sent for Abbé Vignaly and had an interview with him. It was in the evening, so far as I can recollect. Nobody can say what happened at this interview. However, it was reported that the emperor intended that it should be known by the public that he had taken the communion or had made his devotions. M. Vignaly carried the truth to the grave with him.

During the last and very sad evenings almost all the French were assembled about the emperor's bed, and each of them was ambitious to have a look from his unfortunate master. The emperor, seeing Pierron, who was within range of his vision, said to him, calling him by name. "You will tell all my servants that I have made them rich." These words produced such an effect that tears were seen in everyone's eyes,

---

4. The Rev. Mr. Bowater T. Vernon, who was a chaplain at St. Helena till 1823, says that there never was any storm there during Napoleon's captivity. The worst they ever had was a heavy surf or "rollers," which did damage in the harbour, *e. g.*, March 6, 1821.

and each one seemed to say, "Sire, keep your riches; our wish is that you should recover your health and live a long time among us."

One of the following evenings the emperor's fever was strong enough to make him delirious. He asked Pierron, who had been in town during the day, where the ship came from that had arrived that morning. (In fact, one had arrived.)

"Sire, it came from the Cape."

"What did it bring? Are there any oranges?"

"Yes, Sire."

"You must get several dozen."

"I got them. Sire."

The emperor asked the same question several times, then he asked about Doctor Baxter, a physician attached to the governor's staff. "Is it long since you have seen Baxter?" the emperor said to Pierron.

Pierron was about to answer "no" when, at a sign from the grand marshal, he said, "Yes, Sire. He went back to Europe some time ago."

"Ah! I thought he was here."

"No, Sire, he has gone to England."

This doctor, for whom the emperor had an antipathy, was at Plantation House, but when Pierron said that he had gone away it was in order not to disturb his mind. The emperor came back to Doctor Baxter several times during the evening.

During the night which followed this evening he wished to get up. He put his foot on the ground; he wanted to go and take a walk in the garden, he said. We ran to him and were happy enough to arrive in time to hold him and to prevent his falling. He fainted in our arms and we put him to bed, where he recovered his strength by degrees.

Madame Bertrand was anxious about the emperor's health, for she had not seen him for several days, and she came to see him the next day. She had asked him to receive her several times, and each time he had refused. Finally, learning that he was near his end, she came, entered the *salon*, and drew near the bed. The emperor knew her. "Ah! Madame Bertrand!" he said.

"How is Your Majesty?"

"Aie! gently!" replied the emperor, in a weak voice. Though he looked at her, he did not say anything else.

At the place occupied by the emperor's bed there had been a chest of drawers with a bust of the King of Rome on it, and above it hung a full-length portrait of the young prince. This picture had remained hanging. When the bed curtains on the wall side were lifted the emperor could easily see the portrait by raising his eyes. Seeing that he often turned his looks in that direction, it was thought best to take the picture down and put it in another place, where he could not see it. He looked for it for some time, and as he looked by turns at those who were about him he seemed to say: "Where is my son? What have you done with my son?"

The same day, I think, he spoke to Noverraz, who was beginning to get better and had made great efforts to come to see the emperor. "You have changed a great deal," he said, when he saw him.

The next day, I think, toward the middle of the day, Marchand was by the bed, and, observing that the emperor's features were fixed and believing that this was an indication of the approaching end of his existence, kissed his hand and immediately afterward came to the little garden, the grove, where I was, getting some fresh air and walking a little. He told me what he had done and said to me that I might go and do the same thing. We at once went back together into the *salon*, and, with heart oppressed and tears in my eyes, I went up to the emperor's bed and placed my trembling lips on that hand which I had felt so often on my cheeks, and which had recently written my name in his will.[5] My emotion was so great and so acute after this action that I hastened to go away from the bed and the room, for fear that my sobs would arouse the emperor from his doze. Whenever I think of this moment when my lips touched the emperor's hand, I feel my heart beat and my eyes fill with tears.

Doctors Arnott and Antommarchi, seeing that the emperor was very low, consulted whether they should administer a dose of calomel. They agreed, and gave the medicine. Before that there had been a consultation in Antommarchi's room at which Doctors Short and Mitchell were present. They had previously put blisters on the patient's thighs, but had obtained no result. They had not taken hold. The calomel had an effect; it brought about a heavy evacuation of blackish matter, thick and partly hard, which resembled pitch or tar.

As the emperor was extremely weak, it was impossible to move him from one bed to the other, as had been done two days before. He could then get on his night-stool, but now we had to be contented to change the sheet under him, since we were not able to do anything better. This was not an easy operation. In order to lift him I got up on the two bars which formed the sides of the bed, and, passing my arms under the emperor's loins and clasping my hands, I raised him enough

5. Napoleon left Saint-Denis 100,000 *francs*.

for Marchand and someone else to remove the sheet. The position in which I found myself was all the more uncomfortable because the emperor was still very heavy and I had nothing to lean against. In this position he let me feel that he still had plenty of strength, for as I held him up he gave me a blow with his fist in my side, crying out, "Ah! rascal, you are hurting me!" They finally succeeded in washing him and putting another sheet under him. It was I who went to show the English doctors the sheet which had just been taken off, passing it out to them through the window where our Chinaman generally was.

The emperor, who, since his high fever, had had some attacks of delirium, came entirely to himself and talked as if he had only had a slight indisposition. We thought that he was saved, but the doctors told us that the improvement which we saw was only temporary. In fact, our illusion was quickly dissipated, for the next day the emperor was worse than ever.

He could only speak a few words, and with difficulty; his feet were cold. He would ask for a little wine from time to time, which they hastened to give him. He said, after drinking a few drops, "Ah, how good wine is! How good wine is!" The next day or the day after that he already had hiccoughs, which never afterward left him. His pulse could hardly be felt at his wrist; it was necessary to feel his jugular vein. His feet were wrapped in hot cloths to keep them warm. Once, when I put one on which was a little too hot he drew his feet back quickly. A little sugar and water which they gave him sustained what little life was in him. In the afternoon he changed considerably and toward evening his life appeared almost to have ebbed away. The evening passed in the saddest quiet. We expected to see him pass away every moment, and one or another of us was continually going to his bed to make sure that he was still breathing. He was dozing peacefully.

The emperor had been in bed for forty-odd days, and we who had been constantly with him, waiting on him, were so tired, and needed rest so much, that we could not control our sleepiness. The quiet of the apartment favoured it. All of us, whether on chairs or sofas, took some instants of rest. If we woke up, we hurried to the bed, we listened attentively to hear the breath, and we poured into the emperor's mouth, which was a little open, a spoonful or two of sugar and water to refresh him. We would examine the sick man's face as well as we could by the reflection of the light hidden behind the screen which was before the door of the dining room. It was in this way that the night passed.

Toward four o'clock in the morning the little sleep which we had taken had quite removed our drowsiness. We went to the bed. The breath which was escaping from the emperor's mouth was so weak that for a moment we believed that he was no longer alive. We brought the light; his eyes were open, but they seemed paralysed. His mouth was a little open. From that moment we never went away from the bed, and from time to time, pretty often, we gave the dying man a few drops of water which he swallowed with difficulty. The whole day passed without any perceptible change. The two doctors, the grand marshal, and Madame Bertrand, General de Montholon, Marchand, the members of the household were ranged in great part before the bed, and some on the opposite side; they all had their eyes fixed on the emperor's face, which had no other movement than the spasmodic motion given by the hiccoughs.

It was Antommarchi who, standing by the head of his bed, gave him a little water to moisten his mouth, first with a spoon, then with a sponge. He would frequently feel the emperor's pulse, either at his wrist or at his jugular vein. The day before he had placed mustard plasters on the soles of his feet and a blister on his stomach. This produced no effect but to raise his skin in places.

Toward the middle of the day the grand marshal's children came to see the emperor. I think that the eldest, Napoleon, was made sick.

With the exception of a few minutes when one or another went away to take some food, everyone always remained with the emperor, who was soon to pass away.

CHAPTER 18

The Death

Finally, at six o'clock in the evening of the 5th of May, a minute and a half after the cannon-shot at tattoo, the emperor died. The breaths, which had at first been at regular intervals, became progressively farther and farther apart, and the last, slower than those which preceded it, was only the breathing out of a long sigh. Alas! there was left of the emperor nothing but the mortal remains. At this supreme moment all eyes were filled with tears. What a sad and sublime spectacle was the death of a great man, and of a man of Napoleon's stature! If his enemies had been present their eyes, too, would have been moist, and they would have wept over his lifeless body.

As soon as those present had recovered a little from their painful emotion the grand marshal was the first to rise from his chair and kiss the emperor's hand, and all, without exception, followed his example. Then sobs burst forth and tears flowed more freely.

During his last days the emperor had always remained in the same position, lying on his back, with his head straight on the pillow, his right arm stretched out on the bed and the left generally like the right, with this difference, that he sometimes placed his hand on his breast, and that this hand sometimes held the cord which was attached to the knobs on the two posts of the headboard of the bed. His handkerchief was on this cord. His thighs were separated and his heels together. The emperor died without the slightest perceptible convulsion and without the least stiffening; he went out as the light of a lamp goes out.

Immediately after kissing the emperor's hand the Grand Marshal, M. de Montholon, Marchand, and the Abbé Vignaly went into the reception room, where Marchand handed M. de Montholon the package containing the will and codicils. When the seals had been recognized to be intact the Abbé Vignaly returned to the *salon* alone, and the other three proceeded to open the different envelopes. Messrs. de Montholon, Bertrand, and Marchand found themselves named as testamentary executors. M. de Montholon was named first.

By a particular codicil the emperor gave to each of his testamentary executors 50,000 *francs* from the money which he had at Longwood, and directed that to each of his servants should be given a sum larger or smaller, in accordance with their wages and the length of their service, to provide for their return to Europe. By another codicil he left to his executors his money, his jewellery, his silverware, porcelain, furniture, books, arms, and everything which belonged to him at St. Helena. By the same act he desired that his ashes might rest on the banks of the Seine, among the French people whom he so much loved. The emperor had given instructions for his funeral and had designated the spot in which he wished to be buried if the British Government would not allow his body to be carried to Europe.

As soon as the emperor had ceased to live M. Antommarchi had closed his eyes, and soon after had placed a handkerchief under his chin, tied above his head, to close his mouth, which was a little open. A slight contraction which had appeared in the upper lip remained, allowing two or three of the front teeth to be seen. The emperor's head had something of the beauty of the antique medals, and his hands, which were somewhat thin, were of the most perfect model; they resembled the beautiful hands of a woman.

As soon as the testamentary executors had examined the will and codicils they returned to the *salon*. The chandelier was lighted. All the French ranged themselves to right and left of the bed, and Messrs. Short and Nichols, accompanied by the orderly officer, Captain Crockat, who had taken the place of Captain Nichols some weeks before, entered to verify the death. They examined and felt the emperor's body, after which they retired.

To all this movement calm succeeded—the calm of death. Two or three servants remained to watch. All the others went home. It was the first night that we were going to pass without the emperor. Marchand and I were tired and had entire liberty to go and rest, yet, in spite of that, sleep had not the power to take hold of us. We were both buried in the saddest and deepest reflections. This liberty which we were going to have would be only a heavy burden for us poor servants; the condition of easy servitude in which we had lived and to which we were accustomed would have been better. Until now we had had no concern for our future; someone had thought for us, and for us that someone, the emperor, was and ought to be everything. When he was alive, fortunate or unfortunate, we had a support, a stay; now that he was dead, we were left unprotected and abandoned to ourselves. After him there was no one to whom we could attach ourselves. In losing him we lost everything in the world which was dearest to us.

During the evening Marchand, my wife, and I were alone in the *salon*, seated on the sofa, which was near the door of the dining room. My wife had her daughter in her arms. We were talking in a low voice about the emperor, whose body lay a few steps from us. I do not know what caused it, but Marchand took my child, went to the bed, and made her place her lips on the emperor's hand, which was scarcely cold.

When midnight came, Marchand, Noverraz, Pierron, and I took up the body and laid it on the other camp bed. We scarcely dared to touch this body; it seemed to us that it possessed some electric virtue. Our trembling hands touched it only with a respect mingled with fear. Oh, power of the imagination! And yet this envelope of the emperor was as cold as marble.

As soon as the body had been washed and Noverraz had shaved it we placed it on the first bed, which had previously been made up and placed between the two windows. We covered it with a sheet, leaving the face exposed.

When day came two or three English officers entered the *salon* to draw the profile of the emperor's face. Every moment these gentlemen exclaimed, admiringly: "What a beautiful head!—How majestic the features are!" Their exclamations never ceased.

During the morning the governor came to pay his visit. He was accompanied by the admiral, by his staff, and by the principal officers of the sea and land forces. They remained for a few minutes, looking at the emperor, and then retired silently, bowing to General Bertrand, M. de Montholon, Marchand, and the other Frenchmen. Most of the visitors had tears in their eyes as they went away; they were no doubt thinking of the fate of the emperor, who, after being the first man in Europe, had come to die on a lonely rock in the midst of the ocean, and whose body, in a few days, would be covered with earth.

As soon as the governor, the admiral, and their suite had left, a table was set up in the reception room, covered with a sheet, and the emperor's body was laid upon it. It was midday, perhaps, when they proceeded to the autopsy. M. Antommarchi wore the apron and held the scalpel. When the opening had' been made they examined all the parts of the abdomen with care. They observed, among other things, that the liver adhered to the stomach and that this latter had a perforation large enough to pass a finger through. Around this opening there existed many little cavities which one might have said were made by grains of shot which had been fired from a pistol.

When the examination was ended M. Antommarchi took out the heart and stomach, which he placed in two silver vases filled with spirits of wine, and then he sewed up the body again. The doctor, before making the autopsy, had measured the body, had inspected it in its entirety, and had drawn up an official report or description. M. Vignaly had filled the office of secretary.

The cloth on which the autopsy had been made, being stained with blood in many places, was cut up by those present and each one had a piece. The English took the largest part of it.

Before sewing up the body, Antommarchi, taking advantage of a moment when the eyes of the English were not fixed on the body, had taken two little pieces from a rib which he had given to M. Vignaly and Coursot.

When the sewing up was finished we dressed the emperor as he had been in his campaigns—that is to say, in the uniform of the *chasseurs à cheval* of the Imperial Guard; he had on his boots and spurs, with his hat on his head and his sword by his side. No piece of the costume was forgotten. Fearing that the governor might wish to take possession of the emperor's sword, the grand marshal's was substituted for it.

The bedroom, which M. de Montholon had had hung with black, was transformed into a mortuary chapel; the altar was erected against the partition of the dining room. One of the two camp beds, with the curtains raised and attached to the four balls at the tops of the bedposts, formed the sarcophagus. The head of the bed was placed at the foot of the altar and the chandelier from the *salon* was hung in the middle of the room.

The emperor's body was brought from the parlour and placed on the bed, which had been covered with the cloak of Marengo. The head rested on a pillow; on the breast was a silver crucifix. The heart and stomach, in vases, were placed on the front part (the heart in a silver casserole and the stomach in a round cup for a sponge out of the emperor's dressing case). From the manner in which the bed was placed the emperor had his head toward the east and consequently his feet toward the west. The girandoles, the candelabra, and the chandelier were filled with lighted candles and remained so all the time that the emperor's body lay in state.

When everything was ready and in order the Abbé Vignaly said mass, which all the French attended. Attention must be called to the fact that Doctor Arnott or his substitute always remained present. They had received orders from the governor to watch the body, and especially the heart and stomach, which had been removed from it, His Excellency probably fearing that they might disappear or be taken away by means of some substitution.

As the governor had given permission to all the troops of the island, military or naval, to come to Longwood in the afternoon, by a spontaneous movement they all, officers, non-commissioned officers, and privates, hastened there. They arrived at the house of death, some of them in uniform, and some in working clothes, covered with sweat. In spite of the considerable number of visitors everything passed off in the most orderly way. They came in through the valets' antechamber, then the bathroom, the study, and the bedroom, or mortuary chapel, where they remained for a few minutes, after which they went out by the dining room, the salon, and the reception room. During the passage of the visitors the grand marshal was at the head of the bed, M. de Montholon and Marchand at the foot, and the servants ranged on the opposite side, near the windows.

As soon as permission to come to Longwood had been given, all work stopped, for everyone wished to see the great man, the great Napoleon; it was thus that the English soldiers called the emperor. The apartments were not emptied so long as it was light. We remarked that most of the officers and soldiers, after looking at the corpse of the hero, seemed deeply moved by the spectacle which they had before their eyes. We also noticed that a number knelt down after having made the sign of the cross over the emperor's forehead with the thumb of their right hand; they were probably Irish. Among the non-commissioned officers was one who came close to the bed, holding a child by the hand, and saying, as he showed this child the emperor's body, "Come, come and see the great man, the great Napoleon!" This old soldier pronounced these words with so much heart and so much warmth that all those present felt the lively emotion which he felt himself.

At nightfall, as the crowd had melted away, no one was left at Longwood but those who lived there. Two or three servants had the sweet but sad satisfaction of watching beside the Emperor's body.

The next day Abbé Vignaly said mass again, at which several Catholics of both sexes were present from the camp. After divine service the inhabitants of the island arrived, masters and slaves, men, women, and children; they hurried to Longwood from all sides. There was the same crowd as the day before. In a few hours the emperor would be hidden from all eyes.

As Madame Bertrand had the idea that it would be proper to have a cast made of the emperor's face, an English doctor, Mr. Burton, had gone during the morning in search of some calcareous stone from which plaster could be made. The doctor, having found what he wanted with some difficulty, came back to Longwood with a little poor plaster which he had obtained by burning. As soon as the public had gone he and Antommarchi set to work. It order to facilitate the operation they freed the emperor's neck by taking off his collar and cravat. Furthermore, they cut off the hair which still grew on the brow and the temples. It must be said that the rest of the hair had been cut off at the autopsy to be used in making bracelets which were to be sent to different members of the family and in accordance with the order which the emperor had given. In spite of the poor quality of the plaster Antommarchi and Burton succeeded very happily in making a cast, first of the face and then of the rest of the head.[1] It is very unfortunate that they did not think of taking a cast of the hands, for they were certainly beautiful enough to be preserved.

During the evening, May 7th, the coffin was brought, or, to speak more properly, the coffins, for there were three of them, one of tin, upholstered with white satin, a second of mahogany, and a third of lead. A fourth, of mahogany, which was to enclose the first three, was not brought till the next morning.

When everything was arranged we placed the emperor's body in the tin coffin. This proved to be so short that we could not place the hat on his head, so we placed it on his thighs; underneath his legs were placed a number of pieces of silverware—the handsomest— among others a sauceboat in the shape of an antique lamp, knives, forks, spoons, perhaps plates, and a certain number of gold pieces with

1. This mask had a singular history. Antommarchi claimed exclusive credit for making it, and it was only comparatively recently that Burton's share in making it has been established. Saint-Denis's evidence now puts that share beyond any possible question. After the mask was made Burton made a cast from it, which he left at Longwood to dry. Madame Bertrand took possession of this cast (one authority describes her action as "purloined"), and refused. to return it to Burton, who attempted to recover it through the agency of the Bow Street Police Court. It ultimately passed into the hands of Prince Victor Napoleon, and is said to be now in Brussels.

Napoleon's head, both French and Italian. We were obliged to place in the coffin, to the great regret of us Frenchmen, the two vases containing the heart and the stomach (the first had been intended for the empress), but such were the instructions of the English Government communicated to the testamentary executors. The covers of the vases had been soldered on with sufficient care to prevent the alcohol from escaping.

At the moment when the plumber was about to put on the coffin lid in order to solder it down the grand marshal took the emperor's hand for the last time and pressed it with great emotion. In a moment the beautiful head of Napoleon would be hidden from all eyes. What a sad and sublime spectacle was this religious contemplation of the features of him who had been for several of those present the object of their most assiduous care, of their zeal, of their entire devotion and their worship! There were tears in all eyes. When the coffin had been soldered down it was placed in the second, the cover of which was fastened by screws with silver heads. The third coffin, that of lead, having the same form as the preceding ones, contained them and served them as an envelope. As soon as this last was soldered, the mattress and the straps underneath it were removed and the coffin was placed in their place, the bed serving as a frame.

When all the work was finished, as the evening was far advanced, everyone withdrew except the servants who were to act as guard. The most perfect calm succeeded to the bustle. No sound was heard but the noise of the crickets and the rustling of the leaves, shaken by a light breeze. The sentries no longer surrounded the emperor's dwelling; there was no one on watch at Longwood except the officer of the day and Doctor Arnott. So long as the coffins were not closed and soldered the latter had not left the place, and had exercised the utmost vigilance in order that no part of the emperor's body should be removed.

The servants on watch passed half the night walking in the little path which ran beside the windows of the bedroom and study, and half sitting inside, giving way to every sort of reflection, thinking of the past, the present, and the future. The emperor was before their eyes, and he was always the subject of their conversation. Day appeared. The silence of the night gave place to a new activity. The emperor was to leave Longwood during the day, and the earth was to open to receive his remains.

Chapter 19

The Funeral

The French assembled during the morning. Some English Catholics who had been notified came to be present at divine service. Abbé Vignaly said mass, and then the prayers for the dead were read. When this was finished the mahogany coffin was brought and the leaden one was placed in it.

When it was time to prepare for the funeral procession a heated dispute arose between M. de Montholon and M. Vignaly. The latter wished to wear the stole only, as is done when a priest accompanies a dead man; the former wished the *abbé* to wear his chasuble and insisted on it. In spite of the established custom, Vignaly was obliged to submit to the exaction.

About half past eleven the governor and the admiral, accompanied by their staffs, General Coffin, the Marquis de Monchenu and his *aide-de-camp*, and many notables of the island arrived at Longwood, and all, both civil and military, in mourning, drew up on the lawn before the veranda. A sort of car, ornamented with crape and draperies, drawn by four horses, was to carry the emperor's body. It stood in the broad walk at the end of the lawn.

When everything was ready, eight grenadiers, without arms, followed by several persons, entered the reception room and went into the mortuary chapel; they took the coffin and succeeded in putting it on their shoulders with great difficulty. They bent, so to speak, under their heavy burden. They started, passed through the same rooms through which they had just passed, went carefully down the few steps of the veranda and reached the car, on which they placed their precious charge, but not without much difficulty. When the coffin was in place it was covered by a blue pall on which was spread the cloak of Marengo. On this were placed the crossed sword and scabbard.

All the French had followed the emperor's body. The cortege set

BEFORE THE FUNERAL CAR WALKED ABBÉ VIGNALI; BEHIND THE CAR CAME COUNT BERTRAND AND COUNT MONTHOLON ON HORSEBACK FOLLOWED BY THE HOUSEHOLD OF LONGWOOD. NEXT WAS COUNTESS BERTRAND RIDING IN A CARRIAGE WITH HORTENSE BERTRAND.

SOME SOLDIERS FOLLOWED AND THEN SIR HUDSON LOWE WITH HIS
STAFF, AND THE FRENCH COMMISSIONAIRE, MARQUIS DE MONTACHENU

out in the following order: Doctors Antommarchi and Arnott at the head. At a little distance followed Abbé Vignaly, wearing his chasuble, and the grand marshal's son, Henri Bertrand, carrying the holy-water basin. Next came the car, with its horses led by postilions. The four corners of the pall were held by Marchand and Napoleon Bertrand in front, and the grand marshal and General de Montholon behind. The last two, in uniform, were on horseback. To the right and left of the car were the eight grenadiers who carried the coffin. Behind the car was the emperor's horse, saddled and bridled and covered with a black or violet crape. Archambault, in livery and on foot, led it.

Immediately behind the grand marshal and M. de Montholon the emperor's few servants followed in two files, and behind them was a carriage drawn by two horses, in which were Madame Bertrand and Mlle. Hortense, her daughter. After these ladies came the governor and the admiral and all the officers of the staff, among whom were M. de Montchenu and General Coffin. Then came different notables of the island who had been invited or had invited themselves, some on foot and some on horseback. The military had crape on their arms and the civilians, who were dressed in black, had it on their hats.

When the procession had passed the guardhouse we saw the troops of the 66th and 20th line regiments, as well as the island militia, drawn up in line on the little heights which are on the left of the road. Soldiers and officers were in an attitude of sadness, of reflection, of meditation. The soldiers stood with the muzzles of their muskets on the ground, with their hands crossed on the butts and with lowered heads; while the officers held the hilts of their swords level with their chins, the blades turned downward, and, I think, their left hands raised to their *shakos*. The drums were covered with crape; the flags, unrolled and in mourning, were lowered as the car passed, and the band of each corps played funeral airs.

If the emperor's most implacable enemies could have seen his funeral procession passing before the English soldiers sighs would have escaped from their breasts and tears would have moistened their eyelids.

When we arrived at Hutt's Gate we saw Lady Lowe and her daughter, both in deep mourning. The liveliest emotion was depicted on their faces; tears ran down their cheeks.

Opposite the road which comes from Longwood there is a little terrace on which the artillery was in battery; the guns were loaded and the matches burning.

Opening the casket of Napoleon in the presence of Prince Joinville, M. de Roban-Chabot, M. de Las Cases, General Bertrand and General Gourgaud, Abbé Coquereau, and others, before the return to France

After passing Hutt's Gate the head of the procession turned to the right and stopped halfway to Alarm House. There a little road had been made leading to the bottom of what is called Geranium Valley, where many people were already assembled around a clump of willows in which a grave had been dug to receive the emperor's body, not far from the spring to which they went to draw water for the illustrious prisoner.

The procession stopped. Those who were on horseback dismounted. The grenadiers who had accompanied the car again took the coffin on their shoulders, and on the way down everyone marched in the same order as before. When the grenadiers had gone a third of the way they were replaced by eight soldiers of another corps, and the marines, too, wishing to have their share, took the coffin. These last, after covering a third of the distance which remained, laid down their precious load at the edge of the grave.

After the procession had passed, all the troops had followed it and had formed in line on the road which we had just left and which runs along the valley. They were all to be spectators of the sad and imposing scene in which the remains of a great man were to disappear beneath the surface of the earth. The inhabitants of the town, of all conditions and all ages, occupied the bottom of the valley, and groups of men and women, more or less numerous, were ranged on the steep sides of the mountain. The valley looks at this point like a great funnel.

The grave, on the edge of which the marines had just laid the coffin, was dug in the middle of a group of four or five willows; it was some ten feet deep. The four sides of the parallelogram were lined with masonry from top to bottom. A trough of freestone was to be covered with a broad and long flagstone (this stone was one of those which were to be used in the new house). A crab-winch had been set up and the ropes were ready. The surrounding ground was covered with black cloth, which framed the opening to the tomb. When the grand marshal had removed the sword and scabbard and M. de Montholon the cloak and pall, the coffin was placed on two thick oaken planks. Then the priest came forward to the edge of the grave and pronounced the accustomed prayers in a loud voice.

At this moment the servants were on the north side, facing the entrance; the Grand Marshal, M. de Montholon, and the priest were on the two short sides, and the English on the fourth, with the governor, Admiral Lambert, and M. de Montchenu in the middle. When the first prayer was ended they lowered the coffin with the help of the winch, while sighs escaped from the breasts of those present and tears watered the ground where henceforth the remains of the greatest hero of modern times were going to rest. At the same moment the reports of the cannon came three separate times to strike our ears, and these reports were repeated by the echoes of the neighbouring valleys. Silence followed, and the priest, blessing the grave, recited the last prayers. When the religious ceremony was ended the governor asked Generals Bertrand and Montholon whether they were going to pronounce an oration.

When both replied in the negative, on Sir Hudson Lowe's order the winch raised the large flagstone, in the centre of which was a strong movable ring; the stone was hung over the grave, it was lowered little by little and soon it closed the bottom of the vault. Then the workmen hastened down with their trowels; they removed the ring, sealed the stone, and covered it with cement. Everything was finished. Before leaving the valley we each picked a few branches of the willows which shaded the tomb, and with sadness in our hearts we slowly took the road back to Longwood, turning from time to time to cast our eyes toward the spot where lie the emperor's remains.

We learned that after we left the valley the masons continued to work at the bottom of the grave and that then they placed stones to bring it up to the level of the ground, and surrounded it with a border of turf which was protected by a railing. We also learned that the governor had placed a detachment of men commanded by an officer to guard the place.

Plunged in the deepest reflections, we returned to Longwood. This spot, which had been animated by the emperor's presence, was now only a desert. We went looking through the apartments, we wandered through the gardens, we stopped at the spots where he most frequently was, those in which he was wont to rest. We thought we saw him. Alas! it was only an illusion. We shall never see him at Longwood except in our thoughts. He is no more! His body, deprived of life, is down there, shut up in a narrow place shaded by a few weeping willows.

LEONAUR

ALSO FROM LEONAUR
AVAILABLE IN SOFTCOVER OR HARDCOVER WITH DUST JACKET

ESCAPE FROM THE FRENCH *by Edward Boys*—A Young Royal Navy Midshipman's Adventures During the Napoleonic War.

THE VOYAGE OF H.M.S. PANDORA *by Edward Edwards R. N. & George Hamilton, edited by Basil Thomson*—In Pursuit of the Mutineers of the Bounty in the South Seas—1790-1791.

MEDUSA *by J. B. Henry Savigny and Alexander Correard and Charlotte-Adélaïde Dard* —Narrative of a Voyage to Senegal in 1816 & The Sufferings of the Picard Family After the Shipwreck of the Medusa.

THE SEA WAR OF 1812 VOLUME 1 *by A. T. Mahan*—A History of the Maritime Conflict.

THE SEA WAR OF 1812 VOLUME 2 *by A. T. Mahan*—A History of the Maritime Conflict.

WETHERELL OF H. M. S. HUSSAR *by John Wetherell*—The Recollections of an Ordinary Seaman of the Royal Navy During the Napoleonic Wars.

THE NAVAL BRIGADE IN NATAL *by C. R. N. Burne*—With the Guns of H. M. S. Terrible & H. M. S. Tartar during the Boer War 1899-1900.

THE VOYAGE OF H. M. S. BOUNTY *by William Bligh*—The True Story of an 18th Century Voyage of Exploration and Mutiny.

SHIPWRECK! *by William Gilly*—The Royal Navy's Disasters at Sea 1793-1849.

KING'S CUTTERS AND SMUGGLERS: 1700-1855 *by E. Keble Chatterton*—A unique period of maritime history-from the beginning of the eighteenth to the middle of the nineteenth century when British seamen risked all to smuggle valuable goods from wool to tea and spirits from and to the Continent.

CONFEDERATE BLOCKADE RUNNER *by John Wilkinson*—The Personal Recollections of an Officer of the Confederate Navy.

NAVAL BATTLES OF THE NAPOLEONIC WARS *by W. H. Fitchett*—Cape St. Vincent, the Nile, Cadiz, Copenhagen, Trafalgar & Others.

PRISONERS OF THE RED DESERT *by R. S. Gwatkin-Williams*—The Adventures of the Crew of the Tara During the First World War.

U-BOAT WAR 1914-1918 *by James B. Connolly/Karl von Schenk*—Two Contrasting Accounts from Both Sides of the Conflict at Sea D uring the Great War.

LEONAUR

ALSO FROM LEONAUR
AVAILABLE IN SOFTCOVER OR HARDCOVER WITH DUST JACKET

OFFICERS & GENTLEMEN by Peter Hawker & William Graham—Two Accounts of British Officers During the Peninsula War: Officer of Light Dragoons by Peter Hawker & Campaign in Portugal and Spain by William Graham .

THE WALCHEREN EXPEDITION by Anonymous—The Experiences of a British Officer of the 81st Regt. During the Campaign in the Low Countries of 1809.

LADIES OF WATERLOO by Charlotte A. Eaton, Magdalene de Lancey & Juana Smith—The Experiences of Three Women During the Campaign of 1815: Waterloo Days by Charlotte A. Eaton, A Week at Waterloo by Magdalene de Lancey & Juana's Story by Juana Smith.

JOURNAL OF AN OFFICER IN THE KING'S GERMAN LEGION by John Frederick Hering—Recollections of Campaigning During the Napoleonic Wars.

JOURNAL OF AN ARMY SURGEON IN THE PENINSULAR WAR by Charles Boutflower—The Recollections of a British Army Medical Man on Campaign During the Napoleonic Wars.

ON CAMPAIGN WITH MOORE AND WELLINGTON by Anthony Hamilton—The Experiences of a Soldier of the 43rd Regiment During the Peninsular War.

THE ROAD TO AUSTERLITZ by R. G. Burton—Napoleon's Campaign of 1805.

SOLDIERS OF NAPOLEON by A. J. Doisy De Villargennes & Arthur Chuquet—The Experiences of the Men of the French First Empire: Under the Eagles by A. J. Doisy De Villargennes & Voices of 1812 by Arthur Chuquet .

INVASION OF FRANCE, 1814 by F. W. O. Maycock—The Final Battles of the Napoleonic First Empire.

LEIPZIG—A CONFLICT OF TITANS by Frederic Shoberl—A Personal Experience of the 'Battle of the Nations' During the Napoleonic Wars, October 14th-19th, 1813.

SLASHERS by Charles Cadell—The Campaigns of the 28th Regiment of Foot During the Napoleonic Wars by a Serving Officer.

BATTLE IMPERIAL by Charles William Vane—The Campaigns in Germany & France for the Defeat of Napoleon 1813-1814.

SWIFT & BOLD by Gibbes Rigaud—The 60th Rifles During the Peninsula War.

www.ingramcontent.com/pod-product-compliance
Lightning Source LLC
Chambersburg PA
CBHW032051080426
42733CB00006B/239